Stakehol

ONE WEEK LOAN

Edited by Tim Brown

Foreword by Tony Blair MP

Stakeholder Housing
A Third Way

Published in association with the
Labour Housing Group

Pluto Press
LONDON • STERLING, VIRGINIA

First published 1999 by Pluto Press
345 Archway Road, London N6 5AA
and 22883 Quicksilver Drive, Sterling, VA 20166–2012, USA

British Library Cataloguing in Publication Data
A catalogue record for this book is available from
the British Library

ISBN 0 7453 1505 4 hbk

Library of Congress Cataloging in Publication Data
Stakeholder housing : a third way / edited by Tim
   Brown
       p.   cm.
     Includes bibliographical references (p.   ).
     ISBN 0–7453–1505–4 (hbk.)
     1. Housing policy—Great Britain. 2. Housing authorities—Great
Britain. 3. Public housing—Great Britain. 4. Home ownership–
–Great Britain. I. Brown, Tim.
HD7333.A3S72   1999
363.5'85'0941—dc21   99–35171
                                                                     CIP

Designed and produced for Pluto Press by
Chase Production Services, Chadlington, Oxford, OX7 3LN
Typeset from disk by Stanford DTP Services, Northampton
Printed in the EC by TJ International, Padstow

Dedication

This book is dedicated to the memory of Jean Conway, Senior Lecturer in Housing Studies at Sheffield Hallam University, who died in January 1999. Jean made a significant contribution to this book as well as being a good friend and a valued colleague.

Acknowledgements

The author and publishers are grateful for the support of the Barony Group in the publication of this book.

Contents

List of Tables

Foreword

Nothing is more important to individuals and families than a decent and secure home. That is why Labour supports the aspirations of the majority of people to own their own homes and also wants to see healthy social and private rented sectors for those who cannot afford to buy or choose not to.

After 18 years of Conservative government, the problems we inherited were severe: boom and bust in the housing market, massive disrepair in both public and private housing sectors, pockets of severe housing deprivation in our cities and street homelessness as one of the most potent symbols of social exclusion in Britain today.

We have made a start in tackling these problems. By giving operational independence to the Bank of England we have brought long-term stability to mortgage rates. Over the first two years we are investing £900 million in housing and housing related regeneration through the Capital Receipts Initiative. And we have committed an extra £3.9 billion for housing over the next three years, enabling local authorities to begin to tackle the backlog of renovation work and deliver improvements in 1.5 million council homes. We are also setting up a new Housing Inspectorate as part of our Best Value regime with power to tackle poor management of local authority housing and ensure that tenants enjoy high quality service.

Many of the problems are deep seated. We need long-term solutions and joined up thinking across government. That is why I made rough sleeping one of the first priorities of the Social Exclusion Unit and tackling deprivation on our worst estates another. In July 1998, we launched an action plan and target to reduce rough sleeping by two-thirds by 2002. In September 1998, we published a national strategy for neighbourhood renewal. Over the next three years the £800 million

New Deal for Communities will give some of our worst-off local communities the resources to tackle their problems in an intensive and coordinated way.

There is more to be done. The Labour Housing Group has played an important role in raising the profile of housing policy. This book makes a further contribution to the debate.

The Right Honourable Tony Blair MP
December 1998

1

Introduction

Tim Brown

THE DAWNING OF A NEW ERA IN HOUSING AND SOCIAL POLICY?

The May 1997 general election, with hindsight, may become a significant and symbolic date in the development of British housing and social policy. The principles underpinning these changes have become labelled a 'third way' that is radically different from the previously dominant perspectives of the new right and the old left. Leading politicians and academics have made significant contributions to the debate (see Blair, 1998; Giddens, 1998). Furthermore, an ever increasing plethora of ideas and terminology are being used in the debates and discussion on the third way including citizenship, communitarianism, social capital, civic entrepreneurship and stakeholding. The latter is particularly interesting and relevant for the debates on housing and social policy as it reflects an attempt to develop a democratically accountable welfare state involving providers, funders and users collaborating together. Although it is difficult to unravel the complex origins of the stakeholder concept, it is generally acknowledged that its recent use stems from the work of Hutton (1995, 1997a, 1997b, 1997c). He argues that the adoption of a new right perspective with its emphasis on market values after 1979 exacerbated a range of long-term interlocking problems facing British society. These included a financial system that values short-term profit over long-term commitment, a lack of innovation and a failure to develop genuine approaches to partnership at all levels in society. Although his commentary is primarily geared towards the economy, he notes:

> At the heart of the welfare state lies a conception of a just society; a guarantee of some income for the disadvantaged against life's hazards, along with a roof over their heads, access to healthcare and, for their children, the education and training essential to improving their situation. The vitality of the welfare state is a badge of a healthy society; it is a symbol of our capacity to act together morally, to share and to recognise the mutuality of rights and obligations that underpins all human associations. It is an expression of social citizenship. (Hutton, 1995, p. 306)

In many ways, this quotation highlights the essential features of a stakeholding society compared to a shareholding society emphasised by the new right during the 1980s. It also, of course, identifies some of the differences between aspects of the thinking of the old left and new Labour on issues such as public ownership (Hutton, 1997b). Clearly the concept of stakeholding provides a possible basis for a third way for housing and social policy that forms part of a radical centre-left project which could be implemented by the current government.

However, as well as these debates on principles, the period since May 1997 has seen a marked change of style in the process of policy development. The Department of the Environment, Transport and the Regions (DETR) and the Scottish, Welsh and Northern Ireland Offices, for instance, have sought to engage in a genuine debate on the future of housing policy. More generally, there has been an increase in the use of consultation papers and a desire for more open and transparent dialogue. The government has undertaken a wide range of policy reviews with nearly 50 studies related implicitly or explicitly to housing being initiated during 1997. These reviews have resulted in a wide range of consultation papers and Green and White Papers including the Department of the Environment, Transport and the Regions White Paper on modernising local government (DETR, 1998a) and the Department of Social Security White Paper (1998) on welfare policy. But perhaps the most significant of these have been the economic and fiscal strategy and the comprehensive spending review published in June and July 1998 respectively. In style, the focus of these also appears to have moved from ideological rhetoric of the Conservative government to seeking practical solutions. In policy terms, the shift has been towards balancing competitive frameworks with collaboration and partnerships. This is matched with a desire to encourage experiments and a willingness to explore new initiatives prior to legislation. The example of the best value pilots for improving local services including housing by local authorities and registered social landlords (RSLs) in England as part of the modernising of local government can be usefully contrasted with the top–down competitive compulsory tendering regime of the previous government (DETR, 1998b). The emphasis is on working in partnership with other stakeholders especially tenants to develop services that reflect local needs. This can be compared with the new right focus on improving services by opening them up to market competition and the old left approach embracing, at times, a paternalistic top–down bureaucratic approach to the delivery of welfare policies.

At the same time, the long standing tradition of local innovation must not be forgotten or ignored. The editor, for instance, has reviewed local housing and anti-poverty strategies (Brown and Passmore, 1998) and identified a diverse range of locally based initiatives developed by, among others, local authorities, registered social landlords, community groups and tenant organisations. Their importance, although often marginalised and unrecognised, cannot be understated. They have been initiated through bottom–up partnerships rather than a top–down approach, starting with an assessment of local needs leading to the development of projects and schemes that reflect local requirements. Yet many of these local initiatives have struggled to survive because of the lack of support not just in the form of financial resources from the state but also because of an unwillingness on the part of central government to trust local organisations including local authorities.

Indeed, Hutton (1997b) points out that the way forward for the centre and the left is to reawaken a long and honourable tradition based on principles of local cooperation and mutuality. Other writers have begun to explore in more detail some of the principles underpinning the embryonic trade union and labour movement in the nineteenth century. Reference is increasingly being made to key texts such as Thompson (1968) that highlighted the development of community orientated class solidarity incorporating shared values and moral obligations. But it is essential to appreciate that Thompson's argument is based around the concept of the development of class consciousness and a growing appreciation by local working-class communities of the underlying reasons for social inequalities in a capitalist society. This presents an intriguing issue for current thinking on the third way. There is a fundamental emphasis on developing strategies for social inclusion from a bottom–up perspective, yet support for this approach sometimes makes use of radical left wing traditions. Indeed, one might argue along similar lines in relation to a much more recent tradition of local left of centre political initiatives. Local socialism and popular planning in the late 1970s and early 1980s was a rather diverse political movement based around local community renewal and control of resources (Brindley et al., 1996; Boddy and Fudge, 1984). It was nevertheless strongly associated with initiatives by radical left wing local authorities such as the Greater London Council and the West Midlands Metropolitan County Council. Yet current third way thinking seems to disown or ignore these ideas. This has resulted in Wainwright commenting:

> when I hear references to the Third Way, I reach for my sick bag ... what really makes me sick is the use of a discourse from an honourable left tradition (from E. P. Thompson through to Ken Livingstone's GLC) to legitimate policies which take the line of least resistance to those with wealth and power. (Wainwright, 1998, p. 2)

There is thus a diverse set of ideas and views related to the third way. There are at least three interlinked components to these debates: philosophical discussions on principles, government policy initiatives and local action. Each of these aspects has been briefly covered in the preceding paragraphs. A clear picture on what constitutes the third way will only arise through a reconciliation of these three levels of debate. For housing, there is an additional difficulty in that the government and society do not regard it to be as important as other social policy issues such as education and health. Thus discussions on stakeholding and a third way for housing are relatively poorly developed. Furthermore, as has already been pointed out, there is considerable dispute about the nature of the third way and stakeholding. Even supporters such as Giddens have commented that the term, the third way, is of no special significance in and of itself. But what is important is that it is used 'to refer to social democratic renewal – the present day version of the periodic rethinking that social democrats have had to carry out quite often over the past century' (Giddens, 1998, p. viii).

THE PURPOSE OF THE BOOK

The aim of this book is to contribute to the ongoing discussions on the future directions of housing policy and practice. It thus continues the long standing tradition of the Labour Housing Group to raise the profile of housing issues and contribute to new thinking on how housing can form a significant part of the government's agenda for addressing issues such as social exclusion, modernising local government and devolution.

This publication aims to build on the changes in style and substance of government policy making, debates on stakeholding and a third way, and local innovations in housing. It has brought together a wide range of contributors from housing policy and practice. Each of the contributors is an expert in their individual field. What they have in common is not a political belief, but a belief in finding workable solutions to some of the problems that affect Britain's housing and the people who live in it. Most have published widely on their policy area or possess specialist knowledge acquired from work in their field. Thus the publication aims to offer a new perspective on the development of policy and practice under new Labour; a policy approach which commentators are describing as the third way.

It is not, however, intended as a comprehensive and definitive statement on future housing policy. It is acknowledged that a number of topic areas are not fully addressed. For example, the connections between housing and public policy and housing and the economy are not explicitly covered in detail in Part 1. Similarly in Part 3 on stakeholding, the perspectives of employees and of the construction industry are not explicitly discussed. Moreover, the views of a wide range of specific needs groups are not fully analysed. The editor appreciates that there is a lack of comprehensive coverage of a number of important issues, but the book is intended as a starting point for generating a debate on stakeholder housing rather than a definitive policy manual.

STRUCTURE OF THE BOOK

Unlike many housing textbooks, the material is not organised around tenures or on housing activities. This represents a conscious decision to break away from traditional approaches which, we argue, contribute to a narrow and unsatisfactory form of analysis as well as often leading to inappropriate policy and practice suggestions. Indeed, it is suggested that an engagement with debates on stakeholding and the third way requires an approach that emphasises the links with other policy areas, visions for housing, and the views of stakeholders.

The book thus begins with an exploration of what is meant by the third way. This term is defined and reviewed, and its application to housing by new Labour is considered. In particular it is suggested that the third way in housing is contained within the three themes of trust, partnering and stakeholding.

The remainder of the book is divided into three parts covering, first, the links between housing and other issues, second, visions for the future direction for housing, and third, the perspectives of stakeholders. Each part begins with a short introduction highlighting the content and issues The first part may be described as macro housing policy. In this section new Labour's approach to social and economic policy is reviewed. The links between housing and other policy areas are considered, by reviewing health, employment and education policies as well as initiatives for tackling social exclusion as they interact with housing. Consideration is also given to the impact of 'Europe' on housing policy and practice. Finally, a thought provoking perspective is provided through an analysis of housing policy in the USA where much of new Labour's thinking has been developed and implemented since the early 1990s.

The second section explores visions for United Kingdom housing. There are contributions from a politician and academics and professionals on their visions for the four nations. While UK housing policy was managed from Westminster, diversity was not an issue. However, Labour's modernisation of Britain's governance structures through Welsh and Scottish devolution and a peace settlement in Northern Ireland provide an opportunity for distinctive policies to emerge. There are further opportunities for this as Labour takes forward its ideas on regional governance in England.

The third section explores the views of various stakeholder groups. The chapters consider the priorities of stakeholder groups, and how they believe housing policy should be developed at national, regional and local levels. The breadth of views from tenants, local communities, regulators, funders and those concerned about local governance reflects Labour's inclusive approach, and forms a key element of a third way in housing.

Finally, a concluding chapter draws together the key themes and highlights the current issues and state of play regarding housing policy and practice as part of the third way.

REFERENCES

Blair, T. (1998) *The Third Way: New Politics for the New Century* (London: The Fabian Society).

Boddy, M. and Fudge, C. (eds) (1984) *Local Socialism* (London: Macmillan).

Brindley, T., Rydin, Y. and Stoker, G. (1996) *Rethinking Planning* (London: Routledge, 2nd edition).

Brown, T. and Passmore, J. (1998) *Housing and Anti-Poverty Strategies* (Coventry and York: Chartered Institute of Housing and Joseph Rowntree Foundation).

Department of the Environment, Transport and the Regions (1998a) *Modern Local Government: In Touch with the People* (London: The Stationery Office).

Department of the Environment, Transport and the Regions (1998b) *Modernising Local Government : Improving Local Services through Best Value* (London: DETR).

Department of Social Security (1998) *A New Contract for Welfare: New Ambitions for Our Country* (London: The Stationery Office).

Giddens, A. (1998) *The Third Way* (London: Polity Press).

Hutton, W. (1995) *The State We're In* (London: Jonathan Cape).

Hutton, W. (1997a) *The State to Come* (London: Vintage Press).

Hutton, W. (1997b) *Stakeholding and its Critics* (London: Institute of Economic Affairs, Choices in Welfare No. 36).

Hutton, W. (1997c) 'New Labour, New Levers', *Housing*, May, pp. 24–5.

Thompson, E. P. (1968) *The Making of the English Working Class* (London: Penguin).

Wainwright, H. (1998) 'Is there such a thing as a Third Way in Politics? – No', *Guardian*, 2 May, p. 2.

The Third Way

Tim Brown

INTRODUCTION

Apparently Tony Blair's pamphlet on The Third Way is selling well at the Conference Bookshop. But I had to tell them to take it out of the mystery section. (John Prescott, Deputy Prime Minister, speaking at the Labour Party Conference on Wednesday 30 September 1998)

The third way has become a cornerstone of current discussions about the future of society as well as of debates about 'new Labour'. Media interest is intense with an increasing number of interviews with key participants and special features on the topic. During the last few months of 1998, there seemed to be a never-ending spate of publications on the third way including the Prime Minister's own vision (Blair, 1998). In addition, there were pronouncements by leading gurus, such as Giddens (1998a), and more reflective commentaries by, for example, Hargreaves and Christie (1998) and Marquand (1998). At the same time, there was a less sympathetic and more critical response from the left and right of the political spectrum. A special edition of *Marxism Today* (1998) brought together a diverse range of writers from what might be termed the first way. At the same time, the new right (or second way) promulgated further debate by speculating that there was no such thing as a third way and, indeed, arguing that Blair's victory in the general election in 1997 was really a victory for Thatcher's ideas (see, for instance, Novak, 1998).

Interest has not been limited to the UK. Considerable attention has been paid to comparing the political beliefs of 'new Labour' with Clinton and the new democrats in the USA. And the future of social democracy and the renewal of the social democratic project have been widely discussed in Western Europe with the re-establishment of left of centre governments in many countries, culminating in 1998 with the SPD victory in the German general election. This has generated considerable debate as to whether there is convergence or divergence between third way ideas in continental Europe and those in the UK and USA (see, for example, Cuperus and Kandel, 1998; Michel and Bouvet, 1998).

Overall, there is a degree of confusion and mystery over the third way. It is therefore not difficult to concur with Hargreaves and Christie (1998, p. 1) that 'the definition of this new synthesis is only half complete. Some of its themes are becoming clear, but the centre-left is still a long way from having a fully formed ideological position.'

The aims of this chapter are, first, to provide the reader with an overview of the debates on the third way. It thus begins with a current and an historical overview, which is followed by a comparative perspective. The nature of the third way and the elements comprising it are then outlined. Second, the chapter identifies the relationship between housing policy and the third way, and finally it discusses the links with housing practice. It is essential that these relationships be explored, otherwise a major gap emerges between broad concepts and real world practicalities. Debates on communitarianism and on stakeholding (as part of the third way) can appear at best interesting but irrelevant for housing staff and residents faced with the realities of coping with working and living on problem housing estates and in older inner city areas.

Making the connections between the third way, as an alternative to the doctrines of the new right and the old left, and the specific issues facing local communities such as poverty, crime and anti-social behaviour and inadequate welfare services is thus essential. But there is a major gap between discussions on these big ideas and housing policies and practices for tackling immediate problems. Much of the literature on the third way and related concepts is either relatively abstract or focuses on national policies. At the same time, there are an ever increasing number of housing and related studies that identify specific problems and good practice (see, for example, Brown and Passmore, 1998). Moreover the housing profession and housing organisations have not been slow to raise the profile of housing issues by lobbying on a wide range of topics and problems. The Chartered Institute of Housing's campaign for greater investment in housing as part of the government's comprehensive spending review is a useful illustration of this activity (Chartered Institute of Housing, 1997). Furthermore, high profile personalities, such as the Director of the Joseph Rowntree Foundation, have been quick to identify the housing issues facing local communities and draw up a priority list for action (Best, 1997).

Clearly, a major advance in thinking is required so that links are established between the third way and housing policies and practices. Without these links, solutions to local issues may appear to be top–down, paternalistic and often pragmatic and ad hoc. Moreover, the political process and debates will seem to have nothing to offer in terms of an articulate and carefully crafted strategic response to the needs of local communities. Disillusionment and cynicism about policies and practices combined with a growing detachment from political involvement will continue to escalate.

(RE-)DISCOVERING A THIRD WAY?

The phrase 'the third way' has suddenly (re-)appeared as if by magic in the language of those concerned with economic and social policies. The Labour Party's 1997 General Election Manifesto articulated the thinking behind it but without clearly labelling new Labour's 'contract with the people'. The manifesto, building on an earlier draft entitled *New Labour: New Life for Britain* (Labour Party, 1996), highlighted the need for a programme based on a new centre and centre-left politics: 'In each area of policy a new and distinctive approach has been mapped out, one that differs from the solutions of the old left and those of the conservative right' (Labour Party, 1997, p. 3). By mid-1998, there were thus frequent references, sometimes implicit but often explicit, in government discussion papers. The Prime Minister in the Foreword and Introduction to the Green Paper on Welfare (Department of Social Security, 1998) stated:

> We must return to first principles and ask what we want the welfare state to achieve. This is the question this Green Paper seeks to answer. In essence, it describes a third way: not dismantling welfare,

leaving it simply as a low grade safety net for the destitute: nor keeping it unreformed and underperforming: but reforming it on the basis of a new contract between citizen and state, where we keep a welfare state from which we all benefit but on terms that are fair and clear. (p. v)

Similarly, the Green Paper on Public Health (Department of Health, 1998) pointed out that, 'the Government is setting out a third way between the old extremes of individual victim blaming on the one hand and nanny state social engineering on the other' (p. 5).

Furthermore, there was a growing engagement between academics, politicians and their advisers on both sides of the Atlantic on developing the third way. In February 1998, Blair and Clinton jointly ran a seminar to explore new thinking. What they were searching for was a new school of thought to replace the academic traditions of socialism and the new right. Following this high level meeting, there were small-scale policy events attended by 'new Labour' thinkers such as Kelly, Cooper, Radice and Marquand. Secondly, in September 1998, a further seminar was held in New York on the third way involving not just Blair and Clinton but also the Italian Prime Minister, Prodi, as well as leading academics and researchers such as Giddens.

These developments have been underpinned in part by the growing importance of left of centre think tanks since the early 1990s such as the Institute for Public Policy Research and Demos. The latter commissioned and published a number of studies focusing on the third way and related concepts (see, for instance, Hargreaves and Christie, 1998; Leadbeater, 1997). It has also included Perri 6's work on holistic government, which attempts to outline some of the principles underpinning the third way, and states: 'The new agenda for government in the twenty first century is becoming clear. At its heart is the idea and the goal of ever more holistic government, built as much from the bottom up as the top down' (Perri 6, 1997, p. 70). Interestingly, other think tanks, such as the Institute of Economic Affairs which is normally associated with right of centre political viewpoints, have made significant contributions (see, for example, Dennis, 1997; Novak, 1998).

Thirdly, academics, particularly Giddens, have made major inputs into the debate. In recent years, Giddens has published a number of pamphlets and books on the topic, and is now widely regarded as Blair's guru! He has argued, for instance, that the third way can provide a new framework for political thinking which cuts across the old divides of social democracy and neoliberalism (Giddens, 1994, 1998a, 1998b). The third way thus refers to a desire to move out from the strait-jacket of political thinking. It represents an attempt to break free from the traditions of the new right with its anti state and pro market approach, and old Labour with its focus on public ownership. It is argued that such political thinking over recent decades has created ideological breaks to innovative thinking.

HISTORICAL PERSPECTIVE

It is, however, important to appreciate that the third way has been used frequently in the twentieth century to introduce a complex and varied set of alternatives to the traditional political divide between the market and the state. A former Conservative Prime Minister, Macmillan, wrote a book originally published in 1938 on the middle way. A second edition was published in the mid-1960s and included the following statement:

> We do not stand and have never stood for collectivism or the destruction of private rights. We do not stand and have never stood for laissez faire individualism or for putting the rights of the individual above his duty to his fellow man. (Macmillan, 1966, p. xxii)

Both the original text and the second edition set out some interesting middle way principles including an emphasis on the balance between rights and obligations, a sound economy as a basis for social reform, a coordinating role for the state and a minimum wage.

Secondly, there has been an emerging debate among Labour historians and writers on the degree of divergence between old and new Labour. Morgan (1998), for instance, asserts that there is some continuity between the pre and post 1990 Labour Party. He points out that there have been at least three other major shifts in thinking during the twentieth century including a new focus on economic planning and the adoption of Keynesian ideas in the 1930s. The promotion in the 1950s of a social agenda of greater equality represented a significant break with the immediate post-war programme of nationalisation and planning. And the 1960s witnessed a focus on modernisation and the white heat of technology and science.

Thirdly, and at a more local level in the UK, there was much interest in the late 1970s and early 1980s in popular planning as part of an alternative economic strategy. As Brindley et al. (1996) point out, popular planning was a not uniquely socialist idea. Instead it represented a challenge to both traditional free market orientated approaches to urban regeneration and top–down statist strategies. Indeed, Wainwright (1998) has argued that local socialism in the early 1980s was a practical attempt to go beyond both neoliberal and Keynesian economics to develop innovative partnerships with local voluntary bodies and to allocate public resources in a new participatory manner.

Further complexities are created if consideration is given to the neglected history of working-class organisations in the nineteenth century. There is an emerging literature on mutual aid societies, especially working-class friendly societies, in providing welfare benefits for their members. Politicians and writers from right of the political spectrum (such as Gladstone, 1998), as well as from the radical centre (see, for example, Young and Lemos, 1998), claim that the third way focus on provision by local voluntary based community associations, ought to draw inspiration from the early history of the labour and cooperative movement.

The third way can thus be considered a somewhat confusing and problematic term from an historical perspective, and one that carries considerable and varied intellectual baggage with it. Some elements of current thinking on the third way could clearly draw on certain aspects of popular planning in the 1980s such as community architecture, grass-roots involvement in drawing up visions for the future, action zone planning and reinvigorating local neighbourhoods. Giddens (1994) refers to democratising democracy and the importance of self-help groups and social movements, as well as generative politics by which he means allowing individuals and groups to make things happen. But this could apparently equally well draw on ideas from elements of the labour and cooperative movements in the nineteenth century.

COMPARATIVE PERSPECTIVE

The significance of a comparative perspective has already been identified in relation to current debates on the renewal of social democracy. It is also important to consider briefly an historical dimension to these discussions. First, fascist political parties used terms such as a third way in the 1920s and 1930s and argued that socialism and conservatism were obsolete political concepts. Second, in the late 1960s and 1970s, there was frequent reference to a third way between capitalism and the free market and communism and totalitarianism as evidenced, for example, by social democracy in Sweden and socialist self-management in the former Yugoslavia. Considerable interest emerged in alternative models of political economy in the 1970s and 1980s (see, for instance, Barratt-Brown, 1984).

Thus, the third way 1990s style appears to be a rejection of the social democratic model adopted in Sweden and North Western Europe. Indeed, social democratic parties and governments in Western Europe have generally been sceptical of the British Labour Party's embrace of the third way. Walker (1998) implies that there are at least three trajectories for social democracy in Western Europe, all of which could claim to be third ways. These are the third way associated with 'new Labour' in the UK, and the more traditional socialism associated with French government as illustrated by Jospin who states that:

> Capitalism doesn't just suffer from financial hypertrophy, it's structurally weak. As it creates wealth, it concentrates it to excess; as it ensures that production rises continuously, so it tends to exclude more and more men and women from the world of work. Capitalism carries disequilibrium within itself and there is only one counterweight: politics. (Jospin, 1998, p. 20)

Thirdly, there have been debates in countries such as Germany, the Netherlands and Sweden about the possibility of a grand coalition of the centre involving centre-left and centre-right political parties. But some commentators argue that the degree of divergence can be overstated. Michel and Bouvet (1998), for instance, suggest that all countries with centre-left political parties in government are more likely to adopt a modernisation programme for social democracy rather than a shift in the direction towards new democrat liberalism.

Nevertheless, the tensions within social democracy in part reflect the differences which emerged in the 1970s and 1980s between the more liberal market orientated welfare systems in countries such as the USA, Britain, Australia and New Zealand, and the corporatist and social democratic welfare systems in North Western European countries. Yet the similarity in terminology and concepts between welfare states is both interesting and confusing. Inclusion, for instance, appears to be a strong theme within the big idea of stakeholding as developed by Hutton (1995) as part of the third way agenda. It implies both responsibilities and rights for members of society. But as Harloe (1995) has noted, social democracy in Sweden for the last 60 years is underpinned by the concept of the 'folkhemmet' or people's home, that is a vision of a society with social, economic and political citizenship for all. Individuals and households are an inclusive part of Swedish society and gain access to a generous welfare system as long as and only if they accept their responsibilities to the Swedish community.

DEFINING THE THIRD WAY

The third way, nevertheless, reflects a desire to move away from traditional politics of the left and right. New Labour is attempting to shift direction away from the infertile ground of traditional thinking that many acknowledge is outdated. It is attempting to appeal to both the Labour Party's traditional supporters who believe in creating a just and more equal society, and middle-class voters who have been influenced by Labour's election promises on improving education and health and tackling crime. The third way stands for:

> a modernised social democracy, passionate in its commitment to social justice and the goals of the centre-left, but flexible, innovative and forward-looking in the means to achieve them. It is founded on the values which have guided progressive politics for more than a century – democracy, liberty, justice, mutual obligation and inter-nationalism. But it is a third way because it moves decisively beyond an Old Left preoccupied by state control, high taxation and producer interests; and a New Right treating public investment, and often the very notions of 'society' and collective endeavours, as evils to be undone. (Blair, 1998, p. 1)

It thus reflects a desire to repudiate some (but not all) aspects of Thatcherism. Thatcher's arrival in power in May 1979 marked the beginning of the dominance of right of centre political thinking that underpinned economic and social policies in the 1980s and 1990s. But there were conflicting ideas and themes between, for example, neoliberals and neoconservatives (Atkinson and Moon, 1994). The former emphasised issues such as freedom, choice, the free market, minimal state intervention and the importance of the individual, while the latter placed great significance on authority, tradition, stability, morality and order. There is a growing literature from the right of the political spectrum suggesting that Blair's victory in 1997 was really a victory for Thatcherism (Novak, 1998). It is argued that there are important links between the third way and Thatcherism in terms of the focus on economic growth, the repudiation of redistribution and the role of the state in providing welfare from the cradle to the grave. Even more provocatively, Jenkins (1998, p. 20) has argued that Blair is completing the Thatcherite project: 'So far Mr Blair has brought to Thatcherism a touch of magic. He is the icing on the cake – with John Prescott as the marzipan. He is encasing Thatcherism in consensus and sugar-dusting it with joy.'

The third way may thus be as much a slogan of intention as a political ideology. Indeed Giddens (1998b) even suggests that it may be inappropriate to use this term because of its lack of clarity! But he also argues that new Labour has more to offer than just media orientated politics (Giddens, 1998a). He suggests that it reflects important changes in political thinking in parts of Western Europe and North America. Clearly, for example, 'new Labour' is an essential element of the resurgence of social democracy, without being a return to the policies of the late 1940s. It is instead an attempt to popularise social democracy and recast the political map. As such, therefore, it is aimed at changing attitudes, culture and values. It is not just about changing the way politicians think and act, but the way in which business, the state, communities and neighbourhoods and wider society operate.

With only rare exceptions, few in housing have begun to consider the implications of the third way. Yet the debate, as the previous paragraphs have shown, is already taking place and is well developed. It is therefore essential to identify the defining characteristics of the third way in the late 1990s. Useful summaries can be found in Giddens (1994, 1998a, 1998b) who distinguishes the third way from old-style social democracy and neoliberalism (see Table 2.1).

This table, of course, presents an idealised perspective on the third way. The reality may be rather different especially if one attempts to evaluate the concept after such a limited period of operation in the UK. It might be argued, for example, that the scope of government so far in reality has been one of centralisation. Marquand (1998) points out that there is a major tension between a top–down approach by which governments attempt to change social behaviour by regulation and manipulation, and a bottom–up approach focusing on self-government, local autonomy and civic pluralism. He suggests that 'new Labour' can live with this paradox for some time, but implies that, in the final instance, it will revert to a top–down approach.

Table 2.1 The First Way, the Second Way and the Third Way

	Old Style Social Democracy – The First Way	Neoliberalism & the New Right – The Second Way	The 'Third Way'
Politics	Class politics of the left	Class politics of the right	Modernising movement of the centre (e.g. social justice and a cross-class basis of support)
Economy	Keynesian demand management and a confined role for markets (e.g. old mixed economy)	Market fundamentalism	New mixed economy (e.g. a balance between regulation and deregulation and between the economic and the non-economic)
Scope of Government	Corporatism and state dominates over civil society	Minimal state (e.g. state as enabler rather than provider)	New democratic state (e.g. democratising democracy and an emphasis on community)
Nation	Internationalism	Nation-state	Cosmopolitan nation (e.g. a new role in the global system)
Welfare State	Strong welfare state (e.g. comprehensive welfare provision)	Welfare safety net (e.g. residualised welfare provision)	Social investment state (e.g. responsibility and rights of the individual)

Adapted from Giddens (1998a, 1998b)

ELEMENTS OF THIRD WAY THINKING

So far, attention has been paid to the third way as an alternative to the old left and the neoliberalism of the new right. But it is important to appreciate the diverse and interlinked concepts which underpin the third way. They include, for example, citizenship, communitarianism, ethical socialism, social justice, stakeholding, social capital and trust. Each of these big ideas has been used in the debates on the third way, and usefully contributes to our understanding of this ideology.

Modern debates about citizenship are usually traced back to the work of Marshall (1950). He emphasised the importance of social rights as well as political and civil rights. These taken together enable individuals within a society to participate as equals. Civil citizenship includes the rights necessary for individual freedom, and was primarily acquired during the eighteenth and nineteenth centuries. Political citizenship includes the rights to participate in the exercise of power as a member of a body invested with political authority or as an elector of such a body. These rights were acquired largely during the nineteenth and early twentieth centuries. The third element, social citizenship, includes the right to share to the full in the social heritage and to live the life of a civilised person according to the standards prevailing in society, namely a fundamental right to enjoy a reasonable standard of living. This final element only became guaranteed after 1945 in the UK with the rise of the welfare state. It is thus important to note that the concept of social citizenship is strongly linked to old style social democracy. Nevertheless, there has been a resurgence of interest in citizenship in recent years. This renewed interest stems from critical debates about whether social citizenship was ever enjoyed by all sections of society, for instance, women and black and minority ethnic communities. And there is a growing consensus that citizenship, community and society are deeply interrelated ideas. Thus there is an apparent rejection of aspects of individualism and citizenship associated with Thatcherism. Leadbeater (1997) suggests that the days of 'there is no such thing as society' are over. Thirdly, and most importantly, the re-engagement with Marshall's work has reminded us that he was interested in both social rights and responsibilities. Indeed the balance between rights and responsibilities is at the core of the debate about the third way.

Recent interest in communitarianism is particularly relevant in this respect and is associated with the work of Etzioni (1995) on active citizenship. Politicians on both sides of the Atlantic including Ashdown, Blair and Clinton have endorsed it. Etzioni argues that society has seen an explosion of rights over the last 50 years which have been unaccompanied by responsibilities. To address this problem he suggests a shift in focus towards the self, the community and society and away from the state. His four-point agenda consists of a moratorium on new rights, the linking of rights and responsibilities, the acceptance that certain responsibilities are so fundamental as to entail no reciprocal rights, and that rights and responsibilities must change to reflect new circumstances. Hence, overall, there is a fundamental focus on uplifting moral responsibilities. Such views do not sit comfortably with either old style Labour or neoliberalism, and hence their relevance for the third way. Moreover, Tam (1998) argues that communitarianism is an approach beyond the traditional dualism of left and right politics. It represents a progressive attempt to promote an inclusive society based on citizen participation, mutual responsibility, common values and cooperative enquiry. Nevertheless, as with the third way, there is a significant paradox in that there is an emphasis on a reduced role for government but, at the same time, the necessity for greater state intervention through regulation to achieve these ends.

Ethical and Christian socialism adopts a similar stance and is based on a tradition of the independence of each person. It focuses on encouraging everyone to be self-supporting as well as making an independent contribution to the good of all (Green, 1998). The concept has been rediscovered and is particularly associated with Dennis (1997) as well as appearing to have some influence among leading politicians such as Blair and Field. The former has, for instance, acknowledged the importance in the development of his thinking of the work of Macmurray on the relationship between the individual and society. Indeed, in his foreword to Conford (1996), Blair argues that a new settlement is needed between the individual and society, and implies that the third way is the route forward. Field has been particularly influential in the debate on welfare reform from this viewpoint through numerous publications (such as Field, 1995, 1996) and as Minister for Welfare Reform from May 1997 to July 1998. He has developed a powerful critique of the post-war welfare system arguing that the benefit system has created dependency and actively undermined the moral fabric of society. The answer is to remodel the welfare system so that it harnesses the self-interest of individuals through, for instance, moving towards an insurance rather than means-tested welfare system.

Field (1996) uses the term stakeholding to denote a system whereby the welfare capital, created by individuals through their contributions, is owned by them. Thus, individuals have a degree of independence and this ties in with a strong theme in Giddens' work (1994) on the importance of autonomy of the individual in modern society. However, stakeholding has a much wider connotation with the third way. Hutton (1995, 1997) suggests that the fundamental idea of stakeholding is social and economic inclusion rather than equality. Inclusion implies membership; you cannot be included if you are not a member. But membership entails obligations and responsibilities as well as rights. So a stakeholder society and a stakeholder economy exist where there is a mutuality of rights and obligations constructed around a notion of economic, social and political inclusion. Moreover, it requires a combination of new democratic regulation of organisations and new forms of ownership. This goes beyond promoting community organisations and non profit making bodies and requires more consideration of employee ownership schemes as well as incorporating the views of consumers and local communities.

Social justice, particularly that associated with the Borrie Commission (1994), is also an important theme of the third way. Specific emphasis is placed on the welfare system acting as a springboard for individuals and households in their quest for social citizenship. Thus the Commission argued that the choice was not between universal/non means-tested and selective/means-tested welfare systems. Instead it emphasised the need to develop a wide range of different kinds of provision so as to provide windows of opportunity. Of course, it should be noted that the concept of social justice has much wider ramifications. It is, for example, strongly linked with Rawls' theory of social justice (1972). This has been used and continues to be used by centre-left political parties to act as an underpinning philosophy for social democracy with its emphasis on equality unless inequality is in the wider interest, the compatibility of social justice and capitalism, and the need to define justice. Giddens (1998a) argues, therefore, that social justice lies at the core of third way thinking. In particular, he asserts that social justice requires action on rights and responsibilities at the top as well as the bottom of society. In other words, inequality has to be tackled by policies and programmes aimed at challenging the new centres of corporate and professional power in order to achieve social solidarity and inclusion.

Finally, there is growing interest in social capital, and related concepts such as trust, as part of the third way. Hutton (1995) places emphasis on these aspects which are associated with, for instance the work of Fukuyama (1995), Putnam (1992) and Wilkinson (1996). It is suggested that social inclusion and a well functioning community are linked to a more egalitarian society and social capital is a necessary requirement for a successful economy and society. Building social capital requires an emphasis on encouraging civic spirit and entrepreneurship (see Leadbeater, 1997), strong social networks, powerful local communities and neighbourhoods, and effective social movements.

Thus current political thinking is beginning to coalesce around a range of ideas associated with the third way. Blair (1998) has expressed interest in many of the big ideas highlighted in the previous paragraphs including communitarianism, stakeholding and balancing rights and responsibilities. This is manifesting itself in broad areas of social policy such as the government Green Papers on the family (Home Office, 1998), public health (Department of Health, 1998) and welfare (Department of Social Security, 1998). But how do these ideas link into discrete policy areas such as housing?

HOUSING POLICY AND AN HOLISTIC APPROACH

As has been previously noted, there have been relatively few attempts in the UK to relate housing policy to the third way. In the USA, there is already a much stronger focus on relating concepts such as social capital to housing policy (see *Housing Policy Debate*, 1998). Notable exceptions, however, include Goodlad and Gibb (1994), Clapham et al. (1996) and Maclennan with Pryce (1998). The former re-emphasises the links between poor housing, low incomes, inadequate health, poor educational attainment and high levels of crime. But the authors also point out that housing as part of the social justice debate tends to focus on deprived housing estates and the underclass debate. This has two important limitations in that, first, it diverts attention away from other groups and areas such as young people and older inner city areas. Second, and more importantly, it marginalises the resourcefulness of local people; communities are seen as victims of wider structural changes in society with little ability to change their circumstances. Clearly, there is an implicit interest here in moving beyond the blame the victim scenario of the new right and blame the wider society perspective of the old left. It is not surprising, therefore, to note that this study formed one of many policy papers that influenced the Borrie Commission (1994) and hence Labour Party thinking on welfare as a springboard to opportunity. Clapham et al. (1996) develop these arguments in relation to citizenship and housing policy. They suggest that debates in housing on equal opportunities and participation are central to the concept of citizenship. Moreover, they bring forward good practice examples of how to promote citizenship in relation to deprived social housing estates, meeting the needs of young people, and helping the disabled.

Maclennan with Pryce (1998) argue that we are at the start of a third epoch of policy thinking since 1945. The period from 1945 to 1975 can be broadly labelled a welfare state/Keynesian demand management approach, which could well be identified as part of the first way. The second way, as has previously been noted, is associated with Thatcherism and a monetarist view of the economy along with an atomistic and individualist social theory. The authors note that there were benefits from this neoliberal approach for housing policy including greater efficiency in the use of public resources, the use of private finance, and greater opportunity for households to exercise their choice and preference for owner occupation. They also identify key failures including unfair and inefficient rent and benefit policies and lower levels of investment in housing. These have contributed to an erosion of the social 'glue' or social capital. A third epoch is now materialising and this requires the building of a socially inclusive society and promoting innovation. Reference is, therefore, made to the literature on trust and civic entrepreneurship.

An explicit message which emerges from these studies is the need for joined up thinking and an holistic approach to social policy and housing policy. Indeed, it can be argued that an holistic approach is an important and defining aspect of translating the third way into policy making. It is clearly evident in the government Green Papers on the family (Home Office, 1998) and public health (Department of Health, 1998). The latter, for instance, states: 'Our third way is a national contract for better health. Under this contract, the Government, local communities and individuals will join in partnership to improve all our health' (p. 5). The former aims to place families at the centre of society and identifies the role of government as a strategic enabler and coordinator. A wide range of proposals are identified including the establishment of a National Family and Parenting Institute to promote advice and best practice, an enhanced role for health visitors in providing support for families, and the encouragement of mentoring. As Young and Lemos (1998) show, a radical overhaul of housing policy could usefully contribute to supporting the family by, for example, rethinking social housing allocation policies so encouraging households to be rehoused near relatives and friends.

However, the idea of an holistic approach is not new. For example, the Labour Housing Group (1984) and Darke (1992) have argued the case for such an approach. Battle, as Labour Party housing spokesperson, developed this approach under the phrase 'joined up thinking'. He specifically highlighted the links between housing and employment, housing and health, and housing and the environment. He argued that governments needed to recognise that targeted investment in one policy area could achieve positive gains in other areas. Investment in housing provision could meet housing need in areas of stress, but could also create employment opportunities as well as making positive contributions to reducing poor health and improving the environment.

Others have subsequently developed these arguments, in some cases building directly on the ideas of the Labour Housing Group and in other cases pursuing holistic thinking in a more independent way. Examples include the Chartered Institute of Housing (1995) who published *A Point to Prove*, which argued that housing investment could bring spin off benefits to the government in relation to economic prosperity, as well as making a positive impact on tackling health and environmental concerns. Pressure groups, such as Shelter, who have been keen to move housing up the political agenda, have also followed this line of argument. In a series of research papers (such as Power et al., 1995) they have confirmed the positive impact that targeted housing investment can bring. Without settled housing, for instance, educational performance can be affected as children in poor and insecure housing move more frequently and thus suffer the trauma of school changes with its interruption to study and child–teacher relationships. This is in addition to problems of parental stress and lack of space and facilities at home which are not conducive to study.

More recently, the editor has sought to apply these approaches to the issues of poverty and social exclusion as well as evaluating new

Labour's agenda (Brown and Passmore, 1998). Broadening Battle's idea, it is argued that government should take an approach that is action based and partnership focused. Central government needs to involve local government, other organisations and local communities in its work and by targeting investment and using the skills of each agency, multiple gains can be achieved through joined up solutions. Hence an holistic approach is an important feature of the third way policy. Moreover, linking this idea to the third way provides an opportunity to put joined up thinking at the centre of policy debates. Perri 6 (1997) has argued that an holistic approach represents a radical approach for government reform. It embraces:

- integration across the public sector;
- moving away from curing to preventing problems;
- focus on outcomes rather than outputs and measures of activity;
- emphasising persuasion and bargaining rather than control and coercion.

This approach is illustrated by the work of the Social Exclusion Unit launched by the Prime Minister in December 1997. The Unit has a life of two years and had set itself three initial targets by mid-1998; problem housing estates, rough sleepers and school truancy. Reports on each of these topic areas had been produced by September 1998. Its approach, mirroring the themes identified by Perri 6 (1997), has been based on:

- coordination of existing policies at the national and local levels;
- preventing, for instance, the formation of 'problem' estates;
- promotion of good practice; and
- experimenting with new initiatives.

The Unit has brought together civil servants from the major spending departments to tackle issues which cross traditional organisational boundaries. It also involves seconded staff from local authorities, voluntary sector agencies and business.

At the local level, it is argued that, in relation to social exclusion, local government should take the lead (Brown and Passmore, 1998). This is for three main reasons, of which the first is that communication channels already exist between central and local government. Second, local authorities with their developing enabling role and their democratic base are the best placed organisation to coordinate and implement local strategies. Third, local government has access to a wide range of information on poverty and social exclusion, and already provides services to many of those excluded from mainstream society. Local government's track record is, however, variable. Some authorities have excelled in providing responsive and accountable services that are valued by their citizens. Others, however, have become highly bureaucratic or unresponsive to changing demands of local communities. Good practice examples suggest that local government must act corporately, adopt a strategic approach, be research orientated, support a multi agency framework, and involve local communities.

Thus, without realising it, debates on aspects of housing policy such as poverty and social exclusion are being drawn in to discussions on the third way. However, housing policy debates can often appear irrelevant to housing employees and residents at the grass-roots level.

HOUSING PRACTICE AND THE THIRD WAY

Since May 1997, the Labour government has announced and/or implemented a wide range of policies that impact on housing practice at the local level. These include measures designed to tackle crime and anti-social behaviour on estates (through elements of the Crime and Disorder Act 1998). In addition, specific policies for tackling rough sleeping following the Social Exclusion Unit's Report in July 1998 have been announced (Social Exclusion Unit, 1998). There has also been an emphasis on improving the quality of local services through best value. Finally, extra resources, such as the capital receipts initiatives and new deal for communities, have also been committed to tackling poor housing. It is, of course, tempting to suggest that the definition and clarification of the third way will thus develop, not from an abstract idea, but from a summation of what is actually happening. The danger with such a perspective is that the third way becomes merely what the government does, rather than being based on underlying principles and ideas. It is therefore important to try and identify the linkages between the third way and housing practice.

This can be illustrated through ideas such as quality and best value. In recent years, the complex concept of the quality of public services has been widely discussed and debated (see, for example, Sanderson,

1992). It involves at least three dimensions including, first, the technical quality of the service or product. Second, there is the focus on the way in which the customer is treated. Third, there is the more diffuse aspect of the image of the service or product provider. It is only at the intersection of these three aspects that quality is fully achieved. But as Yates (1995) has pointed out, each dimension of quality means different things to different stakeholders. In particular, there are many stakeholders involved in local authority housing provision including consumers, the community, officers, councillors, regulators (such as the Audit Commission) and central government. Central government, as a stakeholder, may be primarily interested in promoting an economic definition of quality associated with a narrow approach to value for money, while local councillors may be more interested in improving the image of the local authority. Hence, there is considerable difficulty in clarifying the nature of quality, but an analysis based on stakeholding exposes the tensions and conflicts over the provision of quality services.

In many respects, the development of best value is closely associated with stakeholding and quality. Social housing landlords (and in general public sector providers) are being encouraged to blend col-laboration with competition and involve consumers, the community and other providers in the development, implementation and evaluation of services (Department of the Environment, Transport and the Regions, 1998). This involvement of multiple stakeholders with competing priorities will result in conflicts. Third way politics is about identifying these conflicts and, through a transparent framework, prioritising interests. A key theme is the emphasis on continual improvement of services. Considerable interest, therefore, exists on methods for comparing service provision between different organi-sations including performance tables and benchmarking. In addition, there is a growing recognition of the importance of charting changing customer perceptions of services through the use of techniques such as focus groups, juries and customer panels. Thus customers are being encouraged to move away from being passive recipients of welfare services to being active stakeholders.

A final example of the growing links between the big ideas associated with the third way and innovative housing practice is the interest in mutual aid and support. Young and Lemos (1998) argue that social inclusion can be promoted and social capital can be built only if housing organisations adopt a fourfold approach. The four elements are, first, rethinking social housing allocation policies by including mutuality points in assessing need. Households in need of support would, thus, gain extra points and these could be transferred to friends and relatives willing to provide the necessary compassion and help. Second, there is the need for mutual aid compacts whereby residents would agree to commit themselves to the principles and practice of working with and supporting neighbours. Indeed, Manningham Housing Association in Bradford is already piloting such a project on one of its new estates. Third, housing organisations ought to work with and support other organisations who adhere to the principles and practices of mutuality. Again, as Brown and Passmore (1998) show, innovative housing organisations are already doing this through supporting credit unions, community businesses and local exchange trading systems. Finally, there is the need to establish and disseminate good practice on mutual aid and support. Young and Lemos (1998) indicate that a mutual aid housing centre should be established to offer advice on best practice.

Hence debates in housing practice about the quality of services, social housing allocation policies, community lettings, tenancy agreements and probationary tenancies, and anti-poverty initiatives are becoming better informed as the links with the third way and associated concepts are further clarified.

CONCLUSIONS

The third way is not a fully developed political philosophy. In many respects, it is currently more of a symbol of a new way of thinking about economic and social policies which is different from neoliberalism and old style social democracy (Giddens, 1998a). It nevertheless draws on a rich range of ideas which are the centre of much critical debate including citizenship, communitarianism and stakeholding. In some areas of government policy such as public health and welfare, the links between the third way and policy and practice are emerging. But this is not the case for housing. This is in part because, between May 1997 and June 1999, there have been no major government pro-nouncements in the form of discussion documents, Green Papers or White Papers. The most obvious and nearest links to housing in relation to the emerging third way can thus be found only in broader initiatives such as welfare reform, the work of the Social Exclusion Unit and modernising local government. As the previous section indicated, there is a strong case for making the links between the big ideas and emerging housing practice initiatives, but these links must be examined in a critically constructive manner.

The following chapters attempt to take the debate forward by making the connections between housing and other aspects of economic and social policy. There is also a focus on developing a vision for housing as part of the third way, drawing on the perspectives of politicians and academics. And lastly, there is an emphasis on the views of stakeholders. The intention is not to produce a definitive statement on a third way for housing, but instead to open up a critical dialogue on this important issue. Thus the final chapter identifies the strengths and weaknesses of a third way for housing and suggests how the debate can be taken forward.

REFERENCES

Atkinson, R. and Moon, G. (1994) *Urban Policy in Britain* (London: Macmillan).

Barratt-Brown, M. (1984) *Models in Political Economy* (London: Penguin).

Best, R. (1997) 'Unlocking the Doors that Cause the Divide', *Housing Today*, 25 September, p. 11.

Blair, T. (1998) *The Third Way: New Politics for the New Century* (London: The Fabian Society, Fabian Pamphlet 588).

Borrie Commission (1994) *Social Justice: Strategies for National Renewal* (London: Vintage Press).

Brindley, T., Rydin, Y. and Stoker, G. (1996) *Remaking Planning: The Politics of Urban Change* (London: Routledge, 2nd edition).

Brown, T. and Passmore, J. (1998) *Housing and Anti-Poverty Strategies* (Coventry and York: Chartered Institute of Housing and Joseph Rowntree Foundation).

Chartered Institute of Housing (1995) *A Point to Prove* (Coventry: Chartered Institute of Housing).

Chartered Institute of Housing (1997) *Housing and the Comprehensive Spending Review* (Coventry: Chartered Institute of Housing, Briefing Paper).

Clapham, D., Dix, J. with Griffiths, M. (1996) *Citizenship and Housing: Shaping the Debate* (Coventry: Chartered Institute of Housing).

Conford, P. (1996) *The Personal World: John Macmurray on Self and Society* (Edinburgh: Floris Books).

Cuperus, R. and Kandel, J. (eds) (1998) *European Social Democracy: Transformation in Progress* (Amsterdam: Federick Ebert Stiftung).

Darke, J. (ed.) (1992) *The Roof Over Your Head* (Nottingham: Spokesman).

Dennis, N. (1997) *The Invention of Permanent Poverty* (London: Institute for Economic Affairs, Choices in Welfare No. 34).

Department of the Environment, Transport and the Regions (1998) 'Modernising Local Government: Improving Local Services Through Best Value' (London: DETR).

Department of Health (1998) 'Our Healthier Nation: A Contract for Health' (London: The Stationery Office).

Department of Social Security (1998) 'A New Contract for Welfare: New Ambitions for Our Country' (London: The Stationery Office).

Etzioni, A. (1995) *The Spirit of Community* (London: Fontana Press).

Field, F. (1995) *Making Welfare Work* (London: Institute of Community Studies).

Field, F. (1996) *Stakeholder Welfare* (London: Institute for Economic Affairs, Choices in Welfare No. 32).

Fukuyama, F. (1995) *Trust: The Social Virtues and the Creation of Prosperity* (London: Hamish Hamilton).

Giddens, A. (1994) *Beyond Left and Right* (Cambridge: Polity Press).

Giddens, A. (1998a) *The Third Way: The Renewal of Social Democracy* (Cambridge: Polity Press).

Giddens, A. (1998b) 'After the Left's Paralysis', *New Statesman*, 1 May, pp. 18–21.

Gladstone, D. (ed.) (1998) *Before Beveridge: Welfare Before the Welfare State* (London: Institute of Economic Affairs, Choices in Welfare No. 47).

Goodlad, R. and Gibb, K. (eds) (1994) *Housing and Social Justice* (London: Institute for Public Policy Research).

Green, D. (1998) *Benefit Dependency* (London: Institute of Economic Affairs, Choices in Welfare No. 41).

Hargreaves, I. and Christie, I. (eds) (1998) *Tomorrow's Politics: The Third Way and Beyond* (London: Demos).

Harloe, M. (1995) *The People's Home* (Oxford: Blackwell).

Home Office (1998) 'Supporting Families' (London: The Stationery Office).

Housing Policy Debate (1998) 'Social Capital – Its Importance to Housing and Community Development', Vol. 9, No. 1.

Hutton, W. (1995) *The State We're In* (London: Jonathan Cape).

Hutton, W. (1997) *Stakeholding and its Critics* (London: Institute for Economic Affairs, Choices in Welfare No. 36).

Jenkins, S. (1998) 'If the Tories Had Won ... ', *The Times*, 29 April, p. 20.

Jospin, L. (1998) as quoted in Walker, D. (1998) 'Tony's Ology for Sceptics', *Guardian*, 22 September, p. 20.

Labour Housing Group (1984) *Right to a Home* (Nottingham: Spokesman).

Labour Party (1996) *New Labour: New Life for Britain* (London: Labour Party).

Labour Party (1997) *New Labour: Because Britain Deserves Better* (London: Labour Party).

Leadbeater, C. (1997) *Civic Spirit* (London: Demos).

Maclennan, D. with Pryce, G. (1998) *Missing Links: The Economy, Cities and Housing* (London: National Housing Federation).

Macmillan, H. (1966) *The Middle Way: 20 Years After* (London: Macmillan).

Marquand, D. (1998) *Must Labour Win?* (London: The Fabian Society, Fabian Pamphlet 589).

Marshall, T. (1950) *Citizenship and Social Class* (Cambridge: Cambridge University Press).

Marxism Today (1998) 'Special Issue', October–December.

Michel, F. and Bouvet, L. (1998) 'Paris, Bonn, Rome: A Continental Way?', in Hargreaves, I. and Christie, I. (eds) *Tomorrow's Politics: The Third Way and Beyond* (London: Demos).

Morgan, K. (1998) 'The Historical Roots of New Labour', *History Today*, October, pp. 15–17.

Novak, M. (1998) *Is There a Third Way?* (London: Institute of Economic Affairs, Choices in Welfare No. 46).

Perri P. (1997) *Holistic Government* (London: Demos).

Power, S., Whitty, G. and Youdell, D. (1995) *No Place to Learn* (London: Shelter).

Putnam, D. (1992) *Making Democracy Work* (Princeton: Princeton University Press).

Rawls, J. (1972) *A Theory of Justice* (Oxford: Oxford University Press).

Sanderson, I. (ed.) (1992) *Management of Quality in Local Government* (Harlow: Longman).

Social Exclusion Unit (1998) 'Rough Sleeping Report' (London: The Stationery Office).

Tam, H. (1998) *Communitarianism* (London: Macmillan).

Wainwright, H. (1998) 'Is there such a thing as a Third Way in Politics?', *Guardian*, 2 May, p. 2.

Walker, M. (1998) 'Swedish Coalition Plan Reflects EU Shift Away from "Third Way"', *Guardian*, 22 September, p. 25.

Wilkinson, R. (1996) *Healthy Societies* (London: Routledge).

Yates, N. (1995) 'Towards an Understanding of Quality in Social Housing' (Leicester: De Montfort University, Unpublished MSc Housing Dissertation).

Young, M. and Lemos, G. (1998) *The Communities We Have Lost and Can Regain* (London: Lemos and Crane).

Part 1

Making the Connections

Introduction

Tim Brown

One of the key themes of the third way and stakeholding is an holistic approach. This can be defined as the horizontal and vertical integration and linkage of functions and activities. As Perri 6 notes:

> Holism is crucial because the fragmented structure of separate health, law and order, education, housing, child protection and social services has consistently failed to make real inroads on the problems of crime, unemployment, poor educational achievement and ill health. (Perri 6, 1997, p. 37)

Governments have generally organised their services on the basis of a top–down functional approach. Organisational reforms have been attempted, such as the interest in corporate and inter corporate planning in the 1970s, but services remain in practice locked within a functional perspective. The organisation of housing services at the local authority level still reflects a desire to administer discrete tasks in a manner that was criticised in the Cullingworth Report in 1969. The lack of coordination between housing activities as well as with other public services remains as much an issue as it was 30 years ago. There have, of course, been a number of attempts to transform the situation in the last two decades through initiatives by various organisations operating at a range of levels such as:

- the establishment in the early 1990s of regional offices of government rather than regional offices of central government departments;

- the introduction of competitive bidding regimes that attempted to enforce coordination between and within organisations, such as city challenge and single regeneration budgets (SRBs);
- reorganisation of local authority organisational structures to create super departments.

However, these initiatives were not particularly successful for a number of reasons. There was a focus on changing organisational structures in the naïve belief that this would change behaviour, and it was assumed that enforcing coordination from above would lead agencies into a situation where they worked in harmony with each other. Thus the fundamental problem with these initiatives was a misunderstanding of how to change organisational behaviour. Indeed, Hudson (1987) pointed out that the simplistic view of the worthy and necessary requirement for coordination fails to appreciate that there are many costs and disadvantages such as loss of control and power, the use of scarce resources and the uncertain benefits of collaboration. He argued that encouraging collaboration through enforcement and regulation is less likely to be successful in the long run than locally based cooperation based on mutual agreements. This closely links into many of the concepts that were discussed in the previous chapter and which underpin the third way and stakeholding, including building social capital and trust. Achieving coordination may well require the encouragement of individuals as managers of change within and between organisations. Again, some of the ideas on third way thinking are useful in this respect such as the interest in civic entrepreneurs as facilitators of change (see Leadbeater and Goss, 1998).

Nevertheless, the difficulties associated with promoting an holistic approach cannot be underestimated. Although there have been attempts, admittedly sometimes flawed, to promote cooperation in the last two decades, there have also been initiatives that have promoted a narrow functional perspective. These include the use of dedicated single purpose agencies such as urban development corporations and housing action trusts, that make coordination more complex. More importantly, the focus during the last two decades on performance measures based particularly on economy and efficiency rather than effectiveness have resulted in a fixation on outputs rather than outcomes. Hence, there has been an interest in league tables of performance on, for example, the quality of local housing strategies in England, and in output measures such as the number of repairs carried out per operative within a set time period. Such measures may be useful for internal management purposes and for promoting competition, but they are not particularly helpful in encouraging coordination within and between organisations.

There is a long way to go in overcoming the narrow functional approach and achieving an holistic perspective. There are, however, an increasing number of examples of a bottom–up approach in promoting a horizontal integration of activities. Leadbeater and Goss (1998) identify a number of locally based initiatives including the role of a primary school in helping to create a more sustainable community in a deprived part of Newcastle upon Tyne. Brown and Passmore (1998) outline a wide and diverse range of local initiatives developed in recent years by local authorities, housing associations, voluntary sector bodies and local communities in tackling symptoms of poverty and social exclusion. But these are unfortunately only isolated examples. Similarly, while the government is encouraging a more holistic approach through initiatives such as education action zones, health action zones and the work of the Social Exclusion Unit, there is still a need to reinforce the links between housing and other services.

The first few chapters in Part 1 explore the links between service areas. Bhatti concentrates on the links between housing and the environment pointing out that only slow progress is being made. It is now over seven years since the earth summit in Rio de Janeiro, yet the environmental dimensions of housing policy and practice are still relatively marginalised. There are interesting examples of joined up and holistic thinking, but it is only recently that environmentalists and housing practitioners have started to engage in meaningful discussions and debates. Conway in Chapter 4 highlights the need to rediscover the links between housing and health. She points out that during the nineteenth and early twentieth centuries these links were well understood and played an important part in influencing policy. These themes need to be emphasised once again so that housing can play its part in improving health conditions. She finally suggests that the Labour government has made a useful beginning during its first two years in office in stressing the importance of the public health agenda.

Chapter 5 by Paterson and Macfarlane analyses the links between social exclusion and the role of social housing providers. They point out that the relationship between residualisation of social housing and poverty and social exclusion are only too evident. But the key question is what can social housing providers do to tackle the symptoms of poverty and social exclusion? They suggest that there are already a wide range of possible actions which can contribute to the role of social housing landlords as social or civic entrepreneurs (see also Leadbeater and Goss, 1998). They also point out that the development of housing related mainstream training and employment initiatives will only address certain features of social exclusion. Therefore there is a need to expand into more innovative areas such as intermediate labour market initiatives and local exchange trading schemes (see also Brown and Passmore, 1998). However, expansion into these areas of activity by registered social landlords will require financial and legislative changes to enable a greater focus on non housing projects. At the time of writing, January 1999, it appears that the government is willing to make the necessary legislative changes but it is less clear if additional resources will be made available.

In contrast, Brown and Maye-Banbury in Chapter 6 explore the badly neglected area of the links between housing and education. As they point out, there has been relatively little research on these links, but education is one of the government's prime areas of concern. Improving educational attainment is one of the main planks of the government's social and welfare policies, but they argue that the government must recognise that improving housing opportunities is also an essential prerequisite for achieving these aims. Moreover, from a similar perspective to Paterson and Macfarlane, they indicate that housing organisations at a local level are already becoming more adept at developing relevant education related schemes with other partners. Nevertheless, there are currently constraints on how far such holistic projects can be developed.

These chapters therefore highlight a variable level of integration between housing and other issues. The relationship between social housing and poverty and social exclusion is reasonably well understood and locally based initiatives exist and are being developed. But this level of development is much less evident in relation to housing and the environment and especially housing and education. As Oxley shows in Chapter 7, there is a European dimension to these issues. Poverty, social exclusion and poor housing conditions are more likely to be tackled if there is economic growth, and closer European integration through, for instance, monetary union may contribute to this situation as well as providing greater opportunities for investing in housing related projects. Even so, there will still be a need to redistribute resources within and between member states. Finally, Chapter 8 investigates the situation in the USA. Goetz points out that the process of implementing the third way started in the early 1990s. As in Britain, housing policy is not regarded as a major political issue and, moreover, the possibilities of implementing third way policies for welfare have been circumscribed in recent years by the political situation in the USA. There has been a lack of a national coherent coordinated approach, but there have been some interesting individual holistic initiatives particularly focused on public housing. Social housing providers in the UK may be able to learn lessons from such projects. But more generally, the experience of the third way in the USA suggests that a degree of caution may be necessary about the ability of governments to develop a third way approach.

REFERENCES

Brown, T. and Passmore, J. (1998) *Housing and Anti-Poverty Initiatives* (Coventry and York: Chartered Institute of Housing and Joseph Rowntree Foundation).

Cullingworth Report (1969) 'Council Housing: Purposes, Procedures, Priorities' (London: HMSO).

Hudson, B. (1987) 'Collaboration in Social Welfare: A Framework for Analysis', *Policy and Politics*, Vol. 15, No. 3, pp. 175–82.

Leadbeater, C. and Goss, S. (1998) *Civic Entrepreneurship* (London: Demos and Public Management Foundation).

Perri 6 (1997) *Holistic Government* (London: Demos).

3

Housing and the Environment

Mark Bhatti

INTRODUCTION

> Act One of the Green movement's paradise play is over, and it is time
> the curtain was lifted on Act Two. (Dobson, 1990, p. 213)

Dobson sensed that by 1990 the era of the environmental critique of
modern society was coming to an end: it was time to propose solutions.
In housing, at that time, most academics, policy makers and practitioners were not yet aware of the environmental impact of housing,
or even that housing policy should play a part in sustainable futures;
they were not even in the audience. By the end of the 1990s, however,
things have changed considerably and there is increasing debate
about environmental sustainability and housing policy and practice.

Even so, we still have a long way to go to the final curtain. As the
recent debate on sustainable housing shows (Williams, 1997), the term
is often used to denote the stability of social and economic processes
underpinning housing policy, not saving the planet. This particular
debate has missed an opportunity to make links across disciplines, and
has failed to engage more directly with the new environmental agenda
(see Bhatti et al., 1994). If future generations are to have a stake, then
we must give them an opportunity to have their say in today's debate
about how to meet our housing needs. This involves undertaking a
re-evaluation of current housing analysis, policy and practice, with

a view towards increased environmental protection. And we must show what green housing policies might look like. The approach being advocated here is that a green housing policy must also tackle inequality and promote social justice; we must not save the planet by making the poor even poorer. Housing is a major arena of activity because it touches every global citizen: after all, every one needs a home!

The integration of social, economic and environmental factors into future housing policy is the next step that needs to be taken if housing is to be sustainable in an holistic sense. An indicators approach is suggested so as to get us beyond the critique and into the realm of developing solutions. This step is even more necessary now that housing has become part of the wider agenda of health, poverty, education, social exclusion and employment. By linking local housing problems to global environmental change, the aim is to develop a green housing policy that includes social, economic and resource issues. The key principle of sustainable development, as applied to housing, is to ensure that our housing needs are not met by making poor people pay, or by compromising future generations and their ability to meet their own needs; the future becomes a major stakeholder in today's decisions. This lies at the heart of green housing policy, and housing must be centre stage in debates about all our futures.

HOUSING AND THE NEW ENVIRONMENTAL AGENDA

The fact that the environment is now being taken much more seriously in housing circles is a culmination of international, national and local events. International activity towards environmental protection has gathered pace since the early 1970s, but it was with the publication of 'Our Common Future', popularly known as the 'Bruntland Report' (World Commission on Environment and Development, 1987), that the idea of sustainable development began to take shape. A new phase was unveiled by the United Nations Conference on Environment and Development (UNCED), known as the Earth Summit held in Rio in 1992, which continued in Kyoto in 1997. In the 1990s, the new environmental agenda has been effectively set whereby sustainability and social justice are the key aims of economic development.

Global warming is perhaps the most important problem facing the world today. Some scientists believe that the climate is changing due to the greenhouse effect. As carbon dioxide (CO_2) is the main greenhouse gas, attention has focused on reducing CO_2 in the atmosphere. The burning of fossil fuels such as coal, oil and gas for the production of energy is the major contributor to CO_2 emissions, and unless energy comes from renewable sources such as wind, wave or tidal power, it will continue to generate climate change. Buildings account for 56 per cent of energy consumption in the UK, of which two-thirds is in the domestic sector. Energy is consumed in the production, exchange and consumption of housing, and design has a major impact on energy use in the home.

Agreements on specific action to reduce global warming were key outputs of Rio and Kyoto. Thus there is a commitment by the UK government to reduce CO_2 emissions to 1990 levels by 2000 and thereafter till 2010; this is effectively a reduction of 20 per cent and requires vigorous action on all fronts, particularly a reduction of energy use in the domestic sector.

By far the most important environmental policy document to emerge is Agenda 21 (see Bhatt et al., 1994), which identifies key problems and the groups most affected, and promotes action by governmental and non governmental organisations with an emphasis on participation by the community. The document provides the basic reasons for environmental action at the international and national levels, and sets a Local Agenda 21 framework for the local level. Internationally the idea of sustainable development, growth of cities and the provision of shelter, have been linked though the United Nations Habitat II conference in Istanbul in 1996. These links are now beginning to appear both nationally and locally.

At the national level there is now more focus on the environment with a review of the UK's sustainable development policy receiving much attention. This will have major implications for housing as international agreements on global warming, for example, feed through to national priorities for reductions in CO_2. Cuts in CO_2 can come about by cutting energy consumption, particularly in the domestic sector, and the Home Energy Conservation Act 1995 (HECA) places an obligation on local authorities to produce plans for a 30 per cent reduction in domestic energy use over the next 10 to 15 years. Up to now HECA has been a planning exercise, but if resources can be made available for local authorities to implement these plans, it could have a major impact on reducing energy use.

Even though global issues have sparked off environmental concern the local level is becoming more and more important. For example, two-thirds of Agenda 21 objectives set at the Earth Summit can only be fulfilled through action by local authorities working with business, the community and voluntary bodies such as housing associations. So Local Agenda 21 includes a major role for local government, the voluntary sector, private organisations and community participation, all working at the local level to develop and implement environmental action plans (Agyeman and Evans, 1994). The changing role of local authorities from being direct providers to enablers, in a number of services including housing, has major implications for environmental action in this context, and could mean a new emphasis on an environmental strategy for housing across all tenures (Brown, 1994). The new environmental agenda therefore challenges traditional housing policies, and pushes national housing debate towards the search for environmentally responsible solutions to housing problems. These new dilemmas signify a much needed discussion about the role of housing in producing wider environmental impacts, as well as the ways in which the housing system could be made more sustainable.

But how are green housing polices to be pursued? The wider environmental impacts of housing relate to the particular way it is produced, exchanged, managed and used. The large number of factors involved, and their complexity, is often a barrier to thinking environmentally about the housing process. The current system of housing provision in the UK has major impacts relating to use of land, pollution, waste, depletion of resources, health and energy use, operating across different spatial levels and time scales. Decisions by individual consumers, the government, the private sector and housing management organisations can affect local and global environmental change. In the context of housing there are five key (interrelated) areas that require attention when formulating a green housing policy. These relate to the planning of cities; housing and neighbourhood; housing design, building and materials; the health of the occupants; and finally, energy use in the home.

SUSTAINABLE CITIES AND HOUSING

Housing is a major item of land use in the urban areas in the UK. The form of towns and cities, whether they are compact or dispersed, can have a major impact on the amount of land used for housing development and associated resource requirements such as transport. In this context land, labour and housing markets often combine to produce severe environmental impacts that affect the overall quality of life in the city. The urban form, which interfaces a home, work, shopping and leisure, may enable sustainable practices, or it may (as is more likely) be a part of the problem in that environmental friendly practices are minimised. The announcement by the previous government (Department of the Environment, 1996) that up to 4.4 million households will need to be accommodated by 2016, introduces a new dimension into the debate about the shape of our cities.

The idea of the sustainable city has focused attention on the long-term trends towards suburban and semi rural developments with more and more pressure on dispersed developments and encroachment on the green belt. The density of residential areas impacts directly on car and energy use; thus low densities encourage car use whereas high densities encourage walking or the use of bicycles. Research has highlighted the negative effects of low density, dispersed settlements particularly in terms of energy use and car pollution (Breheny, 1992). The debate now centres on whether cities should be made more compact by increasing housing densities within existing urban areas. Increasing urban capacity presents a green solution as mixed use settlements cut down on the need to travel and cities become people friendly, but there are dilemmas.

The key argument now is about where new housing should be built, that is brown field versus green field sites, or to put it more crudely, the city versus the countryside. Because of increasing protest from those seeking to protect the latter, the government has recently announced that approximately 60 per cent of new developments will be within the city on brown field sites. This effectively means bringing derelict industrial or other land into use for housing. Apart from the added problem that much of this land is contaminated and expensive to develop for residential use, the dilemma here is to what extent the countryside lobby are seeking to conserve not just the green belt but their comfortable way of life. This policy could mean denying future generations access to decent homes in pleasant surroundings, and the debate has pushed aside the more fundamental question of who new housing is for: low income, or high income households? The outcome of many local disputes now emerging about where new housing should be located could be that figures are revised downwards, and it is social housing that disappears from future provision.

Should we not take this opportunity to green the inner city so that everyone can enjoy contact with nature? Why should poor inner city residents want more overcrowding? The green movement needs to consider the social consequences of trapping more and more low income families in an increasingly congested inner city.

A green housing policy would seek to advocate using the houses that we have more efficiently and effectively by, for example, bringing some of the estimated 1 million empty homes in the UK into use. There are also extra units to be created by converting empty offices into flats, increasing the use of empty flats over shops, and investing in rundown housing (often in the inner city) that can be brought back into use rather than be demolished. The rise in demand is mainly from single person households, so more innovative and imaginative ways of providing housing for this group need to be found. One possible method is to encourage communal living so that densities can be increased in specific areas.

There needs to be innovation in the house building industry, and tighter regulation of how new housing is designed and built, which materials are used and to what standards. So far house builders have been able to accommodate pressures to improve environmental performance, either by ignoring them because they are voluntary, or by ensuring that environmental regulation (for example energy labelling) is set so low that they do not have to innovate (Barlow and Bhatti, 1997). The use of the planning system to deliver sustainable urban development is crucial; this means incorporating environmental appraisal schemes into the planning guidance, so that builders can design environmentally friendly homes (Barker-Wolff, 1994). There is also a role here for the price mechanism to kick-start the building of green homes, either in the form of tax breaks to builders or lower VAT so that consumer demand can be made more effective. Greening the housing market is now on the agenda, and with appropriate institutional pressures and market mechanisms green consumer demand for environmentally friendly and energy efficient homes can be cultivated (see Bhatti and Sarno, 1996).

SUSTAINABLE NEIGHBOURHOODS

These issues relate to the immediate locality or neighbourhood where the design and layout of estates and their location in relation to other services may affect the potential for sustainable practices (URBED, 1995). Recycling schemes or local exchange trading schemes (LETS) may become more viable if they occur within small neighbourhoods. Indeed, as the food in the cities projects have shown, the community can profit from local production of food in between the tower blocks. But there are pressures for residential developments on this land. For example, local authorities are releasing approximately 50 allotment areas per year for housing development, but allotments could be turned into community gardens where groups of people could cultivate vegetables and flowers, selling the produce to local families at low prices. These types of projects are often socially, economically and environmentally beneficial, and most important of all, are controlled by the community. The government can encourage greening the city initiatives by helping to break down departmental barriers and ensuring that funding is flexible. Local authorities can support and fund projects that link housing, employment and environmental solutions.

HOUSING DESIGN AND MATERIALS

The key question in design is how much of the layout of the estate and the design of the house itself can been given over to environmental features. Again this is an important juncture because architects incorporate features which can have negative or positive impacts on the environment. These include:

- siting for maximum solar gain;
- the design of heating and lighting systems;
- spaces for recycling;
- minimising water use;
- specifications for materials that are to be used for construction;
- the durability and flexibility of the dwelling;
- the density and scale of the buildings;
- the disposal of the dwelling at the end of its life;
- how much of the design encourages an environmentally friendly lifestyle.

All these features have a significance throughout the whole life of the house. There is considerable good practice in this area, and simple methodologies such as the Building Research Establishment

Environmental Assessment Method (BREAM) for green building against which to judge new housing are well known. Technology and eco design are not barriers and indeed there are a vast number of demonstration projects and solutions being offered (most within existing technologies). The question really is: why are these solutions not being taken up in the mainstream housing industry? (see Barlow and Bhatti, 1997).

Environmental issues in housing also include production of materials for housing development and refurbishment. For example, land is taken in the extraction of aggregates, stone, iron, clay and wood. The manufacture of primary products into building materials such as bricks, steel, glass, copper and plastics uses non renewable resources and is energy intensive. The house building industry has a major impact on natural sites that can threaten loss of habitat and bio diversity both locally and globally. There is also the environmental cost of transporting these materials from quarries to factories to construction sites.

The polluting by-products of the manufacturing process is also a problem; for example, 90 per cent of the raw material used to produce chemically based paints ends up as waste, much of which is toxic. This is in contrast to paint produced from natural oils, resins and dyes where only 10 per cent of the raw material forms harmless waste. Because houses are not normally designed from a cradle to grave perspective, there are often major problems with the disposal of building materials when the dwelling is at the end of its useful life; most are dumped in land fill sites or, like plastics, tend to be incinerated resulting in toxic gases. A clearer labelling system presenting the negative effects of certain materials would be extremely useful information to occupiers, and it would give policy makers and consumers better guidance as to the wider impacts of housing. There could also be greater encouragement through incentives for house builders to use recycled materials as well as locally sourced products.

HOUSING AND HEALTH

There are health issues (for detailed discussion see Chapter 4) arising from the state of our housing stock (Burridge and Ormandy, 1993; Ineichen, 1993). The microclimate inside the home can cause ill health, arising from cold homes, dampness and pollution, and the effects on the well-being of occupants is an important issue. Modern dwellings are full of synthetic materials including noxious chemicals often contained within a tightly sealed interior full of mechanical and electrical systems. The building and do it yourself (DIY) industries use chemicals in most products such as paints, varnishes, glues, timber treatments and plastics. Many of these chemicals slowly biodegrade over time (or outgas) and the long-term effects of this on occupants are as yet unknown. Sick building syndrome is now widely recognised as a problem in office buildings, but an understanding of similar effects arising out of daily exposure to small quantities of toxic gases in the home has not been developed. This pollution in the home would suggest there is a role for greater information, for instance, on the effects of materials that are traditionally used for DIY or internal decoration.

It is widely being recognised that improvements in housing can lead to improvements in health that may also impact on expenditure on health services (Markus, 1994). The new public health agenda focuses on prevention and moves away from a biomedical model of health (Department of Health, 1998). It seeks to promote action in areas that can enable people to lead healthier lives. In this context decent housing is one key factor which could lead to long-term improvements for a healthier nation (Ambrose, 1997).

HOUSING AND ENERGY EFFICIENCY

In the UK reduction of household energy consumption is seen to be a key factor in stabilising CO_2 emissions thereby relieving the pressure on global warming. Attention is focused on two related measures: first, to reduce the use of fuel, that is energy conservation through the actions of households themselves; second, in making the dwellings more energy efficient, which effectively involves some form of capital investment (Taylor, 1993). The Energy Savings Trust, for example, is targeting higher investment in energy efficiency. But the real dilemma is dealing with the fuel poor who often need to increase energy use to achieve warmth, but cannot afford to do so. A different strategy needs to be developed for low income households.

There is a long-standing joke among energy managers that in Sweden more people die from laughing at the poor standards of the UK housing stock, than die from the cold. In Britain there are between 30,000 and 40,000 excess winter deaths each year caused by the simple fact that on average our homes are not warm enough. Nearly 8 million households in Britain suffer from fuel poverty (Boardman, 1994). Quite simply, these households pay high heating costs because the homes they live in are cold, damp and poorly insulated. Energy inefficient homes provide unhealthy living conditions, as well as generating high levels of greenhouse gas emissions. The three main factors contributing to fuel poverty are substandard housing, rising fuel prices and low incomes. On top of this most households are also socially excluded and may suffer from unemployment with little access to services and facilities that are enjoyed by mainstream society. Combating fuel poverty, or developing a policy for affordable warmth, should be a priority as a number of issues can be tackled at once. The benefits of affordable warmth are that the households become healthier, they have more money to spend on food and other essential items, and landlords or house owners cut down on management and maintenance costs as the stock is improved. Energy efficient investment programmes in Glasgow, for example, have shown there are also benefits to the local economy as local jobs are generated in the insulation industries, and more of the money saved from fuel goes on local goods and services.

Estimates suggest that £1.2 billion is needed annually to improve the UK stock to affordable warmth standards over a 15-year period. Clear direction from 'new Labour' to increase capital investment in the housing stock would produce many benefits, not least the savings in other areas such as the NHS (Boardman and Hunt, 1995). The second problem has been that often the money that is available is not used effectively. This is mainly because the organisations and groups working with poor households do not consider energy issues to be a priority, and there is a lack of inter-agency coordination on fuel poverty issues. And yet improving living conditions by enabling people to keep warm can have a big impact on the general quality of life. Fuel poverty needs to be tackled urgently if the poor are not to suffer new forms of social exclusion. Local authorities, in their new role as energy conservation authorities under the Home Energy Conservation Act (HECA), could achieve much more success if their HECA plans were linked to increased resources.

INDICATORS FOR SUSTAINABLE HOUSING

How are green housing policies to be pursued? What role does local and national government play? Can regulation produce the desired results? Should the housing market be left to green itself? (See Bhatti, 1996, for a discussion on policy instruments in relation to green housing.) If sustainable housing is a goal then we need some way of knowing whether we are moving in the right direction as well as measuring the effects of specific decisions. This means producing indicators that can sensitise housing to specific environmental concerns, as well as linking them to more traditional social and economic goals such as affordability or housing need. As a follow-up to the Rio Earth Summit the Local Government Management Board is coordinating a 'local indicators project' (LGMB, 1994), which should provide decision makers with the tools to develop specific sustainable policies. However, though housing indicators are mentioned there is considerable confusion, and no intensive work has been done specifically on housing in the project. Thus there is a major gap in our knowledge relating to sustainable housing indicators.

The current debate about sustainable housing presents an opportunity for a more holistic and integrated view about the housing system of the future, and for the housing and environmental movements to begin to talk to each other. In remedying this lack of housing it may be useful to take the broad LGMB approach and apply it to housing (see Bhatti, 1998). But what is an indicator and why is it important? A sustainability indicator is a tool by which we can measure and identify progress towards a sustainable society. Such indicators can allow us to make decisions and choices about which path to follow, and which changes in behaviour are required. They need to be linked to both local and global sustainability. Secondly, they should be not more but less sophisticated; thus indicators must be relevant to ordinary people and easy to understand. Their simplicity allows the public to monitor trends and participate in environmental actions. Finally, the production of indicators appears to offer policy makers technical solutions to problems, but it should be noted that indicators cannot tell us how decisions should be made. There are still political processes to go through in achieving sustainability goals.

CONCLUSIONS

We have come a long way since the 1992 Earth Summit with much more awareness now of the ways in which housing has wider environmental impacts. This government is picking up the pieces after decades of neglect of the housing stock. A long-term strategy for investment in improving energy efficiency, especially for those on low incomes, needs to be established. Greater encouragement must be given for green building and design through more information, dissemination of good practice, and financial incentives as well as the setting of higher environmental energy standards for new and existing housing.

Questions need to be raised as to why even the simplest of green solutions are not being implemented, especially when the economic benefits outweigh all other considerations as energy efficiency saves you money! Much is being done, but many projects appear to be marginal, and after the demonstration effect has worn off innovative features are not finding their way into the mainstream. Introducing a green dimension in housing debates also means that there are now new dilemmas to confront, especially in the social housing sector. For example, for a given resource should we build higher quality homes, recognising that fewer units will be completed? Or how far should the green belt be protected if housing needs are rising? There need to be long-term policies for improvement and an emphasis on the social and economic benefits of a green housing policy and practice. Social equality should be the guiding principle of environmental policy so that the houses of low income groups are improved first.

There are still gaps and many barriers to greener housing (especially in the private sector) which can only be removed by increased environmental regulation on the one hand and financial incentives for good practice on the other. In the past, the environmental movement has not fully appreciated the role that housing plays in generating environmental impacts; at the same time the housing movement has largely ignored these green issues. Now at least they are talking to each other, and in some cases actually reading from the same text. Hopefully all those engaged in housing policy and environmental action can be a part of the same play, for the sake of all our futures.

REFERENCES

Agyeman, J. and Evans, B. (eds) (1994) *Local Environmental Policies and Strategies* (London: Longman).

Ambrose, P. (1997) 'Better Housing as Preventative Medicine', *Housing Review*, May/June.

Barker-Wolff, S. (1994) 'Environmental Assessment and the Development Process', in Bhatti, M., Brooke, J. and Gibson, M. (1994) *Housing and the Environment: A New Agenda* (Coventry: Chartered Institute of Housing).

Barlow, J. and Bhatti, M. (1997) 'Environmental Performance as a Competitive Strategy', *Planning Practice and Research*, Vol. 12, No. 1, pp. 33–44.

Bhatti, M. (1996) 'Housing and Environmental Policy in the UK', *Policy and Politics*, Vol. 24, No. 2, pp. 159–70.

Bhatti, M. (1998) 'Squaring the Circle', *Housing*, June, pp. 44–5.

Bhatti, M., Brooke, J. and Gibson, M. (eds) (1994) *Housing and the Environment: A New Agenda* (Coventry: Chartered Institute of Housing).

Bhatti, M. and Sarno, C. (1996) 'Who Greens the Housing Market?', in Rydin, Y. (ed.) *The Environmental Impact of Land and Property Management* (London: John Wiley).

Boardman, B. (1994) 'Energy Efficiency Measures and Social Inequality', in Bhatti, M., Brooke, J. and Gibson, M. (1994) *Housing and the Environment: A New Agenda* (Coventry: Chartered Institute of Housing).

Boardman, B. and Hunt, S. (1995) 'Defining the Problem', in Markus, T. (ed.) *Domestic Energy and Affordable Warmth* (London: E & F N Spon, Watt Committee Report, No. 30).

Breheny M. (ed.) (1992) *Sustainable Development and Urban Form* (London: Pion).

Brown, T. (1994) 'Local Housing Strategies and Environmental Policy', in Bhatti, M., Brooke, J. and Gibson, M. (eds) *Housing and the Environment: A New Agenda* (Coventry: Chartered Institute of Housing).

Burridge, R. and Ormandy, D. (1993) *Unhealthy Housing: Research, Remedies and Reform* (London: E & F N Spon).

Department of the Environment (1996) 'Where will we Live?' (London: HMSO).

Department of Health (1998) 'Our Healthier Nation' (London: The Stationery Office).

Dobson A. (1990) *Green Political Thought: An Introduction* (London: Routledge).

Ineichen, B. (1993) *Homes and Health: How Housing and Health Interact* (London: E & F N Spon).

LGMB (Local Government Management Board) (1994) *Local Agenda 21: Principles and Process* (Luton: LGMB).

Markus, T. (ed.) (1994) *Domestic Energy and Affordable Warmth* (London: E & F N Spon, Watt Committee Report, No. 30).

Taylor, L. (1993) *Energy Efficient Homes* (London and Coventry: Association for the Conservation of Energy and the Institute of Housing).

URBED (1995) *21st Century Homes: Building to Last* (York: Joseph Rowntree Foundation).

Williams, P. (ed.) (1997) *Directions in Housing Policy: Towards Sustainable Housing* (London: Paul Chapman).

World Commission on Environment and Development (WCED) (1987) *Our Common Future* (Oxford: Oxford University Press).

4

Housing and Health

Jean Conway

INTRODUCTION

> The connection between health and the dwellings of the population
> is one of the most important that exists. (Florence Nightingale)

The link between housing and health was recognised by the Victorians,
who introduced improvements to city slums. That connection has been
largely forgotten as general housing standards have improved, major
epidemics have been eliminated and housing has developed as a
separate area of public policy. However, there is now renewed interest
in the relationship between housing and health and a growing
recognition of the need to rebuild the links between services. This
needs to be tackled both strategically and at service delivery level. Much
could be achieved within a relatively short time-scale, given the
political will.

LINKS BETWEEN HOUSING AND HEALTH

The emergence of housing policies in the nineteenth century arose
directly out of a concern with health. The urban slums were centres
of infectious diseases, crime and poverty, which threatened the health
and stability of the cities. During the cholera epidemics doctors saw
at first hand the appalling conditions and were among those who
spearheaded campaigns for public action (Gauldie 1974). It can be

argued that improvements in housing and the environment have had a far greater effect on the general health of the population than any advances in medicine.

Nineteenth-century reformers believed that state intervention in housing would break the link between poor housing and poor health. The removal of the worst slums in the nineteenth century, and again in the 1930s and 1950s, was assumed to deal with unhealthy housing once and for all. During the twentieth century the focus of housing policy gradually drifted away from dealing with poor quality towards other issues such as ownership and management, access and cost. The divorce between housing and health policies was eventually reflected in the establishment of the Ministry of Housing in 1951, separate from the Ministry of Health. Responsibilities for public health have since become fragmented and divided between a wide range of central and local government agencies.

However, despite a century of public health and housing intervention, slum clearance, general improvements in health and near eradication of the main killer diseases, those with the worst health still live in the poorest housing. There is a wealth of evidence to show that good housing remains crucial to good health (Arblaster and Hawtin, 1993; Burridge and Ormandy, 1993; Byrne et al., 1986; Ineichen, 1993). While there have been academic debates about the extent to which studies prove a causal link between housing conditions and health, anyone working with those who live in poor housing is aware of the detrimental impact this has on their physical and mental health. There are also serious economic implications for many other services such as health, education, social services, fire and the police (Barrow and Bachan, 1997). The Department of Health has estimated the cost to the NHS of illness from condensation in the home alone to be £800 million a year (cited in Burrows and Walentowicz, 1992).

In the last decade or so there has been a renewed awareness of the fundamental relationship between housing and health among both housing and health professionals. From the housing perspective there has been a realisation that bad housing conditions persist. The majority of unfit property is older owner occupied housing and improvement activity is failing to keep pace with deterioration (Leather et al., 1994) . Some local authority blocks of flats are also in very poor condition, and are affected by severe dampness, condensation and unaffordable heating. The provision of better heating and insulation improves residents' health and reduces health service costs (Barrow and Bachan, 1997).

From the health perspective there has been a realisation that health inequalities persist. As in housing, the complacency following decades of state programmes has been shattered. The Black Report and subsequent studies have demonstrated widening inequalities in health and that these are related to the environment (Benzeval, 1995; Townsend et al., 1988). At the same time a new recognition of poverty has undermined assumptions about the effectiveness of the welfare state. Bad housing exacerbates the health problems of the poor. They live in the worst housing, can't afford to adequately heat their homes, experience water disconnections and have poor access to adequate health care (Boardman, 1991; Curtis, 1991). Homelessness could be regarded as living in the most extreme form of unhealthy housing and there are shocking figures on morbidity and mortality rates among the homeless (Conway, 1988; Keys and Kennedy, 1992). Yet homeless people have very poor access to health services (Fisher and Collins, 1993; Victor, 1992).

More recently the care in the community policy has brought into focus the essential links between housing and health. This policy depends upon vulnerable people being able to live in healthy homes. But in reality local authorities are often only able to provide accommodation on unpopular poor quality estates which is neither healthy nor safe, and have had to cut back on improvement grants for those in inadequate private sector housing (Heywood, 1996). It is increasingly recognised that poor health limits housing opportunities and those in the worst health struggle to gain access to decent housing (Smith and Mallinson, 1997). There is thus a close relationship between inequalities in housing and in health.

COORDINATION OF HOUSING AND HEALTH SERVICES

To reforge the links between housing and health, agencies need to work more closely together. Almost every housing activity has a health impact and requires cooperation with some part of the health system. This includes the assessment of housing need, which should also take into account health and care needs to be effective. This particularly applies to medical priority assessments for social housing and the acceptance of homeless vulnerable people. From the perspective of other agencies, assessment for community care and hospital discharge of frail and vulnerable people should consider housing needs.

Housing management requires collaboration with a range of other agencies as increasing numbers of vulnerable people live in council and housing association housing. Housing managers are often the first to be aware of a tenant in distress and find themselves providing support beyond basic housing management, while the role of sheltered housing wardens has extended into caring (Clapham and Franklin, 1994).

The quality and quantity of new house building and renovation work has a direct impact on health. Building regulations, fitness standards, improvement grants and the provision of aids and adaptations can determine whether or not a resident can remain independent or must move into residential care. The nature of new housing development also affects the sustainability of the housing stock for future generations (see Chapter 3).

Housing, health and care programmes are most effective with the active involvement of users, whose needs span the services of all these agencies. If agencies respond together they will be far more effective than working in isolation. Inter-agency collaboration has become a popular phrase. Everyone pays lip service to the concept but few are willing to put the necessary effort and resources into achieving it. At the national level until recently there has been no clear agenda or coordination of government programmes within which local agencies could operate collectively. The proliferation of agencies in the last decade, the introduction of the competitive culture, the use of narrow performance indicators and the widespread lack of resources have inhibited inter-agency working. The Labour government is now beginning to change the national agenda and place far more emphasis on collaboration and partnerships.

Local agencies have been working in a non collaborative climate for many years and have not been working together effectively to provide services:

- There is a widespread lack of understanding of the roles and responsibilities of other agencies and the boundaries between them, particularly between the voluntary and statutory sectors.
- There is limited knowledge of what services other agencies provide and who to contact, as well as cultural and professional differences.

- Where there is collaboration at a strategic level this is often not followed through and operated at a service delivery level.
- The involvement of users is unsuccessful at a strategic level and agencies rarely provide a coordinated response to user demands.
- At the level of service delivery there is a lack of communication between those working for different agencies, little knowledge of who does what, difficulties in sharing information, false expectations and often deep mistrust of other professional groups (Arblaster et al., 1996).

There are some good examples of collaboration between agencies to provide specific services but these tend to be ad hoc and are the exception rather than the rule. Nevertheless, these show that there is a willingness to try to overcome barriers on the ground (Means et al., 1997; Arblaster et al., 1998). However, the scope for better inter-agency working will remain limited until central government takes the lead.

TOWARDS A NEW GOVERNMENT AGENDA FOR HOUSING AND HEALTH

Central government must spearhead a new approach which recognises the essential links between services, set a new agenda which breaks down the barriers between agencies, provide flexible resources which support collaboration and generate a new climate of cooperation and understanding. The Labour government is moving in the right direction but the rhetoric must be followed through into practical action.

This new approach to housing and health should apply right across the range of policy areas and can be broken down into four very broad strands: coordinated policy aims, financial measures, better housing standards and administrative arrangements which foster and encourage closer working links.

Coordinated Policy Aims

Shared goals and vision for a broad public health agenda across all government departments are essential. Housing must be a key part of that agenda. It should be recognised that health is determined by factors other than medicine. The Labour government has moved towards this by appointing a Minister for Public Health and a Cabinet Committee of Ministers from twelve Departments. The new public health agenda is an encouraging starting point, with a remit to tackle inequalities in health and the underlying causes (Department of Health, 1998).

While housing has been included as one of the relevant issues, it does not feature very strongly in the government's proposals. Housing must be highlighted as an essential prerequisite to reducing health inequalities. Local authority housing departments should play a key role in:

- the new health improvement programmes;
- the proposed health impact assessments involving measuring the impact of spending in one service area on another, which should be used to highlight the health benefits of housing improvements;
- the health action zones, which should be required to include a focus on poor housing and homelessness.

Health authorities should be encouraged to set specific targets which relate health and housing, such as reducing illness associated with poor housing conditions, and these should be reflected in performance indicators.

Some groups of people have needs which tend to fall between the responsibilities of several agencies and are not a central concern to any. These include street homeless people, refugees, asylum seekers, travellers and those with a severe long-term illness such as HIV/AIDS. Their needs are complex and can only be met through agencies working together. Central government has an important role in raising the profile of these groups and clarifying responsibilities so that the relevant agencies provide a coordinated response to their needs. The appointment of a homelessness czar may be a good model for meeting the needs of other groups of people.

One way to break down the barriers between services is to ensure there is greater understanding of the role of other professions and agencies. The government should require that professional bodies include an understanding of other relevant professions in their qual-ifications. There should be strong encouragement for local joint training programmes, job swaps and forums which bring together those working for housing agencies, health authorities, environmental health and social care agencies in the statutory and voluntary sectors.

Financial Measures

It is impossible to consider improving the relationship between housing and health without recognising the destructive impact of housing funding cuts over the last two decades. These have severely undermined the potential for housing to serve as a positive health intervention. There is a shortage of good quality housing at affordable rents, a shortfall in new building to meet current and future needs, and a lack of spending on private housing improvements to keep pace with deterioration. Investment in housing must be substantially increased, or much of the expenditure on health and care programmes will be ineffective.

The housing lobby has been spectacularly unsuccessful in raising the profile of housing and generating any general outcry about the scale of the cuts in housing programmes. Most health scares which hit the headlines are insignificant compared with the many thousands of deaths every year resulting from home accidents, radon in houses or cold temperatures in the homes of elderly people. There may be more concern if housing is seen as an essential element in the new public health agenda. One mechanism for achieving greater housing investment would be to change the Public Sector Borrowing Requirement (PSBR) rules and adopt the European system of accounting, the General Government Financial Deficit (Hawksworth and Wilcox, 1995). The government should reconsider its rejection of this idea.

The way money is allocated could specifically encourage inter-agency working. Funding needs to be more flexible and joint funding is an effective mechanism for bringing agencies together. Money could be guaranteed for collaborative projects if more were top sliced from all agencies' budgets. Current multi agency programmes such as City Challenge and the Single Regeneration Budget should include health budgets. The new Health Action Zones should be based on pooled budgets across all agencies. Money could be specifically earmarked for joint posts and joint training. The voluntary and independent sectors play a key role in activities which span traditional administrative boundaries and must have more secure long-term funding if they are to fulfil their potential. The different budgetary time-scales for each type of agency make collaboration very difficult and need to be coordinated.

The confusion about what services can be paid for by housing benefit must be sorted out. Housing agencies, which provide intensive management, face a very uncertain future, yet play a crucial role in meeting housing and health needs. Clear guidelines are needed on what housing benefit can and cannot cover and any element of care, which is not included, must be provided for in another way. Support for those with low level and medium level needs who do not fall within the community care provisions is crucial to prevent vulnerable people slipping into greater need and eventually requiring more expensive forms of support.

There needs to be a coordinated policy to tackle fuel poverty, which embraces both capital investment to achieve warm housing and revenue for poor occupiers to pay for adequate heating. Recent increases in funds for home improvement agencies and support for the home energy efficiency scheme are to be welcomed, but these services need to be provided universally and backed up with adequate funds. Cold weather payments are not enough without better thermal efficiency. There would be obvious savings to the National Health Service if fewer frail people lived in inadequately heated and insulated homes.

Better Housing Standards

Housing standards need to be improved to ensure that housing is healthy. The World Health Organisation has proposed a set of healthy housing principles that could form the basis of new standards (Ranson, 1993a). There are no minimum standards for new housing other than the building regulations. After the abandonment of Parker Morris standards in the late 1970s and under increasing financial pressures, both local authority and housing association standards have declined, especially in terms of space. There is concern that this is creating a legacy of inadequate unpopular estates (Page, 1993). Private house building has also been adopting lower standards and well over half of all new private homes fall below the Parker Morris space standards (Karn and Sheridan, 1994). These may become the slums of tomorrow and there is an urgent need for minimum standards in both public and private housing.

This should include a requirement for more suitable housing for those with limited mobility. There are increasing numbers of frail elderly people and greater emphasis on staying at home rather than in hospital or an institution. The extension of the Building Regulations (Part M) to residential building from 1999 is very welcome. These require the provision of certain accessible features and currently apply to public buildings only.

Going beyond these basic requirements, the concept of lifetime homes has been developed to cater for the changing needs of households, and includes an accessible entrance, downstairs wc suitable for a wheelchair, wider doors and circulation spaces and scope for adding a stair lift. Such standards need to be more widely adopted and could be required for a proportion of all new private and public sector housing. The additional cost of building to such standards is very small compared with much greater cost in adapting an existing house for a disabled person or providing residential care (Cobbold, 1996). There are similar arguments for adopting Part M and lifetime homes features into rehabilitation schemes.

Standards for existing housing also need to be enhanced. Government proposals to replace the current fitness standard incorporate a number of welcome features including safety design (Department of the Environment, Transport and the Regions, 1998). There are nearly 3 million known accidents in the home each year in the UK resulting in 2 million people needing hospital treatment and over 4,000 deaths, making up a third of all fatal accidents. Home accidents cost the National Health Service over £300 million each year, to which must be added the cost of lost working time (Ranson, 1993b). Safety in the home should also be reflected in the government's public health strategy, but while current proposals include an aim to reduce accidents, this does not specifically refer to housing (Department of Health, 1998). Housing measures should be seen as a key part of achieving this aim, and local authorities should be given a statutory duty to improve home safety.

One element of a home safety programme should be a local authority duty to licence private rented housing with the enforcement of minimum standards especially in relation to fire risks and carbon monoxide poisoning. The government proposes a licencing scheme for houses in multiple cccupation only but this should be extended to all private rented accommodation and recognised as an essential step in tackling health hazards in the poorest quality housing.

Thermal efficiency is included in the proposed new fitness rating, and this should be backed up by measures and finance to improve energy conservation. The new standard should be made equally applicable to all housing tenures.

Enhanced housing standards are part of a broader agenda for 'sustainable housing' which provides a healthy environment for its residents, is sensitive to the wider environment and will last without great costs for succeeding generations (Bhatti et al., 1994; EDAW et al., 1997). Homes account for 30 per cent of the UK's total energy consumption, produce over a quarter of all carbon dioxide emissions, use non-renewable and unhealthy building materials, and use up land. The government's green agenda must take these housing issues into account (see Chapter 3).

Administrative Arrangements

The government could do a lot to encourage and support better links between housing and health agencies by administrative changes: the ending of competition between agencies to deliver services; the adoption of a wider, more sensitive set of performance indicators, which take into account the broader public health agenda; clarifying the roles and responsibilities of agencies, particularly the voluntary sector; reconsidering geographical boundaries between agencies to reduce the administrative complexity of having to work with a number of different bodies; and a greater requirement for users to be involved at all levels so that the full spectrum of needs is met by agencies working together.

The public health function was held by local authorities until 1974 when it was transferred to health authorities within a public health directorate. This severed a key link in the relationship between housing and health issues on the ground and widened the administrative gap between the services. Wherever this function resides, it should be charged with a responsibility to bring together the relevant services and set a local agenda, which involves both health and housing. This needs to be backed up with adequate resources.

CONCLUSIONS

There is an urgent need to bring housing and health closer together and there is great scope for achieving better links as long as there is the political will to do so. There would be measurable benefits: tackling housing and health inequalities, reducing long-term expenditure on services; delivering more appropriate provision; greater sensitivity to the environment.

The Labour government has given a new impetus to public health and opened up debate about inequalities. The emphasis on partnerships and collaboration is encouraging. However, the real challenge is to translate these statements into a practical programme of action. If housing is to play its part in the new public health agenda housing investment must substantially increase, housing standards must be improved and administrative arrangements must be geared towards inter-agency working.

There needs to be a rediscovery of what the Victorians knew well: that housing and health are inextricably linked and you cannot make progress in health without tackling housing problems. The encouraging new government agenda for public health will be achieved only if housing is placed firmly at its centre.

REFERENCES

Arblaster, L., Conway, J., Foreman, A. and Hawtin, M. (1996) *Asking the Impossible? Interagency Working to Address the Housing, Health and Social Care Needs of People in Ordinary Housing* (Bristol: Policy Press).

Arblaster, L., Conway, J., Foreman, A. and Hawtin, M. (1998) *Achieving the Impossible? Interagency Collaboration to Address the Housing, Health and Social Care Needs of People able to live in Ordinary Housing* (Bristol: Policy Press).

Arblaster, L. and Hawtin, M. (1993) *Health, Housing and Social Policy* (London: Socialist Health Association).

Barrow, M. and Bachan, R. (1997) *The Real Cost of Poor Homes: Footing the Bill* (London: Royal Institution of Chartered Surveyors).

Benzeval, M (ed.) (1995) *Tackling Inequalities in Health: An Agenda for Action* (London: King's Fund).

Bhatti, M., Brooke, J. and Gibson, M. (eds) (1994) *Housing and the Environment: A New Agenda* (Coventry: Chartered Institute of Housing).

Boardman, B. (1991) *Fuel Poverty: From Cold Homes to Affordable Warmth* (London: Belhaven).

Burridge, R. and Ormandy, D. (eds) (1993) *Unhealthy Housing: Research, Remedies and Reform* (London: E & F N Spon).

Burrows, L. and Walentowicz, P. (1992) *Homes Cost Less Than Homelessness* (London: Shelter).

Byrne, D., Harrison, S., Keithley, J. and McCarthy, P. (1986) *Housing and Health: The Relationship between Housing Conditions and the Health of Council Tenants* (Aldershot: Gower).

Clapham, D. and Franklin, B. (1994) *Housing Management, Community Care and Competitive Tendering: A Good Practice Guide* (Coventry: Chartered Institute of Housing).

Cobbold, C. (1996) *A Cost Benefit Analysis of Lifetime Homes* (York: York Publishing Services).

Conway, J. (1988*) Prescription for Poor Health: The Crisis for Homeless Families* (London: SHAC).

Curtis, S. (1991) 'Residential Location as a Gateway to Health Care', in Smith, S., Knill-Jones, R. and McGuckin, A. (eds) *Housing for Health* (Harlow: Longman).

Department of the Environment, Transport and the Regions (1998) 'Housing Fitness Standard: Consultation Paper' (London: DETR).

Department of Health (1997) 'The New NHS: Modern, Dependable' (London: The Stationery Office).

Department of Health (1998) 'Our Healthier Nation: A Contract for Health' (London: The Stationery Office).

EDAW, Global to Local and De Montfort University (1997) *Living Places: Sustainable Homes, Sustainable Communities* (London: National Housing Forum).

Fisher, K. and Collins, J. (eds) (1993) *Homelessness, Health Care and Welfare Provision* (London: Routledge).

Gauldie, E. (1974) *Cruel Habitations: A History of Working Class Housing 1780–1918* (London: George Allen and Unwin).

Hawksworth, J. and Wilcox, S. (1995) *Challenging the Conventions: Public Borrowing Rules and Housing* (Coventry and London: Chartered Institute of Housing and Coopers and Lybrand).

Heywood, F. (1996) *Funding Adaptations: The Need to Co-operate* (Bristol: Policy Press).

Ineichen, B. (1993) *Homes and Health: How Housing and Health Interact* (London: E & F N Spon).

Karn, V. and Sheridan, L. (1994) *New Homes in the 1990s: A Study of Design Space and Amenity in Housing Association and Private Sector Production* (Manchester and York: University of Manchester and Joseph Rowntree Foundation).

Keys, S. and Kennedy, M. (1992) *Sick to Death of Homelessness* (London: Crisis).

Leather, P., Mackintosh, S. and Rolfe, S. (1994) *Papering over the Cracks: Housing Conditions and the Nation's Health* (London: National Housing Forum).

Means, R., Brenton, M., Harrison, L. and Heywood, F. (1997) *Making Partnerships Work in Community Care* (London: DoH and DoE).

Page, D. (1993) *Building for Communities: A Study of New Housing Association Estates* (York: Joseph Rowntree Foundation).

Ranson, R. (1993a) *Healthy Housing: A Practical Guide* (London: World Health Organisation Europe and Chapman Hall).

Ranson, R. (1993b) 'Accidents at Home: The Modern Epidemic', in Burridge, R. and Ormandy, D. (eds) *Unhealthy Housing: Research, Remedies and Reform* (London: E & F N Spon).

Smith, S. and Mallinson, S. (1997) 'Housing for Health in a Post Welfare State', *Housing Studies*, Vol. 12, No. 2, pp. 173–200.

Townsend, P., Davidson, N. and Whitehead, M. (1988) *Inequalities in Health: The Black Report and the Health Divide* (Harmondsworth: Penguin Books).

Victor, C. (1992) 'Health Status of the Temporary Homeless Population and Residents of North West Thames Region', *British Medical Journal*, 305, pp. 387–91.

5

Housing and Social Exclusion

Bob Paterson and Richard Macfarlane

INTRODUCTION

In this chapter, we present a vision for the role of social housing providers in tackling exclusion: summarising what is already being done and setting out the role of the social housing sector as a social entrepreneur. However, before doing this we want to provide a brief context about the ways in which we see social exclusion being tackled.

First, it is clear that social exclusion is a multi-faceted concept involving not only income based poverty, but also a poor quality of life, low self-esteem and a lack of opportunities for social interaction. This requires a multi-faceted response that is concerned with what is provided (such as practical services in housing, the environment, training and employment) and how it is provided. The latter must include the consumers and participants, and provide opportunities for developing their skills, confidence and commitment to the local community.

Second, we cannot tackle social exclusion by the promotion of training and employment alone. As Macfarlane (1997) has highlighted in *Unshackling the Poor*, the growing differential between rich and poor in the UK is related to four factors:

- unemployment, especially among the semi-skilled and unskilled;
- the changing structure of the labour market, especially for the less skilled, which is resulting in lower wages, more part-time

and temporary work, and a continuing high level of job turnover (with jobs disappearing and being replaced with others);
- higher levels of non employment, with rapidly falling activity rates (especially for older men) and higher levels of long-term sickness and disability;
- a benefits system that insists on claimants living in poverty: each step they take to improve their circumstances benefits the state before it benefits the claimant and their family.

There is little evidence to suggest that, despite the will of the current government, the contribution of these four factors to poverty in the UK will change significantly in the future. The European Commission (1994) has predicted a continuation of current levels of job turnover, and the OECD (1995) predicts that the ongoing search for increased labour flexibility will result in more part-time, temporary and self-employed work. Although there is some movement between income levels for those in work, nearly 70 per cent of the poor are long-term poor (Hills, 1998). These trends are in part a response to global trading pressures, and in part a by-product of the determination to restructure public services as a mechanism for reducing or reorienting public expenditure.

The social housing sector has a high (and increasing) proportion of households where training and employment is unlikely to be the solution to poverty. Nearly 40 per cent of households are headed by people aged 65 and over, and where these are replaced it tends to be with families headed by someone who is economically inactive (such as a single parent), and from a manual social class background. Those leaving social housing to buy their own homes tend to be childless couples with both partners working (Burrows, 1997).

The final contextual issue is the lack of congruence between the population who are socially excluded, the population living in the social housing sector, and the population who are job seekers. It is true that there is a large overlap between people living on low incomes and people living in the social housing sector. However, this sector tends to under-represent people whose poverty is related to ill health, as well as poor people from black and minority ethnic communities (Lee and Murie, 1997). Many of these households live in owner occupation or private rented accommodation, and if social housing providers are to take a lead in tackling social exclusion they will need to develop a means of working with this population.

The implication of the above analysis is that while labour market initiatives are essential and must be continued, they are not a sufficient response to poverty and social exclusion in a social rented sector, which houses a high proportion of non workers and those most at risk from low incomes and unemployment. These will be the first people to suffer from any labour market restructuring and economic downturn.

CURRENT ACTIVITIES BY SOCIAL HOUSING PROVIDERS

Here we focus on the activities of registered social landlords (RSLs), a collective term for housing associations, local housing companies, Housing Action Trusts (HATs) and housing cooperatives. These are the social housing providers outside the local authority sector. This focus is in part because RSLs have been asked to deliver the new housing initiatives over the last decade, and in part because the non housing activities of local authorities tend to be the responsibility of other departments (such as economic development, social services, education, leisure, community affairs), or quasi-independent partnership bodies.

As will be clear from the following paragraphs, many RSLs have extended their primary role to include a range of initiatives that aim to tackle social exclusion in its widest sense. Reasons given for this include their origins as community based organisations, the increasing numbers of homeless people they house, the trend towards taking over local authority stock, and housing a high proportion of benefit dependent and vulnerable people (Kemp and Fordham, 1997). However, in financial terms this added value work has been peripheral to their core activity as developers and managers of social housing, and has had to be funded from the surpluses they generate, and from funds obtained from other sources. The exception to this are the HATs, which were established with a more holistic vision and have been able to spend substantial sums on economic and social development for their residents. This wider vision has been adopted for some later regeneration programmes involving housing associations (for example, the Hackney Comprehensive Estates Initiative), although these have tended to have a greater reliance on non housing budgets including the Single Regeneration Budget and European Social Fund than the HATs.

While many RSLs get involved in some housing plus activities, it will be helpful to describe here the work of 50 of these organisations who have become members of People for Action (PFA). They share the common objective of 'enabling local people to improve their opportunities in life and add value to their communities' (Armitage and Macfarlane, 1995). The first list of project factsheets published by PFA covered 74 different projects grouped into 11 different categories. These are summarised in Table 5.1 and reveal some important patterns about initiatives to tackle social exclusion, especially since many of the responses have been developed with community involvement. Key activities are:

- changes to housing and the environment, including estate layout, maintenance and lettings policy;
- changes in the way that housing development and management activities are delivered, including greater involvement of local people (in building, maintenance and management);
- improved social welfare facilities, especially for the non working population (such as children and parents, young people, and the elderly);
- a range of employment and training activities, and services (for instance, child care) that will facilitate involvement in work.

This list can be seen as reflecting the priorities of the local residents (most of whom are not seeking work) and the matters which the RSLs have both the knowledge and resources to tackle.

There are many RSLs that have developed a capacity to deliver projects beyond their traditional core activity of housing provision, but they have limited the scale of what they could contribute by an excessive reliance on funding from external sources. Some have developed small teams who can obtain funding and then initiate and manage projects, but this is a limited resource compared with the scale of the social exclusion being encountered, and difficult to sustain if the organisation sees housing plus as a marginal activity.

It is in this area of resourcing that the HATs have benefited from a different approach. They were established with the promise of multi-million pound investment budgets and a brief to improve the living conditions, social conditions and general environment in their given areas. The HATs have generally given a high priority to their non housing matters, and have obtained government approval to spend significant sums on community development and reducing social exclusion. As can be seen from Table 5.2, Waltham Forest HAT (with

Table 5.1 Activities Undertaken by Housing Association Members of People for Action, 1995

Access to Employment	Running a training centre Providing advice and counselling Preparing a skills register
Community development and capacity building	Establishing a community centre Employing community development staff Child care schemes Community work for local people
Providing/improving shops and workspaces	Living over the shop schemes Building/renovating and letting shops Providing small business units
Resourcing community and tenant projects	Providing funds through a charitable trust Establishing a technical aid fund Providing free office/meeting space Directly funding projects Establishing a credit union
Involvement in urban regeneration partnerships	Involvement in City Challenge partnerships The development of a health centre Involvement in 'safer cities' initiatives 'Care and Repair' schemes
Self-build schemes	Self-build housing Self-build community facilities Youth self-build projects
Construction training	Training for employment on local sites Women into construction Training for self-employment
Local labour in construction (LLiC)	An agency linking people to building jobs Inserting LLiC requirements in contracts Black contractors schemes Local labour repair team
Community based trading operations	Local building company Food cooperative Black builders initiative Estate cleaning and gardening company
European partnerships and funding	Establishing transnational partnerships Participating in a transnational network Obtaining European funding for projects

(Adapted from Armitage and Macfarlane, 1995)

a residential population of approximately 6,000 people) had an annual budget of £1.8 million to spend on housing plus activities in 1997/98, nearly 25 per cent of which was provided for staffing and administration and the remainder split fairly evenly between economic development and social/community development activities. This HAT plans to spend £11.5 million over ten years on its non housing activities: 5 per cent of its total investment.

Table 5.2 Annual Community and Economic Development Budget for Waltham Forest HAT, 1997/98

	£
Staffing/Administration	435,200
Training & Employment Advice	250,000
Training Provision	330,000
Business Enterprise	78,000
Child Care & Youth	206,800
Community Development	500,000
Total	1,800,000

(*Adapted from Waltham Forest HAT, 1997*)

So if we compare the activities of other RSLs with those of HATs we can see a shared commitment to tackling social exclusion through local actions developed with the target community. However, the former have tended to struggle to develop their non housing activities in a highly unstable and fragmented funding market, and without the benefits of an adequate staff team. This has made it difficult to plan and manage their housing plus work. The latter have been able to develop a long-term strategy, and provide a greater continuity of support to their target communities.

SOCIAL LANDLORDS: SOCIAL ENTREPRENEURS

In the previous sections we have described the types of initiative that have been undertaken by socially responsible landlords operating in areas with high levels of social exclusion. But is there a case for RSLs getting even more involved and becoming community regeneration organisations: social entrepreneurs with a much larger remit than just housing?

Social landlords are in a good position to act as social entrepreneurs because:

- they already have a relationship with many of the target client group;
- they are seen as non state and not for profit organisations that are able to have a person centred (non coercive) relationship with clients;
- they have organisational capability: they are used to managing development programmes and administering multi-million pound budgets;
- they have financial strength.

However, although there is a rationale for social housing providers to broaden their operations there are limits to what they will achieve unless they are prepared to invest more of their assets and surplus income in this activity.

RSLs are often the largest financial stakeholders in poor communities. Their combined reserves stood at £6.5 billion in 1997 (National Housing Federation, 1998), of which £2.5 billion is securing loans, and £1.9 billion is set aside for future major repairs. This leaves an accumulated surplus of £2.1 billion. As major investors in areas with high levels of poverty and social exclusion, and the landlords for many excluded families, RSLs have a commercial self-interest in tackling poverty and its many local impacts: if they don't their investments are at risk. In many cases they also have a moral duty deriving from their origins or organisational goals. In these circumstances RSLs need to revise their long-term business objectives. Despite the trend towards tighter margins on their social housing business it is clear that most have the capacity to invest much more of their own resources in the development and delivery of innovative answers to many of Britain's most pressing social problems. This is the direction in which they should now develop.

This is in line with 'new Labour' thinking on building strong communities and tackling social exclusion. To encourage a change of direction by RSLs, the Housing Corporation should provide large social housing grants only where there is a predetermined level (say, 10 per cent of the total development cost) of investment in non housing elements. These housing plus budgets could be part funded by obtaining other public and charitable funds (such as the new deal), but would have to be underpinned by funds provided directly by the RSLs. So housing schemes that were not directly linked to a wider programme of targeted economic and social development would no longer receive social housing grant.

FUTURE DIRECTIONS

So what activities can and should social housing providers be undertaking in order to reduce social exclusion?

Work in the Housing Sector

The first step must clearly be to maximise employment for local people. If there are not sufficient jobs for everyone it is important that residents of areas with high levels of exclusion get their share of those that are around. One way housing providers can do this is by targeting the excluded group in staffing their own activities. Examples here are the recruitment of housing and administrative staff (including training programmes in housing administration), requiring their contractors to provide training and employment for local people, operating maintenance organisations that recruit and train local residents, and adopting self-build approaches wherever possible. In addition, they can introduce monitoring to measure the impact of their initiative, e.g. the proportion of the organisation's wages bill that is paid to the target group. However, targeting jobs may require greater weight to be given to local knowledge in the candidate specification, and the introduction of pre application training for local people.

Access to the Labour Market

However, most of the target community will not want to work in housing or construction, and the scale of in-house employment that can be offered will be small in relation to the scale of social exclusion. So housing providers should also introduce measures to link the target group to jobs in the wider economy. Here the approach must be to map the existing provision of advice, training and job search information, and then supplement this where needed. One of the most effective starting points is to offer one-to-one counselling sessions, backed up by signposting to other services, and the provision of support as people move through the labour market system. This helps overcome the barriers of lack of self-confidence and poor access to information. It is surprising what can be achieved by the provision of this obvious service in a local and non coercive way, but a good service is often too expensive to win funding in a competitive bidding process because it is labour intensive.

Community Business and Intermediate Labour Market Projects

Another approach is to create new services and activities in order to increase employment opportunities. In many cases these will seek to provide improved services for tenants (such as small repair schemes, child care provision, furniture recycling, and cafes), but in others they may need to access a wider and richer market. Intermediate labour market (ILM) projects are one example: here the projects are funded with a mixture of grant and commercial income, and the object is to provide employees with the skills to move on to other employment within 12 months. Funding from the government's new deal programme can be used here.

Tackling Poverty for the Non Employed

But to return to a theme running through this chapter, employment and training initiatives are not a sufficient response to social exclusion. It is our thesis that without a dramatic shift in economic policy many of the socially excluded will remain non employed and poor. So we need to develop activities that improve their quality of life in financial, physical and psychological ways. But this needs to be achieved without relying on a significant increase in public expenditure (which is not likely to be available on the scale and longevity required), or on the provision of many more low skilled but adequately paid jobs (which is unlikely).

Improving the financial position of non workers can be achieved through income generating or cost reduction activities. Increased incomes can arise from the provision of benefits advice and take-up campaigns, and by improving access to casual work within the earnings disregard allowed by the Benefits Agency. An increase in this disregard would be a relatively straightforward way to help the socially excluded to help themselves. Cost reduction activities can include improved household insulation, improved access to credit (through credit unions and other community based financial institutions), non cash service exchange schemes (such as local exchange trading schemes), food cooperatives, collective growing schemes, and campaigns/initiatives to improve low cost public services in the area (for example, transport, luncheon clubs and nursery care).

Improving the Quality of Life

Improvement to the physical conditions can come through landlord activities: renovations, improved security, estate redesign and improved repair procedures (such as estate based warden/caretakers). These may be the result of using rental streams in new ways, or through attracting new public funding to tackle local problems.

Social Inclusion for the Non Employed

The final task is to tackle the way people feel about being excluded. This is important not only as a contribution towards improving the quality of life but also because there are direct links to increased ill health (Wilkinson, 1995). To some extent, this is an issue which needs to be tackled at a national level: while political rhetoric and public policy continue to present non working as socially unacceptable (with even pensioners now being seen as placing an unacceptable burden on the public sector) it is going to be difficult to get the non employed to feel better about their position. However, at the local level, activities can be undertaken that will improve the self-esteem of the non working population, and replace the social interaction that the community of work once provided.

One way of doing this is through the way projects are delivered. The goal must be to increase self-help and voluntary activity. By shifting the role of paid workers from service delivery to volunteer organisers it will be possible to extend the range of services without increasing costs, and provide the rewards of casual employment for the non working population who agree to work as volunteers. This will also help to prepare those who want to return to work (for instance, young parents) to maintain their skills and work habits.

However, research into volunteering shows that people who are unemployed or who are otherwise surviving on low incomes are less likely to be involved in volunteering (Lynn and Davis-Smith, 1992). To attract them, it will be important to provide some rewards such as the provision of personal development opportunities, good quality social interaction, and small financial rewards.

CHANGING THE NATIONAL VISION

It is clear that social housing providers have the potential to play a key role in addressing issues of social exclusion, especially since many of the target group are already their tenants. They have traditionally been seen as the third arm of housing, working in the gap between the public and the private sectors. This third way is increasingly seen by commentators such as Leadbeater (1998) as 'what it needs to be to do the business'.

The need now is to expand their role. There is a growing recognition of the problems of social exclusion, but in many areas where this is a problem there are few organisations that can act as social entrepreneurs. RSLs, as large and financially secure stakeholders, are in a position to undertake this activity: working with local people to develop and manage programmes that deliver additional resources and provide new opportunities for the socially and economically excluded to improve their quality of life.

To do this effectively will require a change to the financial and constitutional positions of RSLs and how the government provides support. RSLs will need to reassess their long-term business objectives and use more of their surplus income to provide continuity for housing plus activities. The government is unleashing the potential of RSLs as institutions, including widening the objectives as set out in Section 2 of the Housing Act 1996, to expressly include non housing activities, but it needs to change the public funding strategy so that funding for housing initiatives is available only where this forms part of a targeted regeneration programme.

These policy changes will help to promote an holistic approach by social housing providers, many of whom were formed with wider community development objectives in the 1960s and 1970s. Then there was full employment but poorer housing. Today many social housing tenants have better housing but no jobs, and live in poverty.

RSLs clearly have a responsibility to become part of the solution to social exclusion. They have a substantial asset base in their housing stock (much of which is in poorer communities), the ability to raise and invest money, and management and financial skills which are often lacking in excluded areas. In short they can become a vehicle for helping Britain's poor get back into mainstream economic life.

REFERENCES

Armitage, R. and Macfarlane, R. (1995) *Good Practice Notes and Fact Sheets* (Birmingham: People for Action).

Burrows, R. (1997) *Contemporary Patterns of Residential Mobility in Relation to Social Housing in Britain* (York: University of York, Centre for Housing Policy).

European Commission (1994) 'Growth, Competitiveness, Employment: The Challenges and Ways Forward into 21st Century' (Brussels: EC).

Hills, J. (1998) *Income and Wealth: The Latest Evidence* (York: Joseph Rowntree Foundation).

Kemp, R. and Fordham, G. (1997) *Going the Extra Mile: Implementing 'Housing Plus' on Five London Housing Association Estates* (York: Joseph Rowntree Foundation).

Leadbeater, C. (1998) as quoted in the *Observer*, 10 May.

Lee, P. and Murie, A. (1997) *Poverty, Housing Tenure and Social Exclusion* (York: Joseph Rowntree Foundation).

Lynn, P. and Davis-Smith, J. (1992) *The 1991 National Survey of Voluntary Activity in the UK* (Berkhamstead: The Volunteer Centre).

Macfarlane, R. A. (1997) *Unshackling the Poor* (York: Joseph Rowntree Foundation).

National Housing Federation (1998) *1997 Global Accounts of Registered Social Landlords* (London: NHF).

Organisation for Economic Co-operation and Development (1995) *The Jobs Study* (Paris: OECD).

Waltham Forest Housing Action Trust (1997) 'The Strategic Approach of the Waltham Forest Housing Action Trust' (London: Waltham Forest HAT).

Wilkinson, R. (1995) 'Health, Redistribution and Growth', in Glyn, A. and Miliband, D. (eds) *Paying for Inequality* (London: IPPC/Rivers Oram).

6

Housing and Education

Tim Brown and Angela Maye-Banbury

INTRODUCTION

> Education and training have become the new mantra for social democratic politicians. Tony Blair famously describes his three main priorities in government as 'education, education, education'.
> (Giddens, 1998, p. 109)

The Labour government is fulfilling its manifesto pledge to put education at the centre of its programme. A range of initiatives, relevant to aspects of housing policy and practice, especially housing plus, have been introduced or reformed since May 1997 including child care (and the associated promotion of after school clubs), education action zones, welfare to work and the new deal. The Chancellor of the Exchequer reaffirmed this commitment in his speech to Parliament on the comprehensive spending review in July 1998. He commented that 'investing in education is essential to secure both a fairer society and a more efficient economy' (*Hansard*, 1998). He also restated the commitments of the Secretary of State for Education and Employment on, for example, setting numeracy and literacy targets for 11-year-olds, establishing new targets for nursery education, cutting truancy, setting improved standards for teaching and inspecting schools. And he confirmed that additional expenditure of £19 billion would be available over three years from 1999. Indeed, in September 1998, the Prime Minster stated that in key public services the goal is to ensure excellent public provision for the next generation. In relation to education this means:

> An unprecedented crusade to raise school standards through investment tied to demanding targets, better training and support for teachers, new resources and approaches to tackle educational exclusion, and rigorous inspection of schools and local authorities. (Blair, 1998, p. 16)

More generally, there is an intense debate over the role and nature of education as part of the discussion on the third way. There is a growing consensus that education policies and practices must reflect the changing needs of society. Bentley (1998) suggests that the post-industrial economy requires individuals who are able to create, use and communicate knowledge in increasingly sophisticated ways, and that increasing affluence has opened up the market for education as a leisure and recreational pursuit. In addition, education is becoming an even more significant passport to individual life chances and mobility. Indeed, as Bayley (1998) notes, in some localities education and qualifications have, in the past, never been seen as the route to the good life, but this is no longer an appropriate belief. Lastly, the growing emphasis on innovation and productivity in organisations places greater priority on learning and skills development.

Although there is this emerging consensus on the fundamental importance of education in a changing world, there is less agreement on the nature of a new education system. One the one hand, there is clear evidence of the expanding role of traditional educational institutions (such as schools and after-hours/homework clubs) along with extending the length of time in which people spend in them (for instance, expanding the number of students in further and higher education). On the other hand, as Bentley (1998) points out, a parallel infrastructure is emerging based on the idea of lifelong learning (including, for example, individual learning accounts). Whether one of these systems (or, indeed, alternative approaches) best meets future education needs can only be answered in relation to discussions on the basic purposes of education. According to Bentley (1998), an education system should, first, strive to promote autonomy for the individual in making choices and decisions. Second, it should promote individual responsibility for oneself and one's family and community as well as wider society. Third, it should promote creativity so enabling, for instance, problem solving, goal achievement and the productive use of knowledge.

There is considerable merit in evaluating the government's actions and proposals within such a framework, but this is not directly within the remit of this chapter. Instead, the focus is on the relationship between housing and education and, in particular, on how the former can contribute to meeting the demands for a relevant education system in a changing society. This is an especially significant issue, as a government which is committed to the mantra of 'education, education, education' could marginalise housing.

This chapter examines the relationship between housing and education in the UK, but at the same time draws on experiences in other parts of Western Europe. It begins by considering the motivational and socioeconomic factors behind learning and the importance of educational achievement in improving housing access in the UK. The chapter then demonstrates how young people with few educational qualifications are over-represented among homeless groups in Western Europe. The extent to which the educational attainment of children resident in temporary accommodation or poor housing conditions is adversely affected is also highlighted. The chapter then considers the nature of local government in the UK, the extent to which the introduction of market principles has impacted on both housing and educational policy and the need to develop a more integrated approach to policy making in the UK. In this context, the importance of joint working between education, housing and social service departments is referred to in the alleviation of homelessness among young people. In addition, attention is drawn to the growing number of grass-roots initiatives on linking education and housing. The chapter concludes by highlighting both the potential for greater links between housing and education policies and the difficulties of realising these opportunities

LEARNING AND EDUCATIONAL ACHIEVEMENT

There exists relatively little research on the relationship between housing and education policy and, more specifically, on the links between low educational achievement and homelessness among young people. A substantial body of research nevertheless exists, which has sought to identify what prompts people to learn. At its most simplistic level, an individual's motivation to learn is either intrinsic or extrinsic. Factors such as an interest in knowledge for its own sake, the desire to succeed and to acquire social acceptance have been cited as key factors in motivating students to learn (Morgan, 1993; Ramsden, 1992). Other attempts to consider the motives for learning have resulted in the development and/or use of paradigms which incorporate an individual's physiological and psychological needs. For example, reference is often made to Maslow (1943) and his hierarchy of needs model when considering motivation to learn. This points to greater possibilities for promotion as well as to the significance of safety, belonging and self-esteem.

Published research such as this is useful in providing a broad framework of analysis for educational research projects. However, it fails to adequately consider any specific socioeconomic factors which, cumulatively, may impact upon someone's ability to learn. More significantly, this research fails to acknowledge the inextricable relationship between specific areas of public policy making such as education, health and housing policy. In this respect, it is instructive to refer briefly to discussions in the 1960s and 1970s on educational disadvantage and social and environmental deprivation. There is a rich mixture of literature ranging from government reports (such as Central Advisory Council for Education, 1967, and Halsey, 1972) through to geographical studies on social areas in cities (for instance, Herbert, 1977). In addition, there has been specific research on the links between housing, health and education (e.g. Kirby, 1979). As Herbert (1977) concludes:

> The school years form a major element in people's lives and have strong formative effects. School itself houses at least one reference group of crucial importance and provides a distinctive social environment. Outside school, there are other environments of at least equal importance – home, neighbourhood and peer groups are the main elements of these. From a very diverse research literature, it can be demonstrated that each of these has some effect and makes some contribution towards a comprehension of educational attitudes and performance. (Herbert, 1977, p. 155)

Similarly, Halsey (1972) points out that the Plowden Report in 1967 on children and their primary schools highlighted the close relationship between educational attainment and social deprivation in the home and the neighbourhood. Moreover, such studies generated considerable discussion on the strengths and weaknesses of positive discrimination through, for example, initiatives such as educational priority areas. It also generated debates on whether education orientated action was attacking the symptoms rather than causes of low educational attainment such as poverty, poor housing and bad health.

In recent years, there has been a slow but gradual resurgence of interest in these debates within the housing profession. The links between poor housing and other aspects of social policy including low educational attainment have been explored, for instance, by the Royal Institution of Chartered Surveyors (1996), the Chartered Institute of Housing (1995), Furley (1989) and by Power et al. (1995). The former concluded that the links between poor housing and educational disadvantage are complex and cumulative, but subject to little research. Poor housing and homelessness 'constitute serious impediments to learning, help to lower health standards and thus increase absences from school and contribute continually to low self-esteem and lack of confidence' (Royal Institution of Chartered Surveyors, 1996, p. 24).

Although only a limited amount of published research exists on the links between education and housing policy, there is a clear relationship between the two. At the most fundamental level, as Bentley (1998) indicates, high educational achievement is generally advocated as a requirement for high earning potential. This is achieved by enhancing an individual's economic autonomy and thus, in theory, facilitating an improved quality of life. Therefore the choices exercised by the consumer and his/her ability to access key services, are often directly linked to educational performance. Arguably, the notion of what constitutes a quality of life is a highly subjective notion, but few would disagree that having a roof over one's head is a prerequisite to having any degree of quality of life. The increased earning power of an individual and the subsequent greater economic autonomy which may be exercised by him or her, therefore, has particular significance for access to housing in the UK. This is especially significant for housing consumers in the UK in the 1990s where the majority of properties are allocated on the basis of ability to pay rather than on the basis of housing need.

YOUNG PEOPLE, HOMELESSNESS AND EDUCATION

In the 1980s and at the beginning of the 1990s, there was a visible increase in the numbers of people, notably young people, sleeping rough in the UK. A consensus exists that radical changes in the welfare benefit system implemented at this time alongside the deregulation of the private rented sector through the introduction of market rents were significant factors in increasing young people's vulnerability to homelessness (Greve, 1991; Maclagan, 1993). The Social Security Act 1988 decreased the amount of benefit available to young people living away from home through the introduction of age related benefits for those under 18 and between 18 and 25 years of age. However, insufficient YTS placements resulted in increasing numbers of 16- and 17-year-olds being disqualified from claiming income support (Kay, 1992). A clear link has been identified between the implementation of the Social Security Act 1988 and a dramatic increase in numbers of young people with no income. For example, Maclagan (1993) pointed to an increase in the numbers of young people with no income from 70,000 in 1988 to 97,000 in 1993. Further, according to the criteria for claiming the Job Seeker's Allowance, introduced in October 1996, claimants may be disqualified from benefit entitlement if they are not defined as available for work or actively seeking work. In addition, there is some evidence to suggest that the implementation of the local reference rent introduced in January 1996, for private sector tenants claiming housing benefit is set below the landlord's rent. This may lead to an increase of evictions of tenants in the private sector (Rugg, 1997). More specifically, Greve (1991) has asserted that the fundamental cause of homelessness among young people is the increasing shortage of affordable rented housing.

Access to a high quality education service has been consistently identified as being significant in preventing homelessness among young people both in the UK and in other parts of Europe. In particular, the lack of educational opportunities alongside other specific factors such as poverty, poor housing conditions and physical and sexual abuse have been cited as being highly significant in increasing young people's vulnerability to homelessness. For example, De Feijter and Blok (1996) point to the way in which low educational achievement may result in young people being disadvantaged in the employment market in the Netherlands. Young people are therefore at risk of being marginalised in the housing market and subsequently forced to occupy the poorest forms of accommodation in the private rented sector in the Netherlands. Further, recent research has suggested that the majority of women occupying refuges in the Netherlands are single women over the age of 30 living in poverty and with few academic qualifications (Maye, 1998). The exclusion of young people from the housing market in the Netherlands is further compounded by the great diversity of dispersed organisations which work with young people who are homeless or threatened with homelessness. Although agencies providing educational, housing, psychiatric or other community services may all be concerned with representing young people in specific ways, the conflicting priorities of these organisations may inhibit inter-agency collaboration. As a result, the cooperation between different care institutions is weak and youngsters run the risk of being sent from one institution to the other (De Feijter and Blok, 1996).

Equally, empirical research undertaken in Portugal points to the over-representation of people with low levels of educational attainment among rough sleepers. A survey conducted in 1996 indicated that one in five rough sleepers in Lisbon were either illiterate or had never attended school. Furthermore, around 80 per cent of people sleeping rough were unemployed and had attended secondary school for only four years or, in many instances, for less than four years (Bruto da Costa, 1996). In Austria, young people who have prematurely left school are over-represented among the homeless (Kofler and Mosberger, 1996).

CHILDREN, HOUSING AND SCHOOLS

In addition to acquiring qualifications, education is crucial in enabling children to develop social and interpersonal skills. In this regard, the nature of the accommodation occupied by a family may interfere with a child's ability to benefit from the environment of school. As the Chartered Institute of Housing (1995) has asserted, while the links between educational attainment and housing conditions may not always be clear, suitable and reliable accommodation is critical in deriving full benefit from any available educational opportunities. In particular, accommodation which is not decent, affordable and appropriate to the needs of the occupant may negatively impact on the extent to which a child may participate fully in school life. For example, a property that suffers from extensive dampness and disrepair may adversely affect the health of the occupier. This may lead to a child's sustained absenteeism from school as a result of illnesses such as asthma and bronchitis which are exacerbated by poor housing conditions (Furley, 1989). Furthermore, research has pointed to the difficulties that children experience in completing homework when resident in temporary accommodation; in particular, bed and breakfast accommodation (Power et al., 1995). Children of homeless families resident in temporary accommodation may have to change schools a number of times, leading to a disrupted and fragmented education (Stone, 1998).

Since families living in temporary accommodation are often forced to move a number of times, schools located in areas with a high incidence of homelessness often have high pupil turnover rates. This in turn leads to additional administration for schools because of maintaining contact with homeless families and increased liaison with other agencies. These extra demands on schools and teachers may adversely affect the progress of all pupils, not just those resident in temporary accommodation. Moreover, as Power et al. (1995) have suggested, poor quality or temporary accommodation may inhibit children in forming a range of relationships and may further stigmatise children who are already traumatised because of the experiences which lead to them being made homeless in the first instance. Similar difficulties may also persist for families offered emergency accommodation before permanent housing is provided by the local housing authority, housing association or, more increasingly, a landlord in the private rented sector. The problems associated with the private rented sector, notably in relation to insecurity of tenure, racial and sexual harassment, illegal eviction and lack of affordability, are well documented (Burrows, 1990; Jew, 1994; Rauta and Pickering, 1992). Living in overcrowded housing conditions and lack of play space may restrict a child's ability to learn (Edwards, 1992).

LOCAL GOVERNMENT

A consideration of the changing nature of local government in the UK is also relevant when evaluating the connection between housing and education. Education and housing services in the UK became subject to a new right perspective and a private sector culture, as a result of the introduction of specific policy instruments by the Conservative government in the 1980s and 1990s. Overall, these policy measures sought to erode the role of local government through restricting essential financial support for the delivery of key services. Indeed, with specific reference to housing policy, it has been suggested that there existed a direct link between attempts to erode the powers of local government and the withdrawal of both revenue and capital support for local government services at this time (Malpass and Means, 1993). Part of this radical ideological shift lay in the promotion of a more responsive service by local authorities for the individual consumer. The advocacy of this more market driven approach to the policy making process to promote notions of strategic enabling rather than direct service provision by the state is manifested in a number of ways in the UK (see Butcher et al., 1990; Thornley, 1991). The prevalence of quangos such as Housing Action Trusts (HATs) and boards of governors in education as the key management agents reflect this shift. Furthermore, the application of performance indicators and league tables in housing and education organisations to evaluate the efficiency, economy, effectiveness and equity of an organisation is considered commonplace in the UK in the 1990s. In this way, housing and educational bodies have both experienced a significant change in the way specific services are managed, funded and delivered. However, the implementation of such methods of evaluation may have a direct impact on those who are homeless or badly housed. For example, pressure on vacancies in temporary accommodation may result in the allocation of hard to let properties in a poor state of repair to homeless households. As Power et al. (1995) have noted, increased emphasis on competition between schools and particularly the publication of league tables of achievement mean that some schools may be reluctant to accept pupils living in temporary accommodation.

At the same time, attempts have been made, specifically in the late 1980s and early 1990s, to transform the face of local government services through reorganisation. Again, the Conservative Party asserted that such a significant change would ultimately provide a less bureaucratic, more responsive service to members of the public. The implementation of local government reorganisation in the UK has potential for providing a more integrated holistic approach to policy making. Collaboration and joint working is an integral part of policy making in the Britain. But as Hudson (1987) and Webb (1991) have commented, much collaboration remains all too often a jumble of services fractionalised by professional, cultural and organisational boundaries and by tiers of government. An examination of the different policies and practices of local education authorities in relation to homeless pupils undertaken in 1995 has highlighted these specific issues. For example, Power et al. (1995) suggest that there is considerable confusion surrounding the roles and responsibilities of the various statutory agencies involved in providing assistance to homeless pupils. As has been noted above with reference to the Netherlands, this lack of inter-departmental homogeneity is not unique to the UK and appears to be equally problematic in other parts of Western Europe. In addition, liaison between local education authorities and housing authorities in the UK is discretionary.

The construction of a robust definition of homelessness is problematic and a range of methodologies have been applied in assessing the level and nature of homelessness using quantitative and qualitative data (see Anderson et al., 1993; Bramley, 1988; Greve with Currie, 1990). As a minimum requirement, local housing authorities are required to record the numbers of applicants towards whom they may have a statutory duty under the provisions of the Housing Act 1996, Part VII. Since the vast majority of such applicants are those defined as homeless and in priority need, these figures include homeless families in the main and therefore exclude the majority of single people without dependent children. Nonetheless, it appears that local education authorities tend to underestimate levels of homelessness in their area (Power et al., 1995). Clearly, it is inherently difficult for local education authorities to devise satisfactory responses in partnership with their local housing authority or other housing provider in meeting the needs of homeless children if they are unable to identify the extent and nature of the problem in the first instance.

LOCAL INITIATIVES

There are, however, an increasing number of housing organisations working with educational bodies, local communities, parents, young people and children. Many of these projects are labelled as housing plus initiatives, but their more immediate significance is that they represent successful local multi-agency approaches for tackling some of the complex issues linking poor educational attainment and inadequate housing provision. They also illustrate how traditional approaches towards education provision can be modified to reflect the changing needs of society and thus go some way towards meeting the requirements identified by Bentley (1998) such as schools as neighbourhood learning centres and contributors to the knowledge economy. Ball (1998), for example, shows how many schools are increasingly becoming more involved with local communities as well as building effective links with parents. She also cites the example of Manchester City Council, which is piloting a project involving three full service primary schools where families and pupils have access to a range of services including health and social services.

Brown and Passmore (1998) indicate that local housing agencies are already contributing to these types of initiatives including pre-school learning and nursery provision, holiday and after school clubs, post school clubs and youth work. Such provision can assist parents who wish to return to the labour market, by providing appropriate child care facilities as well as contributing to the local community and economy through job creation and training provision. An example of nursery provision is the Sunflower Project in Cambridge, which provides 33 places for children aged four months to five years, and is part of a larger project providing housing and training. The nursery is open from 0830 to 1700 on Monday to Friday with parents able to select between a two-, three- or five-day provision. The project was developed by Cambridge Housing Society with support from the Housing Corporation.

In relation to youth work, there is an increasing literature on the role of housing organisations in working with young people on problem estates and on urban regeneration projects (Coles et al., 1998; Fitzpatrick et al., 1998). Particular emphasis is placed on the potential for housing organisations to act as coordinators of a multi-agency approach as well as providing resources in the form of land and buildings and capital and revenue funding. Probably the best example of linking education provision with housing regeneration is in the London Borough of Southwark (Bayley, 1998; Hudson, 1998). As part of their successful single regeneration budget projects, nine education related schemes are being implemented including literacy programmes run by voluntary organisations such as Springboard for Children, homework clubs and mentoring programmes. In addition, a proportion of the borrowing allowed under the capital receipts initiative has been transferred to the education department.

CONCLUSIONS

There exists a clear relationship between education, housing and other policies of local government in both the UK and other parts of

Western Europe. But despite interesting local innovative projects, there is a need for more effective collaboration, and the difficulties of adopting a multi agency approach cannot be underestimated. As Ball (1998) indicates, teaching and administrative pressures on schools brought about by government regulation result in staff having little time to develop links with other organisations, local communities and families. Similarly, the pressures on housing organisations through, for example, compulsory competitive tendering, best value, performance standards and league tables make effective coordination hard to achieve.

It is clear that the provision of decent, affordable accommodation appropriate to the needs of the occupant is crucial in ensuring that children and young people derive the maximum benefit from educational opportunities. It is therefore imperative that the development and implementation of both education and housing policies be viewed as part of the same integrated process. In this respect, a more coherent, holistic approach to government policy making is particularly significant to ensure that housing and education are accessible to all.

REFERENCES

Anderson, I., Kemp, P. and Quilgars, D. (1993) *Single Homeless People* (London: HMSO).

Ball, M. (1998) *School Inclusion: The School, the Family and the Community* (York: Joseph Rowntree Foundation).

Bayley, R. (1998) 'Housing Goes Back to School', *Roof*, March/April, pp. 28–9.

Bentley, T. (1998) 'Learning Beyond the Classroom', in Hargreaves, I. and Christie, I. (eds) *Tomorrow's Politics: The Third Way and Beyond* (London: Demos).

Blair, T. (1998) *The Third Way: New Politics for the New Century* (London: Fabian Society, Fabian Pamphlet 588).

Bramley, G. (1988) 'The Definition and Measurement of Homelessness', in Bramley, G., Doogan, K., Leather, P., Murie, A. and Watson, E. *Homelessness and the London Housing Market* (Bristol: School for Advanced Urban Studies, Occasional Paper No. 32).

Brown, T. and Passmore, J. (1998) *Housing and Anti-Poverty Strategies* (Coventry and York: Chartered Institute of Housing and Joseph Rowntree Foundation).

Bruto da Costa, A. (1996) *Youth Homelessness in Portugal* (Brussels: FEANTSA).

Burrows, L. (1990) *Forced Out: A Report on the Harassment and Illegal Eviction of Tenants* (London: Shelter).

Butcher, H., Law, I., Leach, R. and Mullard, M. (1990) *Local Government and Thatcherism* (London: Routledge).

Central Advisory Council for Education (1967) *Children and their Primary Schools* (London: HMSO, Vols I and II).

Chartered Institute of Housing (1995) *A Point to Prove* (Coventry: CIH).

Coles, B., England, J. and Rugg, J. (1998) *Working with Young People on Estates* (Coventry and York: Chartered Institute of Housing and Joseph Rowntree Foundation).

De Feijter, H. and Blok, H. (1996) 'Youth Homelessness in the Netherlands: Nature, Policy, Good Practice', in Avramov, D. (ed.) *Youth Homelessness in the European Union* (Brussels: FEANTSA).

Edwards, R. (1992) 'Co-ordination, Fragmentation and Definitions of Need: the New Under Fives Initiative and Homeless Families', *Children and Society*, Vol. 6, No. 4, pp. 336–52.

Fitzpatrick, S., Hastings, A. and Kintrea, K. (1998) *Including Young People in Urban Regeneration* (Bristol: Policy Press).

Furley, A. (1989) *A Bad Start In Life: Children, Health and Housing* (London: Shelter).

Giddens, A. (1998) *The Third Way* (Cambridge: Polity Press).

Greve, J. (1991) *Homelessness in Britain* (York: Joseph Rowntree Foundation).

Greve, J. with Currie, E. (1990) *Homelessness in Britain* (York: Joseph Rowntree Foundation).

Halsey, A. (1972) *Educational Priority* (London: HMSO, Vol. I).

Hansard (1998) 'Comprehensive Spending Review', 14 July, Columns 187–194.

Herbert, D. (1977) 'Urban Education', in Herbert, D. and Johnson, R. (eds) *Spatial Perspectives on Problems and Policies: Social Areas in Cities* (London: John Wiley, Vol. 2).

Hudson, B. (1987) 'Collaboration in Social Welfare', in Hill, M. (ed.) (1993) *The Policy Process: A Reader* (Hemel Hempstead: Harvester Wheatsheaf).

Hudson, R. (1998) 'Raising Literacy Standards', *Housing Today*, 29 October, p. 19.

Jew, P. (1994) *Law and Order in Private Rented Housing* (London: Campaign for Bedsit Rights).

Kay, H. (1992) *Conflicting Priorities: Homeless 16- and 17-Year Olds: A Changing Agenda for Housing Authorities* (London, CHAR).

Kirby, A. (1979) *Education, Health and Housing* (Farnborough: Saxon House).

Kofler, A. and Mosberger, B. (1996) *Youth Homelessness in Austria* (Brussels: FEANTSA).

Maclagan, I. (1993) *Four Years Severe Hardship* (London: Youthaid).

McCluskey, J. (1993) *Reassessing Priorities: The Children Act 1989 – A New Agenda for Young Homeless People?* (London: CHAR).

McCluskey, J. (1994) *Acting in Isolation: An Evaluation of the Effectiveness of the Children Act for Young Homeless People* (London: CHAR).

Malpass, P. and Means, R. (eds) (1993) *Implementing Housing Policy* (Buckingham: Open University Press).

Maslow, A. (1943) 'A Theory of Human Motivation', *Psychological Review*, Vol. 50, pp. 370–96.

Maye, A. (1998) Unpublished Preliminary PhD Research Findings, De Montfort University, Leicester.

Morgan, A. (1993) *Improving Your Student's Learning* (London: Kogan Page).

Power, S., Whitty, G. and Youdell, D. (1995) *No Place to Learn: Homelessness and Education* (London: Shelter).

Ramsden, P. (1992) *Learning to Teach in Higher Education* (London: Routledge).

Rauta, I. and Pickering, A. (1992) *Private Renting in England 1990* (London: OPCS).

Royal Institution of Chartered Surveyors (1996) *The Real Cost of Poor Homes: a Critical Review of the Research Literature by the University of Sussex and the University of Westminster* (London: RICS).

Rugg, J. (1997) 'Opening Doors in the Private Rented Sector', in Burrows, R., Pleace, N. and Quilgars, D. (eds) *Homelessness and Social Policy* (London: Routledge).

Stone, E. (1998) *Growing Up Homeless* (London: Shelter).

Thornley, A. (1991) *Urban Planning Under Thatcherism* (London: Routledge).

Webb, A. (1991) 'Co-ordination: A Problem in Public Sector Management', *Policy and Politics*, Vol. 19, No. 4, pp. 229–42.

7

Housing and Europe

Mike Oxley

INTRODUCTION

The European Union has no direct responsibility for housing provision. There cannot, according to the principle of subsidiarity, be a European housing policy as responsibility for housing issues rests with the member states. There is thus supposed to be no European housing expenditure and the only budgets for housing should be national, regional or local. The impact of Europe on housing provision is, however, not dependent on European Union expenditure or policy formation. It is much more significant than this for the impacts come through the multitude of ways in which the European Union influences economic prosperity, the money which individuals spend on housing and the types of housing they spend money on. It has been cogently argued that despite subsidiarity, European integration will have important implications for housing through factor mobility, competition policy and liberalisation of markets, economic growth, lower inflation, cuts in public spending, tax harmonisation and issues of citizenship and social justice (Priemus et al., 1994).

What happens in the future is partly a matter of speculation. As the European Union develops and changes its institutions and its practices, there are likely to be impacts on housing which can be classified in several ways. It is possible to identify these effects as:

- the introduction of the Euro and its impact, whether the UK is in or out, on the borrowing of registered social landlords and the provision of finance for owner occupiers;

- the impact of compliance with the convergence criteria, for membership of European Monetary Union (EMU) on government expenditure on housing;
- the impact of the macro economy, as influenced by EMU, on owner occupation, housing markets and house building;
- the impact of financial constraints on the type of social housing institutions that will predominate in the future;
- the impact of European expenditure on housing as a result of leakage;
- the impact of increased knowledge of the ways in which housing is provided in other countries on the policies and practices in this country;
- it is also important to examine the very significant influences which housing systems may exert on national economies and the effects of housing provision on labour mobility, standards of living and social exclusion.

Governments in Western Europe, throughout the twentieth century, have intervened in housing markets in a variety of ways because of the impact which housing has on wider social and economic issues and because of the recognised inability of housing markets to achieve social objectives. This intervention will continue into the next millennium. The forms of intervention will depend, in part, on how strongly the principle of subsidiarity is enforced. The prospects for the moderation of the principle as well as a consideration of the 'housing and Europe' interactions identified above form the substance of this chapter.

THE EURO AND HOUSING FINANCE

The UK is not one of the eleven initial members of the European Monetary Union (EMU) but will rather be one of the four European Union 'outs' (with Denmark and Sweden, who like the UK have adopted a wait and see approach, and Greece, which does not qualify). From 1999 to 2002 the Euro will coexist with national currencies. Most forecasters expect Denmark and Sweden to join by 2002, with the UK possibly joining early in the next parliament. Greece may then still not meet the qualification criteria related to national debt and inflation (Lloyds Bank, 1998). The EMU will have widespread consequences both for those countries that are in and those that are out. There will, in effect, be a fixed exchange rate between members and both before and after full entry economies are likely to converge in the sense that a number of macroeconomic variables will come closer together. The significant variables are inflation and interest rates. EMU is intended to keep both of these low, and it is expected that, on this score, it will be successful. A consequence of this is likely to be changes in lending and borrowing patterns (*Housing Today*, 1998).

It has been claimed that the relative preponderance of floating rate borrowing, for industry and households, is one reason why the UK's economic cycle does not synchronise well with other European Union states. However, if the UK eventually joins EMU, there is likely to be a shift towards fixed rate borrowing as the risk premium attached to long-term interest rates declines (Lloyds Bank, 1998).

The removal of any exchange rate risk attached to borrowing from financial institutions in other countries will be conducive to more cross-border financing. It is possible, given eventual UK adoption of the Euro, that this will bring increased opportunities for UK registered social landlords to borrow at fixed, and historically low, rates of interest. Indeed registered social landlords already borrow large sums of money from abroad. The Housing Corporation's private finance survey provides a detailed ranking of lenders committed to funding in excess of £10 million. In 1995, 32 banks were listed along with 16 building societies and 13 other financial institutions. There were several foreign banks included in the listing. The French Banque Paribu was ranked fifth and Banque International de Luxembourg was ranked ninth. Several German banks were also included. A further survey of the opportunities for European banks to lend to social housing organisations concluded that some of the best opportunities, at relatively low risk, exist in the UK (Boelhouwer, 1997). These opportunities will expand.

There are also opportunities in the other direction: UK institutions may be more likely to fund social housing in other European countries. The extent of this opportunity is, however, limited in some countries, for example France and Belgium, where social landlords arrange loans through special intermediary financial organisations. More generally, the extent to which the opportunities are realised depends on knowledge of the operations of each other by both lenders and borrowers in different countries. Increased reliance on borrowing from capital markets is common to social landlords across the European

Union. As mutual understanding of financing requirements and financial harmonisation increases, inter-state boundaries will become irrelevant to these financial flows.

This scenario can be extended, logically, to the financing of owner occupation. Here the history and sophistication of specialised lending for home ownership by UK institutions should put them in a strong position relative to, say, German and Dutch lenders. For home owners and housing associations, however, whether borrowing comes from an organisation based in London or Frankfurt will be less significant than the effect of the EMU on the cost and the terms of the borrowing. If EMU achieves its objectives, borrowing should be cheaper and available at more stable rates of interest.

CONVERGENCE CRITERIA AND NATIONAL GOVERNMENTS' EXPENDITURE ON HOUSING

As the private funding of housing in Europe has been increasing, so national governments have been reducing the volumes of public expenditure devoted to housing. Within this reduction a major shift has occurred in favour of housing allowances which go to households and away from production subsidies which have gone to housing suppliers.

EMU convergence criteria require that governments' borrowing requirements amount to no more than 3 per cent of GDP and that total government debt is no more than 60 per cent of GDP. In the run up to entry this has created a climate of fiscal austerity in which public expenditure on housing has been particularly vulnerable. Governments' direct expenditures on housing have, in any case, been falling in Europe over the last 20 years or so. This has been largely a consequence of governments believing that housing shortages have been greatly diminished and a reasoning that subsidies to support housing construction are less necessary than in earlier decades. This restraint on government expenditure to promote housing supply is likely to continue unless politically convincing counter-arguments are advanced.

The public expenditure constraints have thus been reinforced rather than initiated by compliance with convergence criteria. The impact of this restraint has been different in the UK than in other countries because of the extent to which social housing provision has relied on institutions whose expenditure counts as public expenditure. This has led to arguments for freeing more council housing from the limitations of the public sector borrowing requirement.

Technically, how much governments spend on housing is largely a consequence of institutional arrangements and accounting procedures. If social housing institutions are part of the public sector, public expenditure will be higher than it would be with organisations like housing associations who provide housing with some government assistance. Thus public expenditure on housing might be reduced simply by changing the institutions providing housing.

It is common for housing benefit type payments not to be counted as part of public expenditure on housing but to be part of the social security budget. One trend, which has persisted for over 20 years, has involved less public expenditure on housing construction and more, relatively, on housing allowances. This has been common to most European Union states. The efficiency and equity of payments to support supply verses payments to assist household budgets are issues which need to be re-examined in the context of both national and EU expenditures.

MACROECONOMICS AND HOUSING

Reduced and reducing expectations of rising inflation will have important consequences for housing markets. The owner occupation market in the UK has thrived on inflation. It has been argued that in the past:

> Housing has had a symbiotic relationship with inflation. High and persistent general inflation has fostered high house price inflation and thereby promoted the idea of ownership of property as a speculative investment. Meanwhile, high house price inflation may have helped to stimulate general inflation. (Bootle, 1996, p. 67).

The real value of mortgage debt has been eroded, repayments have fallen relative to incomes, and house prices have risen, in many years, ahead of inflation. These circumstances have combined to make housing a very good investment for households who have been able to obtain mortgages. At least, this was clearly the story until the 1990s. Experiences in the first half of the decade of falling house prices, negative equity and increased job insecurity have darkened the image of housing as a good investment.

If EMU is successful, it will result in lower inflation and low and stable interest rates. It has already had an impact in that expectations of inflation have been dampened. The investment as opposed to the occupation demand for home ownership may have thus been diminished. However, while this may reduce the turnover within the existing stock and limit the extent of increases in house prices, it might have very little influence on the overall level of home ownership. Trading up to take advantage of inflation may be diminished but entering the market as a first time buyer may be promoted by steady interest rates and plentiful supplies of mortgage funds.

The UK housing market is adjusting slowly to a new era of more stable economic circumstances and the change from the boom and bust cycles of the past. This will have consequences for the motivations of house buyers and the activities of house builders. Buyers will be more concerned with housing as a place to live rather than as an investment. It is possible that builders will have less opportunity to gain profits from rising land prices, resulting from house price inflation, and will have to make a greater proportion of their return from the construction process. Making large gains from the hike in land values associated with developing green field sites will become less probable in the future. This could be a stimulus for efficiency gains in house building and also help to tip the balance a little more favourably in the direction of brown field developments and an increase in the dwelling stock through conversions.

SOCIAL HOUSING PROVIDERS AND THE SUPPLY OF RENTED HOUSING

Despite the popularity of the right to buy and the large volumes of council housing that have been transferred to housing associations, the vast majority of social housing in the UK is owned and managed by local authorities. Indeed, over half of all rented housing in the UK is in the local authority sector. Only around 4 per cent of the housing stock is owned by housing associations. This is quite a different situation compared to the rest of the European Union (Oxley, 1995). Indeed, a study for the Chartered Institute of Housing considered the various types of social housing landlords in France, Germany, the Netherlands and Sweden. It found that outside the UK:

> The principal agencies providing social sector housing are either public or private corporations under international accounting conventions, and in every case the borrowing of those agencies falls outside the primary measure of government financial deficits adopted in the country in question ... Council housing in the UK stands alone as the only case where a government body is itself the direct provider of the majority of social sector housing. (Hawksworth and Wilcox, 1995, pp. 42–3)

The study concluded that the resulting borrowing and spending constraints in the UK had an adverse effect on housing investment.

Getting around the financial constraints imposed by the public sector has been the driving force in the development of ideas about, and eventually the reality of, local housing companies. These are still evolving and there is no standard model for their constitution, but the creation of new forms of social housing that achieve social objectives without the constraints of public ownership will be a very important aspect of the housing agenda over the next few years (Wilcox et al., 1993).

There is scope, however, for more radical developments which blur the division between the private and the public sectors (Oxley, 1999). In Germany, for example, such a division is difficult to recognise because a variety of landlords, including private sector providers, deliver social housing. The German example shows that the ownership of housing is less important than who has access to the housing and the terms on which that access is available. German providers have signed up to social housing agreements which give them the privileges of cheap loans in return for rents being held below specified levels and tenancies being granted to low income households. More generally, the distinction between private and social renting is much less clear in other Western European countries than it is in the UK (Oxley, 1995).

The private rented sector has declined throughout Europe since 1945. However, the sector, at only around 8 per cent of the housing stock, is lower in the UK than in any other EU state. Political initiatives to revive the private rented sector have been unsuccessful. There are many reasons for the smaller private rented sector in the UK. The success of owner occupation and the availability of social housing are important in this context. Two other factors are also significant. One is the lack of depreciation allowances for residential investment in the UK and the perceived lack of attractiveness of residential investment by financial institutions. Fiscal reforms which make the provision of rented accommodation more financially attractive could be significant, and incentives to encourage investors to engage in social rental agreements could increase the supply of rented housing in the UK.

A move in this direction which might make the UK more European in its tenure pattern, and in the nature of the ownership of its social housing, could also have a positive effect on the overall level of housing investment. The proportion of national income going into housing investment has, for many years, been lower in the UK than in almost all other European Union countries (Feddes and Dieleman, 1996). Housing investment as a proportion of national income averaged 3.3 per cent in the UK from 1990 to 1994. In Germany the comparable figure was 6 per cent and in France 4.9 per cent (Ball and Grilli, 1997). Housing investment in this sense means money going into new housing developments and improvements to the existing stock. Low levels of investment are in the long run a key factor in producing poor housing conditions.

HOUSING, SUBSIDIARITY AND LEAKAGE

In the absence of direct expenditure on housing by the European Commission, housing organisations have benefited indirectly from European funds that have leaked into housing. Thus housing associations have benefited from funds aimed at projects with, for example, employment generating, training or urban regeneration objectives. Several examples of the success of housing organisations in obtaining such funds have been recorded. European structural funds are related to specific objectives and targeted at regions that have unemployment rates or levels of industrial decline compatible with these objectives. There are, in particular, examples of housing organisations in Scotland and Wales that have benefited from European funding (see Brown and Passmore, 1998, pp. 107–8; Stirling, 1998).

The application of the subsidiarity principle involves inconsistencies that stretch its rationale to the limits. The EU is concerned with labour mobility, unemployment, social exclusion and inequalities.

These are all areas where there are housing consequences and sometimes housing causes. FEANTSA is among several Europe-wide alliances which have called for the subsidiarity principle, with respect to housing, to be reviewed. (For an example of FEANTSA's activities and views, see Mugnano, 1998.) Despite such lobbying it is unlikely that a European housing budget will develop. However, the EU will continue to have more than a watching brief on housing provision in member states. Housing ministers do meet annually to consider progress on housing themes. The European Commission sponsors the periodic production of data on housing in the European Union. More needs to be done at the EU level if the connections between housing and a wide range of economic and social objectives are to be better understood. This will help to reduce the likelihood of housing circumstances in a member state impeding the achievement of EU objectives and of housing markets suffering adverse effects from European-level actions.

This better understanding should involve more European-level research into the relationships between housing provision and economic and social prosperity and a much improved set of EU housing data. Despite the efforts of the Commission, we know very little of a meaningful nature about a plethora of differences between countries including variations in housing quality, access to housing, housing costs and housing expenditures. The evidence which is available from a growing volume of academic research into housing systems in Europe points to a vast diversity in housing conditions, tenure types and forms of government intervention. Any attempt to replace subsidiarity by harmonisation in housing policies would have to be abandoned before it began. A common currency is an easier proposition than a common housing policy.

TYPES OF SUBSIDY

There are, however, many common trends in housing policy in several EU states. The major shift that has been noted from subsidising building production to subsiding the costs of housing consumption, can be supported by the political rhetoric of subsidising people not buildings. But it can be a very expensive and inefficient way of improving housing conditions and making housing affordable for low income households. In the UK, the volume of public resources supporting housing has changed little in real terms since the mid-1970s. The composition of the spending has, however, changed dramatically, with direct support for council housing falling and housing benefit rising to become the largest and fastest growing part of the housing budget (Hills, 1997, p. 69). Most other EU states that have housing allowances are also faced with a burgeoning bill. Many are searching for reforms to reduce the size of the bill (for example, the Netherlands; see Priemus, 1998).

If housing allowances are to help low income households meet their housing costs there is a good case for reforms which do two things. First, there is much sense in helping all households in need irrespective of whether they are tenants or low income home owners. Second, a closer integration with other welfare assistance would streamline the fairness and administrative efficiency of the system. A universal housing allowance available to all households would replace, in the UK, housing benefit and the last vestiges of mortgage interest tax relief. Such an allowance and its equivalent in other countries would be financed by member states. The magnitude of such payments could be less if production subsidies kept down housing costs and helped to ensure an adequate supply of decent housing. Such expenditure would be directly related to real investment in housing.

Where real housing investment, which improves the quality and quantity of the housing stock, also promotes economic growth, urban regeneration and increased prosperity there is no reason why such support should not, in selective cases, come from EU funds. This would not amount to abandoning the principle of subsidiarity but would be a pragmatic recognition of the very significant links between housing investment and wider aspects of well-being and the quality of life.

CONCLUSIONS

Throughout Europe, improvements in living standards will continue to be constrained by two main housing issues: housing investment and housing affordability. These are no longer determined by decisions taken only within member states. They are determined by, and help to determine, economic success and well-being across international boundaries. The recognition of this within the EU will be entirely compatible with EU objectives such as economic growth and social cohesion.

For the UK, more stable housing markets and the growth of social housing institutions which are at arm's length from government will be promoted by both European integration and learning from other countries. Poor housing conditions and poor people are linked throughout Europe, as they are throughout the world. Improving housing conditions and tackling poverty is easier with economic growth but it also requires redistribution of resources. Within Europe we will have to accept that some of that redistribution is within member states but some is between EU partners.

REFERENCES

Ball, M. and Grilli, M. (1997) *Housing Markets and Economic Convergence in the European Union* (London: Royal Institution of Chartered Surveyors).

Boelhouwer, P. (ed.) (1997) *Financing the Social Rented Sector in Western Europe* (Delft: Delft University Press).

Bootle, R. (1996) *The Death of Inflation: Surviving and Thriving in the Zero Era* (London: Nicholas Brealey Publishing).

Brown, T. and Passmore, J. (1998) *Housing and Anti-Poverty Strategies: A Good Practice Guide* (Coventry and York: Chartered Institute of Housing and Joseph Rowntree Foundation).

Feddes, A. and Dieleman, F. (1996) 'Investment in Housing in Ten Northwest European Countries, 1950–1985', *Tijdschrift voor Economische en Sociale Geografie*, Vol. 87, No 1, pp. 73–9.

Hawksworth, J. and Wilcox, S. (1995) *Challenging the Conventions: Public Borrowing Rules and Housing Investment* (Coventry: Chartered Institute of Housing).

Hills, J. (1997) *The Future of Welfare: A Guide to the Debate* (York: Joseph Rowntree Foundation).

Housing Today (1998) 'Update: EMU, the Housing Market and Social Housing', 18 June, pp. 1–3.

Lloyds Bank (1998) *Economic Bulletin*, No. 19, February.

Mugnano, S. (ed.) (1998) *Current Trends in Social Welfare and Access to Housing in Europe* (Brussels: FEANTSA).

Oxley, M. (1995) 'Private and Social Rented Housing in Europe: Distinctions, Comparisons and Resource Allocation', *Scandinavian Journal of Housing and Planning Research*, Vol. 12, pp. 59–72.

Oxley, M. (1999) 'Institutional Structure of Housing Finance in the UK', *Urban Studies*, April.

Priemus, H. (1998) 'Improving or Endangering Housing Policies? Recent Changes in the Dutch Housing Allowance Scheme', *International Journal of Urban and Regional Research*, Vol. 22, No. 2, pp. 319–30.

Priemus, H., Kleinman, M., Maclennan, D. and Turner, B. (1994) 'Maastricht Treaty: Consequences for National Housing Policies', *Housing Studies*, Vol. 9, No. 2, pp. 163–82.

Stirling, T. (1998) 'Slicing the European Cake', *Housing*, June, p. 17.

Wilcox, S., Bramley, G., Ferguson, A., Perry, J. and Woods, C. (1993) *Local Housing Companies: New Opportunities for Council Housing* (York: Joseph Rowntree Foundation).

8

An American Perspective

Edward G. Goetz

INTRODUCTION

Housing policy has not been a central concern of the Clinton Administration, the President's major initiatives in domestic policy being in welfare reform, health care and budget deficit reduction. Just two years into his first term, the Republican takeover of both the House of Representatives and the Senate led to serious talk in Congress of abolishing the Department of Housing and Urban Development (HUD). The combination of both the President's lack of interest in housing policy, and defensiveness within HUD after the Republican efforts to eliminate the agency have eliminated the possibility of any major expansion of public sector activity in housing. In fact, the innovations in housing policy during the Clinton years have been directed at reducing costs and streamlining housing assistance programmes. Clinton's housing policy has been characterised by the recycling of old policy approaches, shifting spending emphasis from certain tools to others, and modifying programmes and approaches that have been around Washington for decades. At the same time, however, many of the minor adaptations have allowed the Clinton team to put its own identifiable stamp on American housing policy. In most cases, the emphasis of the Administration has been towards implementing various aspects of the third way.

President Clinton has rarely made pronouncements related to housing and urban development matters. Therefore, high profile and explicit discussion of the third way in housing policy in the USA is rare.

However, the President's two appointees to HUD, Cisneros (from 1992 to 1997) and Cuomo (since 1997) have more frequently used the vocabulary of the third way to describe agency initiatives.

HOUSING OBJECTIVES AND THE CLINTON ADMINISTRATION

The Clinton Administration has attempted to achieve four broad policy goals in the arena of housing and community development. The first is to address the severe problems of physical and social decline in the nation's worst public housing projects. Problems of crime, drug abuse and social alienation characterise the country's worst public housing projects. Second, the Administration has consciously attempted to increase the rate of home ownership in the country, both as a means of generating macro economic activity and enhancing local communities. Third, the Administration has attempted to increase the income diversity of central city neighbourhoods by encouraging greater mobility on the part of public housing recipients. Fourth, the Administration has used HUD as a test case for its efforts to reinvent government. It should, however, be noted that the reinvention of HUD was as much a response to Republican efforts to eliminate the agency as it was a proactive effort at bureaucratic reform. These reinvention initiatives, usually led by Vice President Gore, have been efforts at defining bureaucracy in an era in which big government is no longer possible or, according to the Administration, desirable. In addressing each of these major policy problems, the Administration has incorporated several elements of the third way.

BALANCING RIGHTS AND RESPONSIBILITIES IN PUBLIC HOUSING

A central element of the third way is a call for greater personal responsibility in community affairs through a balancing of the rights and responsibilities of citizens. In relation to housing policy, this tenet has been most directly expressed in two initiatives; the first is the crackdown on drug use and criminal behaviour among public housing tenants, and the second is the continued emphasis on self-sufficiency programmes for residents of assisted housing.

In relation to anti-crime efforts in public housing, a number of policies have been developed. Although the United States has been engaged in a vigorous war on drugs for many years, the Clinton Administration has increased the emphasis on eliminating drug related crime problems from public housing. The first effort in this arena actually occurred during the Bush Administration with the passage of the Public Housing Drug Elimination Act of 1988. Recently, the programme has provided between $250 and $300 million per year to local housing authorities to fight crime and drugs. Under Clinton, the federal government has stepped up these efforts through the creation of 'operation safe home' and the 'one strike and you're out' policy.

'Operation safe home' combines the efforts of federal, state and local housing agencies and law enforcement agencies in fighting crime in public and assisted housing. Local task forces have been set up around the country to facilitate anti crime efforts. Between 1995 and 1998 the programme has led to the seizure of $25.5 million worth of illegal drugs, 1,860 weapons, including 200 assault weapons, and $3.6 million in drug money, according to HUD. The 'one strike' policy dates to the President's State of the Union address in 1996, in which he declared: 'Criminal gang members and drug dealers are destroying the lives of decent tenants. From now on, the rule for residents who commit crime and peddle drugs should be one strike and you're out.' The policy was formally adopted by Congress and enacted in March 1996. It includes efforts to toughen tenant screening in order to deny admission to public housing for those who have engaged in illegal drug use and other criminal activities. In addition, under the programme, HUD encourages the use of lease provisions that explicitly prohibit drug related and criminal activity, making it easier for local housing agencies to evict residents.

Anti-crime measures in public housing have created some controversy among those who complain about the infringement on the civil rights of poor, usually minority households living in the targeted public housing. Of particular concern is the fact that in many cases innocent family members are denied subsidised housing because of the illegal acts of another household member or guest (Saffran, 1996), or that residents relinquish some of their civil liberties as a result of stepped up surveillance and crime prevention activities (Miller, 1998). The response on the part of public housing officials emphasises the responsibilities of the individual to the community and the need to create safe communities for the majority of residents who are law abiding. The denial of assisted housing to a family that cannot follow tenancy rules is seen both as a means of improving the living environment for neighbours, but also as giving another needy family the opportunity to live in subsidised housing. Indeed, aggressive anti-crime activities in public housing are consistent with a de-emphasis of individual rights in the face of community benefits, a central tenet of communitarian thought.

Promoting the economic self-sufficiency among public housing residents is also a recurring theme in Clinton housing policy. Like anti crime efforts, programmes to increase the self-sufficiency of public housing residents (and thereby decrease their dependency on welfare) pre-dated the Clinton Administration. Nevertheless, self-sufficiency is strongly aligned with other Clinton Administration efforts at welfare reform and redefining rights and responsibilities to the larger community. HUD has grafted the self-sufficiency effort on to its main programme of public housing redevelopment, HOPE VI. All public housing redevelopment projects using HOPE VI funding must include an element of social spending aimed at providing a range of social service supports to residents, focused on facilitating the transition of these families out of public income assistance programmes and into employment (Epp, 1996). HUD's continued emphasis on self-sufficiency is part of the Administration's larger effort to reduce welfare dependence, an objective that serves the purpose of reducing the size of government and establishing new expectations about the work responsibilities of poor households.

CITIZENSHIP AND SOCIAL CAPITAL

A second major element of third way thinking that has permeated Clinton's housing policy is an effort to make housing and community development policy serve the purpose of enhancing citizenship and the connection of residents to their communities. Operationally, this is being promoted through efforts at creating (or in some cases re-creating) social capital within urban communities and communities of public housing. There is, according to one Administration official, a 'growing consensus that social capital constitutes an important new dimension for community development' (Lang and Hornburg, 1998). The claims made for social capital are plentiful: it can result in higher quality housing and lower crime rates (Saegart and Winkel, 1998), it can lead to greater neighbourhood stability (Temkin and Rohe, 1998), it improves the economic conditions for poor and minority households (Briggs, 1998), and it may even provide communities with the ability to respond to federal efforts to devolve social policy to the local level (Lang and Hornburg, 1998). There are three policy initiatives that are being used by HUD to increase social capital in assisted housing: expanding home ownership through the National Homeownership Strategy, creating better community design through the HOPE VI public housing redevelopment programme, and mixing incomes in assisted housing through residential mobility programmes.

In relation to expanding home ownership, according to the announcement of the National Conference on Homeownership Zones in 1996:

There is no better foundation for rebuilding communities and restoring self-sufficiency than homeownership. Home is where our connection to our community, our city, and our country begins. And that is where HUD's homeownership strategy and Homeownership Zones begin. Imagine the decaying neighbourhoods in your community; then imagine these neighbourhoods transformed. New brick homes and new homeowners, all with a stake in the community. Neighbours sit on porches and share stories and smiles. Row after row of new houses spur revitalisation and economic development. There is energy and hope.

Home ownership has always been a central element in American housing policy (Hays 1995).

The focus on home ownership has reflected a general consensus, supported by a great deal of research (see Rohe and Stewart, 1996, for a review), that home ownership produces positive results for families and communities. According to the research evidence, home ownership is related to greater levels of voluntary and political organisation activity, greater levels of interaction with neighbours, greater commitment to one's neighbourhood, greater neighbourhood stability and less residential turnover, and stability in property prices. Whereas in the past, home ownership programmes have been pursued because of their appeal to middle-class constituencies (Hays, 1995), the Clinton Administration clearly emphasised the communitarian benefits of home ownership. The National Homeownership Strategy (NHS), announced in 1995, is aimed at achieving home ownership for 67.5 per cent of the American population by the end of the year 2000. This would mean an increase of 8 million home owners during that period and bring the home ownership rate in the USA to an all-time high. The NHS is a collection of 100 separate action items involving an extensive network of public and private partners. Among the action items is an initiative called home ownership zones. Created in 1996, home ownership zones are designated areas of blight that will receive HUD funding for land purchase and infrastructure improvements to facilitate the development of new home ownership housing. In the first year, HUD distributed $100 million to local home ownership zones. The programme has not, however, received funding for the past two fiscal years.

In relation to enhanced community design, the Clinton Administration, especially through the efforts of Cisneros, has enthusiastically endorsed the notion that aspects of community design can strongly influence the connectedness of residents to their communities. This idea has been the driving force behind much of the physical redevelopment of distressed public housing projects that has taken place during Clinton's terms in office. The fate of the nation's worst public housing projects became an item of public policy deliberation with the creation of the National Commission on Severely Distressed Public Housing (NCSDPH) in 1989. NCSDPH was formed by Congress to establish recommendations for dealing with older, generally high rise public housing projects that had become physically decayed and were characterised by high levels of social distress. The conclusion reached by the Commission is that the USA public housing programme systematically created neighbourhoods of isolation, alienation and fear, devoid of any meaningful community social interaction (Spence, 1993). The Commission's recommendations led to the creation of the HOPE VI programme in the autumn of 1992, just months before Clinton took office. HOPE VI, or the Urban Revitalization Demonstration programme, is aimed at producing the physical and social renewal of severely distressed public housing communities. Under Clinton, the programme's objectives have been to transform these public housing projects into vital and integral parts of their neighbourhoods and to create an environment that encourages self-sufficiency in residents (Epp, 1996).

HOPE VI, as implemented in cities across the nation, usually involves the demolition of high rise public housing towers, and their replacement with lower density, mixed income developments. Central to the success of HOPE VI projects is reducing the concentration of poverty in the public housing neighbourhoods, and invoking design elements that foster community building and the creation of social capital. Many HOPE VI projects endorse the precepts of new urbanism, an architectural and design movement aimed at capturing the best elements of older American communities that fostered face-to-face interactions among neighbours. The tenets of new urbanism are strongly supported by communitarians as a way of re-engaging people in their communities. As support, the new urbanists point to the stability of older American neighbourhoods, even those troubled with poverty, and the resources within these communities to deal with problems that do arise (for a dissenting view, see Bennett, 1998).

These communities of the past are contrasted with the desolate and isolating landscape of the modern ghetto (and more specifically, the modern public housing project) in which neighbours are isolated from each other and for which it is possible to say that no real community exists. The new urbanism informs both community design and architecture. In the realm of landscape design, the emphasis is on narrower streets, sidewalks, parks and public gathering places, and a street layout that integrates residents rather than isolating them (Langdon, 1997). Identifiable, clearly demarcated (and therefore defensible) space (such as lawns marked by hedges or small fences) also produces greater watchfulness of outdoor areas. In terms of architecture, the emphasis is on porches, a friendly front and a more human scale to structures (Bothwell et al., 1998). These design features are thought to produce a series of positive outcomes for the community, including:

> upholding central principles of good citizenship; vigorous involvement in a geographic community; interchange with people with different stations in life; a healthy combination of guidance and independence for youngsters; responsive local government; and local support of culture, charity and philanthropy. (Langdon, 1997, p. 36)

Critics, on the other hand, argue that this is simply a form of physical determinism and point to the range of positive outcomes that was expected for the now discredited super block or campus approach to public housing (Bennett, 1998; Von Hoffman, 1996). Nevertheless, former HUD Secretary, Cisneros, declared that the new urbanism would be a central element in the department's attempts to rebuild communities for the poor. These design elements have been used in a number of HOPE VI public housing redevelopment projects, as well as incorporated into HUD's home ownership zone initiative.

The last policy element being used to foster social capital in communities of assisted housing is income mixing of residents. As important to some in pinpointing the cause of decline in American public housing as design, is the fact that federal policy has constrained the ability of local public housing agencies to rent to a wide variety of income groups (Spence, 1993). The tenant preferences mandated by Congress during the 1970s and 1980s resulted in a less differentiated public housing population and one that increasingly came from the very bottom of the income distribution. This extreme concentration of poverty, in turn, results in a series of social pathologies that ranges from drug abuse and criminal activity to teenage pregnancy, dropping out of school, and low labour force attachment (Jargowsky, 1996). According to Wilson (1987, p. 144), the lack of a sufficient number of higher income families in poorer neighbourhoods:

> made it more difficult to sustain the basic institutions in the inner city (including churches, stores, schools, recreational facilities, etc.) in the face of prolonged joblessness. And as the basic institutions declined, the social organization of inner-city neighborhoods (...sense of community, positive neighborhood identification, and explicit norms and sanctions against aberrant behavior) likewise declined.

As a result, according to this argument, a mix of income groups within a neighbourhood is necessary for the maintenance of social institutions and social organization, such as social capital (Spence, 1993; Epp, 1996; Temkin and Rohe, 1998). This has been a main element of the HOPE VI redevelopment projects, and it is also the rationale for so-called mobility programmes that facilitate the movement of subsidised low income households out of neighbourhoods of concentrated poverty (see Briggs, 1998). Income mixing was also incorporated into HUD legislation in 1998, allowing a greater degree of moderate income households in public housing projects. Most mobility programmes around the USA, including the federal moving to opportunity (MTO) programme, are modelled after the Gautreaux programme in Chicago. The Gautreaux programme was the result of a US Supreme Court decision in 1976 that required HUD and the Chicago Housing Authority to provide metropolitan-wide housing opportunities to public housing residents. The programme provides Section 8 vouchers and certificates (housing allowances) to public housing residents to be used in non concentrated parts of the Chicago metropolitan area. While concentration is defined in racial terms in the Gautreaux programme, in the federal MTO programme, concentration is defined by reference to the percentage of families below the poverty level. Thus, the federal programme is an income integration programme.

In addition to MTO, HUD has begun to settle several discrimination lawsuits (similar to Gautreaux but covering other cities) by agreeing, in most cases, to tear down concentrations of public housing and replace them either with lower density housing, scattered site public housing or housing allowances that are to be used in non concentrated areas. In many cases, the consent decrees entered into by HUD and the local housing authorities produce special agreements that resemble a combination of HOPE VI redevelopment of public housing and MTO type mobility programmes.

REINVENTION OF GOVERNMENT

The third way puts a premium on reorienting government bureaucracies to decentralise public activities and increase the consumer friendliness of government. The Clinton Administration has undertaken several efforts to reinvent government, none more extensive than HUD. In 1995, the Administration unveiled its 'Reinvention Blueprint' for HUD that laid out three major reforms:

- removing subsidies from public housing authorities and making them compete with the private market;
- consolidating 60 major categorical programmes into three block grants;
- restructuring the Federal Housing Administration to respond more quickly to market cues.

Implementation of the Blueprint has been piecemeal and is ongoing. In 1997, Secretary Cuomo revealed a management plan for the agency. The document, called 'HUD 2020', features the creation of two different types of customer service centres to connect HUD more directly to the people and groups it serves. The plan also attempts to streamline operations and eliminate fraud and waste.

CONCLUSIONS

The policy initiatives described in this chapter are not the only recent housing initiatives that reflect themes of the third way. Smaller initiatives such as the creation of Community Development Financial Institutions and HUD's support of communities of faith in urban redevelopment efforts also reflect the desire to rethink the connection between government and communities. What is striking about these efforts is that the core idea for the policies virtually all pre-date the Clinton Administration. Clearly, support of home ownership has been a long standing American housing policy. Anti-crime initiatives in public housing are not new in the Clinton Administration, nor are mobility programmes or even HOPE VI. The third way, at least in housing, has not produced any qualitatively different type of housing programme or policy in the USA. Instead, the contribution of the third way seems to be in the manner that these programmes are used and combined, the objectives they are meant to meet, and the way in which they are framed in official rhetoric.

REFERENCES

Bennett, L. (1998) 'Do We Really Wish to Live in a Communitarian City? Communitarian Thinking and the Redevelopment of Chicago's Cabrini-Green Public Housing Complex', *Journal of Urban Affairs*, Vol. 20, No. 2, pp. 99–116.

Bothwell, E., Gindroz, R. and Lang, R. E. (1998) 'Restoring Community through Traditional Neighborhood Design: A Case Study of Diggs Town Public Housing', *Housing Policy Debate*, Vol. 9, No. 1, pp. 89–114.

Briggs, X. S. (1998) 'Brown Kids in White Suburbs: Housing Mobility and the Many Faces of Social Capital', *Housing Policy Debate*, Vol. 9, No. 1, pp. 177–221.

Epp, G. (1996) 'Emerging Strategies for Revitalizing Public Housing Communities', *Housing Policy Debate*, Vol. 7, No. 3, pp. 563–88.

Hays, R. A. (1995) *The Federal Government and Urban Housing: Ideology and Change in Public Policy* (Albany, NY: State University of New York Press, 2nd edition).

Jargowsky, P. A. (1996) *Poverty and Place: Ghettos, Barrios, and the American City* (New York: Russell Sage Foundation).

Lang, R. E. and Hornburg S. P. (1998) 'What is Social Capital and Why is it Important to Public Policy?', *Housing Policy Debate*, Vol. 9, No. 1, pp. 1–16.

Langdon, P. (1997) 'Can Design Make Community?', *The Responsive Community*, Vol. 7, No. 2, pp. 25–37.

Miller, S. R. (1998) 'Order and Democracy: Trade-offs between Social Control and Civil Liberties at Lake Parc Place', *Housing Policy Debate*, Vol. 9, No. 4. pp. 757–74.

Rohe, W. M., and Stewart, L. S. (1996) 'Homeownership and Neighborhood Stability', *Housing Policy Debate*, Vol. 7, No. 1, pp. 37–81.

Rossi, P. H. and Weber, E. (1996) 'The Social Benefits of Homeownership: Empirical Evidence from National Surveys', *Housing Policy Debate*, Vol. 7, No. 1, pp. 1–35.

Saegert, S. and Winkel, G. (1998) 'Social Capital and the Revitalization of New York City's Distressed Inner-City Housing', *Housing Policy Debate*, Vol. 9, No. 1, pp. 17–60.

Saffran, D. (1996) 'Public Housing Safety Versus Tenants' Rights', *The Responsive Community*, Vol. 6, No. 4, pp. 35–9.

Spence, L. H. (1993) 'Rethinking the Social Role of Public Housing', *Housing Policy Debate*, Vol. 4, No. 3, pp. 355–68.

Temkin, K. and Rohe, W. H. (1998) 'Social Capital and Neighborhood Stability: An Empirical Investigation', *Housing Policy Debate*, Vol. 9, No. 1, pp. 61–88.

Von Hoffman, A. (1996) 'High Ambitions: The Past and Future of American Low-Income Housing Policy', *Housing Policy Debate*, Vol. 7, No. 3, pp. 423–46.

Wilson, W. J. (1987) *The Truly Disadvantaged: the Inner City, the Underclass and Public Policy* (Chicago: University of Chicago Press).

Part 2

Visions for Housing

Introduction

Tim Brown

The previous chapters highlighted the importance of housing policies in tackling a wide range of social and welfare issues. A coordinated approach is also required in ensuring that policies reflect the needs of local communities. There is, however, a dilemma between balancing the development of a top–down holistic approach so as to ensure that a third way approach is achieved and the encouragement of a bottom–up approach building on initiatives arising from local action.

The Conservative government introduced many reforms including new types of regulation and greater competition within the public sector to increase efficiency. Much of the rhetoric underpinning these measures was based on the benefits of adopting a market orientated approach so freeing individuals and organisations from the bureaucratic nature of state involvement. But one of the unintended effects was that attempts to create a more market orientated system resulted in even greater degrees of government intervention that stifled individual and community initiatives. The complex and ever increasing set of regulations and guidance on compulsory competitive tendering of services including housing management illustrated this problem.

Is there not a danger, therefore, that the third way will become an overtly top–down prescriptive approach dictated by central government? This, despite some of the principles underpinning the third way that place great emphasis on individual rights and responsibilities, the role of local communities and, according to Giddens (1998), the importance of democratising democracy. Indeed, it might be argued that some aspects of the third way, such as communitarianism, place fundamental importance on local communities as the building block for social capital as well as the development of a balance between rights and responsibilities. Nevertheless, supporters of a communitarian perspective, such as Tam (1998), argue for instance that governments should be committed to inform and involve citizens in state activities. Thus the key issue is the balance between a top–down and a bottom–up approach, but that the former must not be prescriptive and detailed.

The contributors to the second part of the book include a politician, a housing professional and academics. Each of them attempts to develop a broad vision for housing that enables local innovation to flourish. More importantly, each reflects the changing governance of the UK since 1997. Many housing textbooks have previously adopted a Westminster centred approach to policy, and often failed to reflect on the different housing agendas in Northern Ireland, Scotland and Wales. Prior to 1997, this type of approach was often inexcusable, but now it is simply irrelevant. The emerging peace settlement in Northern Ireland with its implications for elected representatives directly responsible for housing, and the establishment of national assemblies in Scotland and Wales in 1999, require a new approach for thinking about housing issues. Furthermore, the formal establishment of regional development agencies in England in 1999 and possibly in the medium term the creation of regional elected assemblies raise interesting issues on the governance of housing. What are the implications for local government? What will be the consequences for quangos such as the Housing Corporation? What will be the reaction of local communities? It may well be that there will be important lessons for England from the experiences over the next few years in other parts of the UK.

The Minister for Housing and Local Government in Chapter 9 highlights the importance of housing within the government's broader agenda. She stresses that the legacy of the previous government's policies place limitations on what can be achieved in the short term. Even so, during the first two years of the Labour government many important decisions have been made that will shape the long-term development of housing policy as part of an holistic approach for tackling poverty and social exclusion. These decisions are based around a series of principles, which she believes reflect third way thinking. They include making the housing system work for everyone, empowering people and communities as stakeholders, helping to build sustainable communities and improving public services.

The chapters on Scotland and Wales, by Goodlad and by Stirling respectively, reflect a rather different starting point. Both authors highlight that Westminster has never fully acknowledged the specific issues and problems facing both countries. Moreover, despite the rather different legislative and organisational context, especially in Scotland, these issues have never been fully reflected in housing policies and practices even though there have been many interesting local initiatives. Not surprisingly therefore both Goodlad and Stirling speculate on the implications of the establishment of national assemblies. They suggest that there will still be a strong influence from Westminster on aspects of housing policy (and the powers of the assembly will be greater in Scotland than in Wales). But both authors are optimistic that in future housing policies are more likely to reflect specific national needs and the requirements of local communities.

Gray and Paris in Chapter 12 reflect on the uncertain situation in Northern Ireland. They comment that it will take a long time for 'normal politics' to emerge and that the governance of housing will continue to operate within a turbulent political environment. A number of changes in housing policy have been suggested by the present government including the possibility of the transfer of housing and planning powers away from the Secretary of State. Also the future of the Northern Ireland Housing Executive remains unclear. But as Gray and Paris argue, it is essential that new administrative structures build on rather than dissipate the strengths of the Executive.

REFERENCES

Giddens, A. (1998) *The Third Way* (Cambridge: Polity Press).
Tam, H. (1998) *Communitarianism – A New Agenda for Politics and Citizenship* (London: Macmillan).

9

A New Vision for Housing in England

Hilary Armstrong MP

A NEW VISION AND A PRACTICAL RESPONSE

The Labour government is committed to developing a new and radical framework for housing. We need to throw out a lot of baggage from the past, develop a clear vision for the future, and set clear and achievable goals. The overall aim of the government's housing policy is to offer everyone the opportunity of a decent home and so promote social cohesion, well-being and independence. Good housing policies are important in themselves. But under Labour, housing has moved much closer to the centre of social policy. For example, housing policy is:

- an important element in a wide range of government policies, such as strengthening the family, meeting welfare to work objectives, and tackling social exclusion;
- the catalyst for the government's drive to renew and regenerate our poorest neighbourhoods;
- the foundation on which to build sustainable and cohesive communities where people are enabled to enjoy safe, decent and productive lives.

The task of developing a new vision for housing must run alongside the practical job of tackling the mess inherited by the government in

May 1997. Let us not forget the reality of Labour's inheritance in housing:

- Investment had reached an all-time low, the consequence of a continuous squeeze throughout the Tory years.
- There was no strategy for dealing with the very poor condition of the housing stock in all tenures.
- Social housing was perceived to be part of the problem not part of the solution. Council housing in particular was stigmatised after years of neglect.
- Despite all the talk, tenants were kept on the margins and at arm's length from real decision making.
- The private rented sector had been deregulated, a process funded at enormous cost in housing benefit with few gains in terms of improved conditions and better management.
- The leasehold regime was even more muddled following half-hearted attempts at reform.
- No attention had been paid by government to the dysfunctional features of the home ownership market which adversely affected so many home owners as consumers.
- A balanced housing strategy had been abandoned in favour of an ideological obsession with breaking up council housing.

THE LABOUR GOVERNMENT'S EARLY PRIORITIES

Since the general election there has been intense speculation about the future shape and direction of housing policy. The government has been flooded with ideas and proposals that have been both valuable and valued. The government wants to encourage further debate, especially around the long-term future role of social housing.

In the first phase after the election, the government's approach has been to act where possible; to change and develop policy where necessary; and to consider the future carefully. Manifesto commitments have been kept firmly in view. In some areas we have been able to move quickly. In others a longer period of consideration has been necessary, especially through the intensive and successful comprehensive spending review. There are a number of areas where legislative change is necessary, but the pressure of parliamentary business has made it impossible to bring forward early housing legislation.

Nevertheless, the government has made swift progress to improve the housing chances and choices of people. Some of the most important initiatives taken include:

- The early release of nearly £1 billion through the capital receipts initiative brought housing investment back from the brink, improving 300,000 homes for 300,000 families and providing new homes in the social rented sector.
- Following the comprehensive spending review, making available an additional £3.9 billion for housing over three years, so meeting in full our manifesto commitment to provide extra resources for housing from accumulated capital receipts.
- Reshaping the housing investment programme process, moving away from crude bidding for ever declining funds and placing a new emphasis on the development of local housing strategies and local partnerships, and ensuring a fairer distribution of investment resources linked more closely to need.
- Pushing forward the agenda for achieving best value in housing, with a strong emphasis on tenant involvement and community consultation.
- Developing a tenant participation compact to ensure that tenants are fully involved in the management of their housing everywhere.
- Putting substantial extra resources into the rough sleepers initiative and extending it beyond London to cities and towns across the country and then, following an investigation by the Social Exclusion Unit, making the strategy to bring rough sleeping down to as near zero as possible a priority across all government departments.
- Reversing one of the most disgraceful acts of the Conservative government by restoring access to permanent housing for homeless people.
- Launching a consultation exercise to find a way of dealing with the cross-subsidy from housing revenue accounts to rent rebates (now about £1.4 billion a year) in response to widespread concern about the unfairness of the poor subsidising the poorest.

There have been dozens of other decisions that mark a radical shift away from the Tory inheritance. Of course, it's just the start. It is in the nature of the beast that housing will not be put right in a few short months. But there are grounds for optimism that the framework is being put in place, and that housing will be a success story for the government during the next election and the one after that.

Not all of the important announcements affecting housing come out of the Department of the Environment, Transport and the Regions (DETR). Given the central importance of housing finance to housing policy, the Chancellor of the Exchequer's policy statements on the 'golden rule', the future of the public finances and the outcome of the comprehensive spending review have been vital to the development of housing policy.

The separation of current and capital spending is perhaps of greater significance to housing than any other policy area. The comprehensive spending review has released significant additional resources to get the job under way. With the introduction of best value, resource accounting and long-term asset management plans, there will be opportunities for greater flexibility and innovation to generate prudent and sensible investment, and so address years of underinvestment and infrastructure neglect. The government has started to tackle many of the barriers to efficiency and effectiveness that have been identified in recent years.

THE PRINCIPLES UNDERLYING THE GOVERNMENT'S APPROACH TO HOUSING

Achieving the government's overall aim for housing will involve all the partners in the housing world. But the government has specific areas of responsibility that are the cornerstones on which our housing policy will be built:

- It is the government's responsibility to seek to make the housing market work for all the people, to protect the vulnerable and reduce the scope for exploitation.
- It is the government's responsibility to seek to empower people as stakeholders in the homes and communities where they live.
- It is the government's responsibility to seek to maximise the effectiveness, efficiency and accessibility of public services serving those communities.
- It is the government's responsibility to seek to strengthen communities, their stability and sustainability.

Making the Housing Market Work for Everyone

The housing market does not and cannot accommodate the needs and aspirations of all. Government must intervene, but intervention must be targeted and strategic, empowering and enabling, not centralising and controlling. Making the housing market work for all means protecting the vulnerable and creating opportunities for self-help and independence. It is an essential element in our effort to overcome social exclusion. This is why tackling the problems of neighbourhoods which face multiple deprivation and tackling the problem of rough sleeping were two of the first three priorities for action given to the Social Exclusion Unit by the Prime Minister. The government's national strategy for neighbourhood renewal is to be achieved through an extensive programme of work which involves virtually all of the Whitehall departments working together to develop practical solutions.

At local level, local authorities will have the key strategic housing role. This is why the government has heavily revised the housing investment programme (HIP) guidance and developed strategic joint commissioning between local authorities and the Housing Corporation for registered social landlord (RSL) schemes. Too many local authorities still see strategy as an add-on to the real job of managing council housing. To be effective, authorities should separate their strategic and housing management functions. Strategy means moving away from a service by service and tenure by tenure approach to a comprehensive, corporate focus, working closely with a wide range of partners.

Never again must ideology become an excuse for inactivity. In making the market work for all, we must back practical ideas to raise the quality of the housing stock, free of the ideological obsession with tenure. The government will not force councils to transfer stock but if it generates additional funds, if it is viable, and if it is what tenants want, then transfer is an appropriate option. What matters is what works.

Housing needs are far from homogeneous around the country, indeed local conditions probably vary more now than at any time since the Second World War. It is vital that authorities carry out comprehensive assessments of needs and requirements to inform their housing strategies and investment decisions. Increasingly, local authorities will need to cooperate in subregional or conurbation-wide assessments to ensure that neighbouring authorities are supporting and not undermining each other's efforts. In each area of the country there is a difficult balance to be struck between investing in the existing stock and investing in new social housing. Decisions on the best balance should be taken as far as possible at the local level, taking account of the available resources.

The most obvious failure of the housing market occurs when people are left homeless or living in overcrowded, unfit and inappropriate properties, and are unable to exercise a genuine choice within the housing market. Rough sleeping is one of the most visible, serious and disturbing manifestations of social exclusion. We are committed to reducing to as near zero as possible the numbers of people sleeping rough in Britain. The Social Exclusion Unit's report on rough sleeping, commissioned and launched by the Prime Minister in July 1998, set out a considered and coordinated approach to tackling rough sleeping into the next century.

The homelessness legislation, which the Conservatives forced on local councils in 1996, disrupted a long established consensus on how to deal with the needs of homeless families and vulnerable individuals. It compounded market failure with bad politics. The government took early action to restore access to permanent housing for homeless households, and will publish a revised code of guidance on homelessness and allocations. This will provide councils with new directions on the discharge of their duties towards the homeless, and give guidance on issues such as joint working between social services and housing departments, on preventative measures, and on action to help single homeless people gain access to the housing market.

To make the housing market work we also have to address the problems in the private rented sector. If the market is to work in the interests of all then we must see an improvement in both quality and value in the private rented sector. There are some good private landlords who value their tenants as well as their properties and proceed in a fair and sensible way. Their efforts and commitment are appreciated. However the benefits of the modest expansion in the private rented sector following deregulation have failed to trickle down to those on lower incomes with the least power in the market. Some properties, particularly those in multiple occupation, are not just squalid and in disrepair, they can be a potential death trap. There is understandable public concern at the sight of landlords failing to deliver acceptable conditions, or even the benefit of basic health and safety, while continuing to receive housing benefit payments. They are exploiting those least able to exercise choice in the housing market, and they are exploiting the taxpayer who often picks up the bill for their high rent and low value housing.

Under Labour, the rights of landlords will be respected and upheld but they must do right by their tenants. Where necessary the government will intervene. For example, the government is developing options for a scheme which will prevent exploitation of tenants who have paid deposits that are not honoured by landlords. The government would prefer a voluntary approach, where all landlords recognise their responsibilities. But we will legislate if voluntary action means landlord inaction. When there is an opportunity to legislate, the government will meet the manifesto commitment to introduce universal licensing for houses in multiple occupation (HMOs). In the interim, the government has encouraged local authorities to use their existing powers, for example to set up HMO registration schemes, more extensively.

Nearly 70 per cent of people in this country own their own home. For another 10 per cent, it is their preferred long-term housing choice. The government is in favour of home ownership where it meets individual or family aspirations and where it is affordable. The government will intervene to reduce the level of risk and uncertainty which is borne by millions of ordinary people in the process of buying and selling and obtaining loans. The aim is to speed up the buying process and to beef up the protection for home buyers. The government wants to see more mortgages with flexible repayment arrangements, allowing increased repayments during the good times and lower payments, even contribution holidays, when times get tough, and an industry-wide standard for mortgage protection policies.

Making the market work for all also means reducing the scope for leasehold exploitation. Despite 30 years of legislation, serious problems persist for many leaseholders. There has been an accumulation of quick fixes, sticking plaster solutions, rather than a consistent and coherent framework of leaseholder rights. The government is consulting widely on options for change.

It stands to reason that the housing market is not working efficiently and effectively if large swathes of housing are unfit for human habitation. It is vital to raise the quality of housing, not least because it is often the case that the poorest people are living in the lowest quality homes. Raising standards across all housing means having a reliable yardstick against which to assess the worst conditions. The government's proposal to develop a home fitness rating as a replacement for the current fitness standard has been widely welcomed. The rating will measure health and safety risks in the home and provide a more effective mechanism for identifying and targeting action on the worst housing.

Empowering the Individual

The government's housing policy must not just strengthen the market place; it must also empower the individual. Home ownership provides people with their own stake in the housing market. We will focus on giving all social housing tenants a similar stake in the communities where they live.

For too long, the benefits system has combined with a paternalistic approach to council house allocations, to create a system where some families, over two or more generations, have exercised little or no choice within the housing market. The state has made choices on their behalf: where they will live; how much is their rent; even, although this is now largely a thing of the past, what colour the front door had to be. Choice and freedom must not be the preserve of the private sector alone. For the next century, the government will ensure that social housing tenants have far greater choice and power, self-reliance and personal responsibility. Tenants will be empowered to get involved in the management of their homes and to work in real and meaningful partnerships with their landlord. Many housing authorities, and many housing associations too, have a good track record here; but too many others do not.

As with regulation of private landlords, the first approach is to encourage voluntary action. We should not have to legislate for something which should be a central feature of the practice of all social landlords. But the government will use the law if necessary to empower local people as stakeholders in the management of their housing.

The way forward must be to enable tenants to become involved effectively and to the degree which they choose. The tenant participation compact between local authority tenants and landlords will set out common standards for tenant involvement across the country and provide a framework within which both tenants and landlords can work. It will draw together common standards for tenant involvement and set out what is possible, what is desirable, the council's role and minimum standards for tenant participation. In parallel moves, the Housing Corporation is strengthening its policies on tenant involvement in housing associations.

Tenant empowerment is not a fashionable add on; it is one of the four cornerstones of the government's housing philosophy. It needs not just the commitment of government but the support of all landlords, with the emphasis on an equal partnership between landlord and tenant, based on trust, openness and willingness to cooperate.

Best Value in Housing

Alongside efforts to make the housing market work for all and to empower people as stakeholders in their homes and communities, the government has a responsibility to ensure that public services are of high quality and high value. Poor quality services have a major impact on the public reputation and self-respect of local communities. House prices fall if good quality schools are not available, if the streets are not clean, if the public realm is not cared for, if transport links are poor, if crime is rife, if the quality of life is low. In some parts of the country, where tenants do have some choice, they are beginning to vote with their feet and move to better areas.

Weak housing management often compounds the problems facing tenants on the most deprived social housing estates. Excellence in estate management should be the target of all and mediocrity and poor performance should be unacceptable to all. This is the aim of best value, which will apply to housing management and the whole housing service, backed up by a housing inspectorate within the Audit Commission Standards Inspectorate. The Housing Corporation will apply a parallel regime to registered social landlords.

Of course housing management alone does not determine the quality of life on estates. The duty of best value will apply to all local services. It will challenge the existing quality, service delivery and performance standards of public services and provide the opportunity to develop innovative programmes for service improvement. The government will not leave local people to endure mediocre standards of public service. Neither will we tolerate service failure. Locally, housing managers will often be well placed to lead the transformation which is needed.

The government aims to create a culture of reform and reward to boost public service performance. We will link housing investment programme and capital receipts initiative allocations to the quality of local strategies and to performance. Good performers will receive more and poor performers will receive less. Those helping to improve public service will be rewarded by this government for their efforts. Where all else has failed, the government will retain powers to take over the management and delivery of services from failing local authorities.

Strengthening Communities

The fourth cornerstone of the government's housing policy is to strengthen communities, their stability and sustainability. This government believes in strong communities where power, wealth and opportunity are widely shared. The government's belief in the good society, the strong community, stands in stark contrast to the 'no such thing as society' politics which left so many communities damaged by high unemployment, low educational achievement, high crime and few opportunities. To address the long-term market failures in the areas with the most severe deprivation, it is necessary to combat their long-term social and economic decline. Links between housing, regeneration and other social policies are vital.

The 'new deal for communities' (launched in September 1998) is beginning to tackle social exclusion in the most deprived neighbourhoods by improving the opportunities and life chances of local residents. It will bring housing and regeneration spending together to achieve improvements which last, extend economic opportunities for local people through training, skills and employment development, improve neighbourhood management and the delivery of local services. It is an ambitious project but it could alter the landscape of decline in Britain's most deprived areas.

Government does not always have the solution. Indeed, in many of these areas, central and local government may have been part of the problem. The 'new deal for communities' will therefore focus resources in support of local partnerships and decision making, which fully involves the communities from the outset. It will strengthen the capacity of communities to take key decisions about the regeneration priorities in their area and support strategies which tackle them effectively.

The first stage involves a number of pathfinder projects in some of our most deprived communities. Their role will be to inform the development of the full initiative and the government's broader strategy on tackling social exclusion. Stable communities are only possible where residents feel safe and secure, not just locked in their own homes but safe for the children to play and the elderly to get together. This is why the government has placed such emphasis on tackling young offenders and the problem of disruptive neighbours. It is the job of government to help to restore order to communities wrecked by crime and the fear of crime.

In addition, the government intends to create more sustainable communities by ensuring a wider mix of public and private housing development, different types of tenure and mixed use. This cuts both ways as planning guidance should ensure more affordable housing within private developments, and revised local strategies should ensure more shared ownership and low cost home ownership within social housing schemes.

Of course, council allocation policies have to continue to ensure social housing goes to those in the greatest need. However, the government wishes to encourage councils to drop unnecessary restrictions on entitlement to appear on a housing register or be considered for housing as part of a planned programme for creating more mixed and sustainable communities.

CONCLUSION

The development of effective housing policies is central to a wide range of social issues and programmes. Good housing is essential in tackling social exclusion and in building prosperity for individuals and communities.

In the years ahead, the task is to create a housing market which is better able to meet the needs and deliver the aspirations of the people; a housing market in which people have a greater personal stake; a housing market served well by public services; and a housing market which contributes to the creation of stronger communities and a stronger economy.

10

Challenges and Opportunities: A Scottish Vision for Housing

Robina Goodlad

INTRODUCTION

Housing policy in Scotland is at a junction created by the convergence of recent economic, social and political as well as constitutional developments. The establishment of the Scottish Parliament provides a timely opportunity to focus on the housing needs and aspirations of the people of Scotland. Accountable to them, it can create the housing policy framework required for the achievement of empowerment, quality and security for all citizens. This chapter outlines the housing issues the new Parliament faces; it considers the challenges for housing policy and suggests how the new opportunities might be used creatively to improve housing opportunities for all, especially those least able to operate in the market.

CHALLENGES FOR THE FUTURE

Conditions, Finance and Tenure

Scotland has a distinctive history, geography and legislative tradition which mean that housing conditions and housing policy differ in important respects from the rest of the United Kingdom. The most striking feature is the tenure structure, with a lower incidence of owner occupation – 60 per cent in 1997 – than in the rest of the United Kingdom. Local and public authorities own more than one in four houses (28 per cent in 1997), compared with 54 per cent in 1976. Tenure change since the 1980s was driven by the right to buy but also by a growing proportion of new housing in the private sector and by stock transfer, usually to community based housing associations and cooperatives, pioneered primarily as a device for securing investment and tenant involvement.

Scottish Homes received a growing proportion of public spending on social rented housing (relative to local government) in the period from 1989 to 1996 (see Table 10.1). Housing associations were able to lever a growing level of private funding into their projects until cutbacks in the last two years of the Conservative government prevented further expansion.

The Conservatives have left a damaging legacy by transferring public spending from bricks and mortar subsidies to individual rebates and allowances (housing benefit). In addition, spending on housing fell as a proportion of all government spending. As a consequence, there are serious and emerging housing condition problems, although the Scottish House Condition Survey 1996 reports a reduced level of below tolerable standard housing, from 4.7 per cent in 1991 to 1.3 per cent in 1996. More than nine in ten dwellings fail the national home energy standard. Dampness and condensation are found in 41 per cent of private rented housing and in 34 per cent of public rented housing. Some council housing suffers from serious disrepair, with 16 per cent of tenants in housing with repair costs greater than £1,200 (Scottish Homes, 1997).

The worst neighbourhoods tend to contain also the largest concentrations of unemployment and poor health. Efforts to tackle the problems include new housing partnerships, programme for partnership and the new deal for training and jobs. The Labour government's New Housing Partnerships are a significant initiative to tackle the problem of low investment in the council sector by using private finance. What is 'new' about the model is the greater stress on tenant involvement, the deployment of £278 million arising from the comprehensive spending review from 1999 to 2002 (in addition to the £45 million already committed in 1997 to 1999) and the commitment to dealing with residual debt. Proposals are not limited in scale and might include whole stock transfers, providing arrangements for community participation are in place at all levels.

Table 10.1 Trends in Housing Spending and Subsidy: Key Indicators (£ millions)

Type of public spending	1989/90	1991/92	1993/94	1995/96	1996/97	1997/98
Local Authority Capital† (council housing)	486	476	475	579	421	299*
Local Authority Capital† (private sector)	157	111	119	121	91	59*
Scottish Homes**	205	235	303	316	293	199*
Private Finance Levered In	10	87	149	199	170	130*
Mortgage Interest Tax Relief	470	420	300	200	n.a.	n.a.
Exchequer Subsidy to Local Authority HRA	65	56	36	22	19	15
Housing Benefit (to LA tenants)	364	446	524	562	601*	586*

(Adapted from Wilcox, 1997, various tables)

Notes: *estimate; n.a. not available; **i.e. mostly capital grants to housing associations; †strictly provision for rather than actual spending; mostly financed by borrowing.

Owner occupation retains its hold on the public imagination, but bitter experience by some owners and evidence from the Scottish House Condition Survey suggest caution about quality and sustainability. Tax breaks, on a smaller scale, and discounts under the right to buy continue to boost the sector but expenditure on private sector repair and improvement grants has reduced by one-half since 1995/96. The consequences are serious for particular client groups and house types, for example, some ethnic minorities. The growth of owner occupation has highlighted the incoherence of public support for the tenure. Creating an appropriate policy framework will be a challenge complicated by the split in functions and financial instruments between UK and Scottish levels.

Discrimination and Disadvantage

Much housing policy is already targeted on groups whose housing situation – without public policy – would be compounded by disadvantage or discrimination. As a result, just over one in eight (14 per cent) public sector tenants and a similar proportion of housing association tenants (15 per cent) are long-term sick or disabled, a much higher proportion than in any other tenure (Scottish Homes, 1997). This could be considered a triumph for the targeting of public provision were it not that too much of the public sector stock is in need of urgent repair or is located in unattractive and problematic neighbourhoods.

Some citizens benefit less than others from the targeting of policy. In particular, some housing providers have a poor track record in addressing the needs of black and minority ethnic communities who suffer very poor conditions and overcrowding compounded by serious discrimination and harassment. The work of Scottish Homes and a few local authorities and housing associations needs to be built on by others. Similarly, some local authorities are more vigilant than others in tackling homelessness. At a Scottish level, policy under Labour shows more continuity than change, although the rough sleepers initiative has been extended with an additional £1 million to £16 million in phase one and £14 million for a second phase has been announced. As tenure change continues, the needs of homeless people should be met by ensuring access to council or other rented housing. In addition, solutions need to be found to a multiplicity of social and employment problems at local and regional as well as individual level if homelessness is to be prevented.

Management and Participation

The development of tenant participation has been limited in Scotland in the absence of any statutory rights for tenants. Small advances have been made in the face of deterioration in the overall status of tenants. Now, however, there is a strong focus on tenant participation by the new government. Proposals developed by a working party, including tenants' representatives, propose to grant public and housing association tenants new rights to involvement. The Scottish Office also intends to involve tenants in formulating national housing policy (Scottish Office Development Department, 1998).

Two other issues have dominated debates about management. First, managerialism combined with a belief in markets has been replaced by the new government with an emphasis on excellence in service delivery, to be achieved through best value within the public sector if possible but in the private sector if necessary. Second, neighbour disputes have at times consumed more column inches in Scotland's newspapers than any other issue. Amidst the controversy, too little attention is given to the potential of a variety of existing management and legal remedies less draconian than those now proposed.

THE OPPORTUNITIES

We now consider how these challenges for Scottish housing policy might be addressed at national and local levels.

The Parliament

Overall, the Scottish Parliament has been given a substantial housing role. In addition, it has powers over all the key elements of area regeneration including land use planning and the work of Scottish Enterprise. Broadly, three matters are reserved to Westminster:

- the tax system;
- the regulation of banks and building societies; and
- the social security system, including housing benefit.

However, 'The Scottish Block will include expected expenditure on housing benefit and council tax benefit at the time the Scottish Parliament comes into operation' (Dewar, *Hansard Written Answers*, 20 January 1998, col. 488). It is housing benefit relating to council tenants which is involved here, creating, in the short term at least, an incentive to promote more stock transfers.

The housing role can be seen as falling into two parts: strategy and legislation. While it is tempting to argue that there should be a minister responsible for housing alone, it is more important that there be coherence in the links with area regeneration, health, social work, land use planning, local economic development and education.

The Parliament's housing strategy needs to clarify roles for local authorities, housing associations, Scottish Homes (or any replacement bodies), voluntary organisations, private developers and financial institutions. In addition, the Scottish Executive and Parliament will face some difficult dilemmas in devising its housing strategy in relation to the balance in development between urban and rural areas and green field and brown field sites, and between policy priorities such as energy efficiency, new building, rehabilitation, homelessness and support for particular tenures.

The Scottish Executive and the minister responsible for housing will implement the Parliament's housing strategy through activities such as setting the housing budget in competition with other areas of expenditure, deciding on the allocation of capital consents and grants between local authorities and other housing developers or tenures, dealing with planning appeals, ensuring the registration and monitoring of housing associations and other registered landlords, funding voluntary organisations, consulting pressure groups and responding to local authority housing plans. The Parliament and Executive are likely to be judged on two key issues: the future of the council stock and owner occupation.

In relation to the first, strong tenant involvement is as essential as investment. While some on the left of the political perspective will set their face against transfer on ideological grounds, most tenants and local authorities will be willing to consider the conditions under which they would find housing associations, local housing companies and other transfer options acceptable for their worst estates. Local authorities can continue as landlords where the stock is good, the tenants are satisfied and the prospects of investment and good management are sound.

Elsewhere, the proposals most likely to succeed are those that attract private funds, provide comparable rents, ensure tenant involvement and good management, and provide a route to spread existing debt burdens across tenants and the wider community. In large transfers, there is a risk that transfer to one body would fail to achieve the improvements in management, morale and tenant participation that usually follow the creation of neighbourhood based housing organisations and, second, would make it harder to put right any future management failures. The interests of housing management staff and direct labour organisations come second to tenants but their future should not be ignored. The new Scottish government should examine the issues that arise for workers in public–private partnerships to ensure proper consultation and protection for the right to organise.

The new Parliament will have to ensure that present intentions for tenant participation are realised with legislation and promotion. In relation to other management issues, delivering best value will be a challenge for local government which at times may become a challenge for national government, uncertain when to intervene. Finally, striking an appropriate balance in the measures used to deal with neighbour disputes while maintaining civil liberties will be an important issue.

Second, the issue of the future housing conditions of Scotland will increasingly depend on the capacity of individuals and families to sustain good quality housing in the private sector. The public resources available for owner occupation would be better targeted on the people most in need, requiring the Parliament to seek Westminster or Whitehall cooperation to implement parts of their strategy. But subsidy is not everything. Owner occupiers may need assistance, for example in working out a scheme for maintenance, achieving improvements in energy efficiency or coping when times are hard. Flexible tenure, allowing people to move more easily between owning and renting, should play an important part here as should a variety of forms of housing advice.

The Parliament will also have substantial legislative powers. It should take the opportunity to:

- review the right to buy and amend it, or the discounts applying to it;
- introduce a new unified tenancy package for all social rented sector tenants, including a new right to participation;
- strengthen and change the strategic housing role of local government; and
- reform the law relating to feudal land ownership rights and planning.

Scottish Homes

Scotland's national housing agency has a number of functions, all of which need scrutiny in the changed conditions of Scotland at the turn of the century. The landlord role has been phased out substantially, amidst controversy about lack of choice, leaving fewer than 20,000 houses remaining. The policy of disengagement can be promoted by Labour for what it is: there is now no case for a Scotland-wide public landlord and transfers should take place to another form of collective ownership, community based landlords, who are tenant managed or on which there is strong tenant representation.

Scottish Homes has shown more enthusiasm for its development funding role, applied mainly to the task of supporting the development activities of housing associations. Increasingly grants have been allocated in collaboration with local authorities and it is proposed below that the task of allocation should be transferred to local authorities.

Regulation has gone hand in hand with funding, but experience in other sectors suggests that regulation and funding should not be carried out by the same body, since this can create divided loyalties as between consumers' interests and funding imperatives. A Scottish Homes without development funding could, therefore, become a highly appropriate body to regulate housing associations and alternative landlords, including local authorities. The boundary between this role and the work of the (Scottish) Accounts Commission would need to be rethought.

Scottish Homes staff have built up a strong record in research and in local market analysis. Such analysis will continue to be required at Scottish level. In addition, it is important that this expertise be spread to the diminishing number of local authorities who have been slow to appreciate the value of local housing systems analysis. Research and analysis are essential if the Parliament is to carry out the role envisaged for it and Scottish Homes has shown it has the skills for such work. Scottish Homes staff could also play a role in promoting innovation in housing management, planning and development, including the promotion of alternative landlords. Whether the officers concerned are technically civil servants or not is probably less important to all but them, perhaps than their line of accountability, which must be to the Executive or Parliament.

Local Government

Under the Conservatives, no positive vision was apparent of what the housing role of local government might be. There are three ways in which the Parliament could change this. First, the role and purpose of local authorities should be redefined so that they become the lead agency in community governance. Local authorities might have a duty to promote the well-being of communities and a new power of community initiative to respond to local needs, similar to the recommendation of the joint Convention of Scottish Local Authorities (COSLA) and Scottish Office Community Planning Working Group (Scottish Office and COSLA, 1998).

Second, a new housing act should clarify and update archaic provisions, for example in relation to the private sector, renewal, housing advice, strategic planning, needs assessment and regulation. The Convention of Scottish Local Authorities and individual local authorities recognise there is no going back to the post-war position of local authorities as large-scale housing developers and have argued for a more positive future (COSLA, 1998).

Third, local authorities should have responsibility for the funding of housing development and renewal by housing associations and other agencies. One view is that local authorities should have this responsibility but only after giving up their landlord role. An alternative view is that a separation could be created between landlord and enabling functions by restoration, at least temporarily, of the block allocation for expenditure on non council housing. Either option would create some confidence among housing associations that resources would not be applied inappropriately to capital investment in council housing when it would achieve greater value in the housing association sector, though local authorities would have to work hard to provide the reassurance that they have the skills, expertise and commitment to housing associations to take on this role.

CONCLUSION

This chapter has reviewed the challenges and opportunities facing the Scottish Parliament and argued that it will be able to make a real difference. The main challenges for Scottish housing policy are:

- the serious disrepair in the housing stock in all tenures except housing associations;
- the needs of the worst neighbourhoods in the public rented sector;
- to produce coherence and targeting in policy for owner occupation;
- to resolve (within the UK) the problems associated with housing benefit;
- to ensure better targeting of policy and financial support on socially excluded groups;
- to make best value work effectively over time in public and social rented housing; and
- to give tenants new legal rights to participation and to ensure their implementation.

The main opportunities are:

- to provide coherence in housing governance, recognising links with area regeneration and other policy fields;
- to consolidate the initiatives taken to promote regeneration of the worst public sector estates;
- to sustain good quality housing in the private sector with better targeting on the people most in need;
- to use the Parliament's legislative powers positively to review the right to buy, tenancy conditions, and land and planning law;
- to make regulation and monitoring of all social and public landlords the responsibility of a slimmer Scottish Homes or a new agency;
- to ensure a research and analysis capacity, accountable to the Parliament; and
- to enhance the housing role of local authorities with development funding and community planning and by clarifying the powers and duties of local housing authorities.

REFERENCES

Convention of Scottish Local Authorities (1998) *Housing into the Millennium: A New Agenda for Councils* (Edinburgh: COSLA).

Scottish Homes (1994) *Action for Race Equality* (Edinburgh: Scottish Homes).

Scottish Homes (1997) *Scottish House Condition Survey 1996* (Edinburgh: Scottish Homes).

Scottish Homes (1998) *Framework for a National Strategy for Housing Information and Advice* (Edinburgh: Scottish Homes).

Scottish Office and COSLA (1998) *Report of the Community Planning Working Group* (Edinburgh: Scottish Office and COSLA).

Scottish Office Development Department (1998) *Partners in Participation: Consultation on a National Strategy for Tenant Participation* (Edinburgh: SODD).

Wilcox, S. (1997) *Housing Finance Review 1997/98* (York: Joseph Rowntree Foundation).

11

A Vision for Wales

Tamsin Stirling

INTRODUCTION

This chapter outlines a vision for the future of Welsh housing. In housing, as in many other policy areas, Wales starts from a different place than the other countries of the UK. Acquiring a better understanding of the nature of the difference of Wales will be a key aspect in developing appropriate policy and investment responses in the future. From May 1999, the National Assembly for Wales takes on a range of responsibilities with respect to housing. The powers of the Assembly include developing secondary legislation and guidance, making decisions on investment and the development of policy and strategy. Such powers could be exercised to the considerable advantage of people living in poor housing conditions across Wales. The Assembly also needs to work with Westminster on areas that require primary legislation.

This chapter starts by identifying the key components of the existing Welsh housing environment and summarises the housing inheritance of the National Assembly for Wales. It then moves on to identify two key current themes for housing in Wales and sets out three potential strands to the future development of Welsh housing policy.

BACKGROUND

The Welsh Context

Wales has certainly suffered from being the 'and' in England and Wales. Unlike Scotland, Wales has worked with the same primary legislation as England. Many former Department of the Environment consultation papers were simply issued by the Welsh Office in the same form, while legislation and policy initiatives have often seemed inappropriate. There is a reasonably widespread feeling that Westminster has not understood the problems of the country and that, particularly under the last administration, both legislation and policies were clumsily applied. In many instances, Wales has been an afterthought. The advent of the National Assembly for Wales offers the chance to change this; for housing policies in Wales to be based on the reality of the problems and concerns of Wales and its communities. So what is different about Wales?

Wales is distinctive: geographically, culturally, linguistically, demographically and economically. All these characteristics, and others, have had impacts on the housing landscape. The geography of Wales affects people's ability to travel quickly from one part of the country to another. Varied topography means that certain housing types have become prevalent in different areas, such as the terraces of the South Wales valleys. The distribution of first-language Welsh speakers varies markedly across the country and concern for Welsh speaking communities presents particular challenges for housing policy. In many areas, such concern interacts with questions about how rural communities are to survive and prosper.

Average household incomes are lower in Wales than in the rest of the UK. This is due to a combination of low rates of economic activity, high levels of benefit dependency (including long-term sickness) and low incomes for many people who are in work. There appears to be a trend of an increasing gap between Wales and the rest of the UK. In 1996–97 household incomes in Wales declined in relation to the UK average (Williams, 1998). An employment history associated with heavy industry, in decline for some decades, has had severe impacts in particular areas. The current structure of the economy shows that there is a continuing reliance on manufacturing and that both wages and productivity in this sector are high. In stark contrast is the service sector, which is underdeveloped and characterised by both low wages and productivity.

In housing terms, Wales is also distinctive. The country has the highest level of owner occupation in the UK at over 71 per cent and outright ownership is also higher. Its housing stock is older than that in the rest of the UK; 36 per cent of homes were built before 1919 compared to 26 per cent in England. The results of the last Welsh House

Condition Survey showed that over 13 per cent of all homes were defined as unfit, with an estimated cost of £565 million to bring them into good repair (Welsh Office, 1994). At the time of writing, the results of the Welsh House Condition Survey which was carried out in 1998 are still awaited. The problems presented by a greater proportion of home owners who are, on average, poorer and whose homes are, on average, older and in poorer repair, cannot be ignored if the National Assembly is indeed to 'improve the quality of life for all the people of Wales and promote social inclusion' (Welsh Office, 1998b).

It should also be noted that Wales is not a homogeneous country. There are significant differences between rural Wales, the south Wales valleys, urban areas and the north Wales coastal strip. The regional structures of the Assembly should have sensitivity to these differences at their heart; they will have a key role in ensuring that the diverse needs of Wales are addressed.

The Housing Inheritance of the National Assembly

The extent of housing problems in Wales has been described as a crisis (Chartered Institute of Housing in Wales and Shelter Cymru, 1996). In reality, the picture painted by housing is as varied as for any other policy area. There have been considerable successes and notable failures. Wales has perhaps avoided some of the worst excesses of past housing finance and policy systems such as large-scale high rise estates. But significant problems exist.

The only study of housing need at a national level was carried out by Holmans (1996). This concluded that the already high level of owner occupation in Wales is only likely to increase slowly from present levels and that an overall shift from building for private owners to building for the social rented sector is needed. The study indicated that between 4,000 and 5,000 new homes for rent are required each year up to 2011. This contrasts with just under 3,000 new homes which have been built by housing associations in 1998–99. This national picture of need masks local variations; patterns of need at a local level are becoming increasingly complex. Housing can be built quickly if there is an increase in demand, but as houses are fairly permanent features of the landscape, when demand decreases, housing lags behind (Chartered Institute of Housing, 1998). The current distribution of housing in Wales reflects its economic history, whereas current demand reflects the present and, to some extent, the future. In some areas, there may well be a surplus of housing for rent, but it is in the wrong places and/or is not of an acceptable quality. There are certainly areas of Wales where the demand for homes in the public sector seems to have decreased. The phenomenon of low demand needs further investigation, but available evidence suggests that the division of investment in housing between new build and addressing problems within the existing stock is no longer appropriate.

The housing needs of particular groups in Welsh society, such as rough sleepers, young people and black and minority ethnic groups, have historically largely been ignored. Work is currently being undertaken to find out more about levels of rough sleeping in the 22 unitary authorities so that appropriate strategies and provision can be put in place. A number of Welsh local authorities have developed single homeless strategies. However, it seems perverse that the current homelessness legislation, designed to protect vulnerable households, does not cater for single people, particularly young single people who are penalised by the benefits system and often excluded from the workforce. The needs of black and minority ethnic groups across Wales are not well understood (Franklin and Passmore, 1998). Mainstream provision is often not sensitive to the needs of specific minority ethnic groups; homes of an appropriate size, location and design are crucial. Key issues for all the above groups are knowledge about their needs, sensitivity to their needs and the ability to develop a range of housing solutions.

The picture of underinvestment in the housing stock of Wales is, if not a crisis, certainly a cause for concern. The total repair bill for Wales' housing was estimated, by the 1993 Welsh House Condition Survey, to be £1.2 billion (Welsh Office, 1994). A recent study estimated the costs of putting local authority homes across Wales into a reasonable state of repair at a minimum of £740 million (Chartered Institute of Housing in Wales, 1998a). Current Welsh Office estimates of the backlog of repairs needed in local authority stock is £600 million, with a further £400 million required for improvements. In addition to disrepair and unfitness, there are other elements of the quality of Wales' housing stock that may be inadequate for current and future needs, such as energy efficiency, accessibility and adaptability for independent living.

KEY CURRENT THEMES

Two linked key themes for housing, present and future, are considered here. The first of these is how housing fits into wider debates and objectives about promoting an inclusive Welsh society, while the second is the need to put communities first, to acknowledge their needs and work towards meeting their aspirations.

Housing and Social Exclusion

The current government agenda of tackling social exclusion is clear. What is also clear is that housing needs to be a core element of this agenda. After all, having no home is the most extreme form of social exclusion. Social exclusion is often also identified with local authority and housing association estates:

> This research has identified patterns of social exclusion shared by local authority estates in the region (South East Wales). These estates, often in hilltop locations, demonstrate characteristics of high unemployment, high rates of lone parenthood, poor housing stock, physical and social isolation and social stigma. (Adamson and Burns, 1998)

However, social exclusion is not just about homelessness and social housing. In Wales, there is a significant proportion of owner occupiers on low incomes whose housing does not meet their needs and, in many cases, prevents them from participating in society. A key issue for the future is how housing can play its full part in tackling social exclusion rather than contributing to it.

The link between housing and other areas of policy is key to the exclusion agenda. Housing has long been recognised as a key determinant of health as 'adequate housing is a vital component of better health' (Welsh Office, 1998c). There are also links between housing and educational achievements, employment opportunities and levels of crime. The National Assembly for Wales is charged with a statutory responsibility to produce a scheme for sustainable development. Sustainable development and tackling social exclusion are inextricably linked. Again, sustainable development cannot be achieved if housing is ignored. It will also not be achieved without developing links between housing and land use planning, transport and economic development, as well as with health and social services. The rhetoric of joined up thinking needs to develop into joined up action between housing and other areas, based on an understanding that the scope of housing policies and strategies is far wider than the provision and management of social housing.

Putting Communities First

Shelter is a fundamental human need. For people without a decent home, initiatives to provide them and their families with better education and health care and facilitate access to training and employment will not succeed. A first step in putting communities first is a recognition of the potential contribution of housing to the wider agenda being pursued by the government. One of the recommendations of the People Building Communities Working Party states: 'That the Welsh Office acknowledges the pivotal role of housing in the battle against social exclusion and in pursuit of sustainable development' (People Building Communities Working Party, 1998).

The housing agenda of the National Assembly of Wales should have as its aim the provision of decent, affordable housing for all the people of Wales, so that they can fulfil their potential and participate fully in Welsh society. Indeed, the Welsh Office has already committed itself to the aim of offering 'everyone in Wales the opportunity of a decent home' (Welsh Office, 1998b). Achieving this aim is a long-term objective, as is moving housing from its current position to one where it can properly contribute to the wider agenda. 'To deal with social exclusion on the required scale, the objectives of the (social exclusion) strategy should underpin all aspects of housing policy' (Clapham, 1999). As part of this process, a reappraisal is needed of where housing is built in relation to employment opportunities and other facilities and in relation to the type of land on which it is built. Detailed consideration is also needed as to what housing is built or refurbished in terms of size, accessibility, standards of energy efficiency and adaptability, design and impact on the landscape. In addition, significant changes are needed to the housing finance and benefits systems. Currently, they combine to produce a crippling poverty trap with high marginal tax rates, provide little or no support for low income home owners and feature imbalances between capital and revenue subsidies for housing.

The advent of the National Assembly for Wales presents an unmissable opportunity for housing. It is an opportunity to look at housing in an holistic way and to establish a national policy agenda, which responds to the actual housing problems and opportunities of Wales. It is also an opportunity for such a national agenda to clearly make the links between housing and other policy areas addressing economic, environmental and social issues. There are potentially three strands to future development of housing policy in Wales: meeting needs in better ways; improving housing services; and finding the money for housing.

FUTURE POLICY DEVELOPMENT

Meeting Housing Needs in Better Ways

The starting point for meeting needs in better ways is information. Better quality information is needed on a whole range of housing issues in Wales and certainly some of the work needed requires to be supported financially by the Welsh Office and the National Assembly. For instance, we must develop a better understanding of the links between housing and other government priority areas such as health and education, so that this can influence investment decisions in the medium term. In addition, a comprehensive housing survey, which includes assessment of both the condition of the existing stock and a measure of need for additional homes for rent, is required at a national level so that it can inform overall expenditure decisions and feed into planning guidance. Local authorities should be required to carry out regular assessments of need and demand at community level, rather than at an authority-wide level. This would lead to a better under-standing of localised housing markets and the phenomenon of low demand.

In order to meet various types of housing need in better ways, there are seven key points to consider:

- Addressing homelessness: Current homelessness legislation needs reform. It is limited in scope both with respect to who is helped and how they are helped. Local authorities should be required to have a strategy in place for all homeless people at risk, including young single people. Such a strategy should encompass the provision of independent advice, advocacy and support and outreach work. It would also link into strategies for improvements to the private sector, dealing with empty properties, access and low demand (Shelter Cymru, 1998).

- Improving owner occupation: A wide range of measures must be put in place to improve owner occupation. Such measures can be divided into those which are appropriate at the point when people buy their home, those aimed at people who are already owners but who get into difficulties and those to assist people who are forced to give up their homes (Chartered Institute of Housing, 1997). For instance, housing credit schemes funded by the withdrawal of mortgage interest tax relief should replace the current housing benefit scheme (Welsh Local Government Association, 1997).

- Improving the private rented sector: The private rented sector is significantly smaller in Wales than in England. Very little is known about the sector, except that there are considerable problems of disrepair (Welsh Office, 1994). Current proposals for a licensing scheme for houses in multiple occupation (HMOs) aim to address the worst of these problems. However, there are considerable difficulties in defining an HMO; most people living within the private rented sector do not know if they are living in an HMO or not. In addition, the private rented sector tends to fluctuate in size with changes in the housing market making a further case for licensing across the whole sector to improve standards and protect vulnerable people.

- A single form of tenure for social housing: There are currently a number of legal differences between the tenancy agreements of tenants of local authorities and those whose landlord is a housing association. The introduction of a single form of tenure for the social rented sector would equalise both the rights and the responsibilities of social landlords and tenants. It would also apply to tenants of potential new social landlords such as local housing companies, which may evolve through transfer of local authority stock.

- Sustainable investment in housing associations: The issue of affordability is a vexed one. Grant levels for housing built or refurbished by housing associations should be increased so that rents decrease. This means that fewer homes will be built for the same investment of public money. However, we must move away from the numbers game if housing investment is to achieve sustainable results. The same debate applies to the standards to which housing is built or refurbished. Lifetime homes standards should be incorporated into all new homes so that they are accessible to everyone in the community.

- Housing contributing to a wider agenda: If housing is to contribute effectively to a wider agenda, housing organisations need to be enabled to do so. In particular, secondary legislation is needed to extend the activities in which housing associations can become involved.

- Further research leading to the development of a black and minority ethnic community housing strategy for Wales.

Improving Housing Services

Communities experiencing social exclusion need, if anything, better services from statutory agencies than more affluent areas. However, this is often not the case in reality: 'The community suffers an appalling level of service provision that is both a consequence of its social exclusion but also is one of its major causes' (Adamson and Burns, 1998).

This presents an enormous challenge to all agencies, but perhaps particularly to the 22 unitary authorities across Wales, who have a key role in taking forward strategies to tackle exclusion and poverty. As best value develops, authorities will have to question whether they are best placed to deliver particular services to communities. Where authorities do continue to deliver services, support will be needed so that these services can be continually improved. Housing organisations can be supported by the Welsh Office and the National Assembly in a number of ways. Dissemination of information and examples of good practice does not occur in any structured way at the moment. This should be rectified and, in addition, funding be made available for innovation and good practice developments by housing organisations.

The future framework for regulation should provide a stimulus for improved services. The government's 'better regulation task force' has identified five principles of good regulation; transparency, consistency, targeting, accountability and proportionality (the linking of risk and protection to the cost and burden of regulation). Whatever framework for regulation of local authorities and housing associations emerges in Wales, it should include service users in its operations and an effective system of redress where services are failing.

Service users have a strategic role to play working with individual housing organisations to improve housing services. The current requirement on housing associations to take a strategic approach to tenant participation should also apply to local authorities. In particular, the involvement of tenants in strategic discussions before plans are drawn up is crucial if participation is to be genuine (Tenant Participation and Advisory Service Cymru and the Welsh Tenants' Federation, 1998). The National Assembly for Wales itself should also ensure that there is genuine consultation on policy decisions that will affect communities such as strategic decisions about where investment will, and will not, be made.

Finding the Money for Housing

The money needed to build and improve housing across Wales cannot all come from the public purse. However, there is a view that housing should be considered as a primary area for public investment because of its potential role in producing a better living environment for the people of Wales, promoting social inclusion and good health (Chartered Institute of Housing in Wales, 1998b). The principles of best value and the community action planning process, at the heart of the People in Communities programme, indicate that the priorities of local communities should be incorporated into decisions about the future allocation of resources at both national and local levels. Much work is needed to make this a reality.

There is a need for bringing private finance into housing; and a number of opportunities exist for doing this:

- In the short to medium term, support for pilots of various models of stock transfer should be provided by the Welsh Office and the National Assembly. Practical guidance should also be provided to local authorities on the process of stock transfer to prevent expensive duplication of basic work.
- In the longer term, public sector borrowing requirement (PSBR) definitions should be revisited so that there is wider scope for different models such as local authority owned corporations.

- Notwithstanding the negative findings of a recent survey on equity release, such initiatives and loans for owners whose homes are in need of repair, improvement or adaptation, should be explored in the Welsh context (Joseph Rowntree Foundation, 1998). A particularly problematic issue is the very low value of homes in some areas of the country even after they have been improved.

In addition, funding opportunities should be made available for the wider role for housing to enable linkage with other programmes. A recommendation from the People Building Communities Working Party (1998) is that 'the Welsh Office consider funding mechanisms for activities which might enhance the sustainability of investment in housing'. Housing organisations themselves should be encouraged to access sources of funding which have, to date, perhaps been under-utilised, such as European funding. Housing organisations working in areas of Wales that achieve Objective 1 status have considerable opportunities to do this.

CONCLUSION

The current structure of housing policy and finance works against housing achieving its potential in tackling exclusion. Despite this, many housing organisations are achieving much with communities across Wales. The above proposals represent a long-term proposition to move towards a more sustainable housing future for the people of Wales. It is essential that Westminster, the National Assembly for Wales, local government, housing associations and the voluntary and private sectors all play their part in working towards this aim.

REFERENCES

Adamson, D. and Burns, D. (1998) *Pen-yr-englyn Social Exclusion Audit – Interim Report June 1998* (Pontypridd: University of Glamorgan/Rhondda Cynon Taff).

Chartered Institute of Housing (1997) *Sustainable Home Ownership: New Policies for a New Government* (Coventry: CIH).

Chartered Institute of Housing (1998) 'Low Demand for Housing – Discussion Paper' (Coventry: CIH).

Chartered Institute of Housing in Wales (1998a) *Improving Council Housing in Wales: Finding the Money* (Cardiff: CIH in Wales).

Chartered Institute of Housing in Wales (1998b) 'Opportunities for Change – Consultation Response' (Cardiff: CIH in Wales, unpublished paper).

Chartered Institute of Housing in Wales and Shelter Cymru (1996) *Housing in Wales: Problems and Solutions* (Swansea: CIH in Wales and Shelter Cymru).

Clapham, D. (1999) 'A New Housing Vision for Wales', in Passmore, J. (ed.) *Labour Housing Group Pamphlet 1* (London: LHG).

Franklin, B. and Passmore, J. (1998) *Developing for Diversity: The Needs of Minority Ethnic Communities* (Cardiff: Taff Housing Association).

Holmans, A. (1996) *Housing Demand and Need in Wales 1991–2011* (York: York Publishing Services).

Joseph Rowntree Foundation (1998) *Failure: Equity Release* (York: JRF).

People Building Communities Working Party (1998) *Sustainable Communities for the Future* (Cardiff: Tai Cymru).

Shelter Cymru (1998) *New Approaches to Homelessness* (Swansea: Shelter Cymru).

Tenant Participation and Advisory Service Cymru and the Welsh Tenants' Federation (1998) *Count Us In: A Report on Tenant Participation in Wales* (Cardiff: TPAS Cymru and WTF).

Welsh Local Government Association (1997) *A Housing Manifesto for Wales* (Cardiff: WLGA).

Welsh Office (1994) *Welsh House Condition Survey 1993* (Cardiff: Welsh Office).

Welsh Office (1998a) *Welsh Housing Statistics* (Cardiff: Welsh Office).

Welsh Office (1998b) *Comprehensive Spending Review: Modern Public Services for Wales* (Cardiff: Welsh Office).

Welsh Office (1998c) *Strategic Framework – Better Health, Better Wales* (Cardiff: Welsh Office).

Williams, P. (1998) *Wales in Housing Finance National Markets Review 1998* (London: Council of Mortgage Lenders).

12

A Vision for Northern Ireland

Paddy Gray and Chris Paris

INTRODUCTION

Housing provision and management in Northern Ireland have been politicised and controversial for over 30 years (Murie, 1992). The 1960s civil rights movement sought reform of a range of discriminatory social policies, particularly arguing that local councils allocated public housing on sectarian lines. Direct rule since the early 1970s, together with the removal of all housing and planning powers from local government, created a form of governance of housing that is unique in the UK.

One statutory authority, the Northern Ireland Housing Executive, has dominated social housing provision and management since 1971. The Executive is responsible to the Department of the Environment, Northern Ireland (DoENI), which has controlled all government housing policies. A close-knit housing policy community has evolved, with many individuals occupying multiple roles. As in most policy arenas in Northern Ireland, housing has benefited from a relatively generous treasury subvention; this has been reflected, since the early 1980s, in significantly higher levels of public housing construction than in Britain.

Much remains uncertain at the time of writing. Developments in the peace process, culminating in the Good Friday Agreement in 1998, the referendum and elections for the new Northern Ireland

Assembly, suggest that a new governance structure is emerging. This would mark the end of the democratic deficit in an administrative state in Northern Ireland and require locally elected politicians to make decisions about policy directions and the allocation of limited resources. Some commentators have argued that continuing peace will result in greater prosperity, more inward investment and growth in tourism. Others, however, have argued that the treasury subvention may well be lost, together with thousands of (mainly Protestant) police jobs, and that under peaceful conditions the Northern Ireland economy would become 'just another part of the European periphery, with no particular reason to perform better than anywhere else' (Bew et al., 1997, p. 118).

Whatever happens in the economy, and to resources available to the Assembly, it will take a long time for normal politics to emerge in Northern Ireland. Political parties remain structured around sectarian divisions and Northern Ireland residents are still refused admission to the Labour Party. Considerable potential remains for disruption of the Assembly and of movement toward a more settled civil society. The governance of housing in Northern Ireland will thus continue to be carried out in uncertain and occasionally turbulent times.

PUBLIC HOUSING POLICIES AND PROGRAMMES

The Northern Ireland Housing Executive (NIHE) faced a huge task in its early years, having to deal with poor housing conditions in a context of civil unrest, and political and economic turmoil. It took over all public housing management, allocation and building from the Northern Ireland Housing Trust, Belfast Corporation, three development commissions and 60 local authorities (Brett, 1986). By 1973 it was responsible for 155,000 homes. This regional comprehensive housing authority still dwarfs other social providers today with its stock of over 140,000 dwellings.

The Executive has enjoyed widespread local support for its success in non discriminatory housing allocation and the transformation of housing conditions through new building, slum clearance, redevelopment and rehabilitation programmes. It has also played a key role in rehousing families affected during periods of intense violence, paramilitary activity and property destruction. Sectarian divisions in housing provision, however, have increased despite the Executive's successes and Catholics and Protestants largely occupy separate spaces (Boal, 1996). Residential segregation is most intense between public housing estates, due to applicants' desire to live among co-religionists rather than being the outcome of Executive allocation policies.

Many key Conservative housing reforms in Britain did not affect the province, especially large-scale voluntary transfers (LSVTs), HATs and compulsory competitive tendering (CCT) in housing management. Even so, the role of the Executive has been changing due to external pressures: its budget has been reduced; new construction fell dramatically from the heady levels of the late 1970s and early 1980s; planned maintenance and stock upgrading has been delayed and rescheduled; new management approaches were imposed; and a high level of sales reduced the overall stock and speeded up residualisation. By the mid-1990s, therefore, the Executive was downsizing in an environment of increasing uncertainty.

Housing policy in Northern Ireland underwent a major review, for the first time since 1971, in the mid-1990s. A lengthy review process aroused many fears in the housing policy community, especially regarding the role of the Executive. Such fears were summed up in July 1996 by the SDLP housing spokesperson, McGrady, commenting on the DoE housing policy review document *Building on Success: The Way Ahead* (DoENI):

> The one body that through a quarter of a Century of turmoil and strife has been able to renew the face of public housing in Northern Ireland while at the same time gaining an almost unique reputation for fairness is about to be destroyed. (cited in Minton, 1996, p. 1)

Subsequent reform proposals partly followed the British model and were being implemented at the time of the May 1997 election. Despite McGrady's fears, the government proposed retaining the Executive as the main strategic housing agency in Northern Ireland and even to give it additional strategic and regulatory functions, especially regarding housing associations. It was also proposed, however, to transfer new social housing development to housing associations. Other possible changes included large-scale voluntary stock transfers to other housing agencies.

Reform proposals were put on ice following the election of the new Labour government. Lord Dubs, a Minister of State in the Northern Ireland Office, announced that he would endorse some of the issues in the review but put others on hold. He endorsed the transfer of new build to associations, the transfer of regulatory functions governing associations from the DoE to the Executive, the introduction of a common waiting list and a common selection scheme, the introduction of competitive bidding among associations, the introduction of voluntary purchase grant for housing association properties, and retaining the Executive to determine overall housing need and develop strategies and programmes to meet that need.

OTHER RENTAL HOUSING

The rented sector in Northern Ireland includes a tiny private rented sector (about 4 per cent of the stock today), over 40 registered housing associations (under 1 per cent of the stock), and a few small other social landlords. The private rented sector has declined dramatically in Northern Ireland, despite limited rent restriction.

Most growth in rental housing provision, outside the Executive, has been in housing associations which effectively date back to the 1976 Housing (Northern Ireland) Order (largely based on the Housing Act 1974). Three-quarters of their rented stock was purpose built after 1976 and most of the rest was rehabilitated or converted after that date (NIHE, 1998). The registration, monitoring and financing of associations was vested in the DoE. Tenant selection policies had to be approved by the DoE, which also set rent levels in line with comparable Executive property (in contrast to the fair rents system in Britain.) Registered housing associations are eligible to receive housing association grant (HAG) from the DoE. Subject to DoE regulation, they have built accommodation for which the Executive had to confirm need and they have allocated dwellings on the basis of selection schemes approved by the DoE.

The government had indicated in 1976 that the Executive would be responsible for mainstream housing and associations should confine their activities to more specialised fields including sheltered housing for less active senior citizens, community based housing renewal, single person housing, supported special needs housing and new types of tenure such as equity sharing. Most associations concentrated on one specialism and they collectively produced about 1,000 rented and a further 800 equity sharing homes per year during the 1980s. The funding basis of associations changed with mixed funding in

1991 (three years after Britain). Exchequer support for housing associations has remained about constant but most projects have been awarded a lower rate of grant. Associations borrowed over £35 million from banks and building societies between 1991 and 1997 (Gray, 1997).

As in Britain, housing associations had a relatively easy ride under the Tories, as their preferred provider of new social housing. Some have become very professional, with excellent management systems and diverse property portfolios; others remained small and some have avoided scrutiny. Some associations have enabled elderly home owners to capitalise their assets and move into subsidised rented sheltered accommodation, some of which is difficult to let. The equity sharing programme has declined significantly during the 1990s and is probably past its 'use-by' date.

Increasingly, again as in Britain, housing association accountability has been the subject of debate. Questions are asked about the use of public funds, the role of committee members, the domination of boards by full-time paid officials, and the growing financial complexity of associations' operations. Board members are still selected by associations in Northern Ireland without outside involvement or regulation; in some cases, indeed, they may be hand picked by association directors. Unlike the Executive, few housing associations have enjoyed cross-community support. Some have been strongly identified with unionist or nationalist political traditions. They have begun to shed symbols which associated them with one grouping or another, some by changing their names, but their past associations with particular interests remain in the minds of the community. As associations in Northern Ireland take on an increased role, so they must come under much greater scrutiny in order to ensure that they can be seen to provide and manage social housing in a fair and equitable manner and with effective targeting of public funds in line with agreed policies. It is, clearly, time for a thorough and rigorous review.

OWNER OCCUPATION

The owner occupied sector has expanded faster than other UK regions during the 1990s and now accounts for about 68 per cent of the housing stock. The expansion of home ownership has been assisted by the sale of more than 70,000 Executive dwellings, mainly to sitting tenants through the voluntary house sales scheme. Public sector stock is currently being transferred in Northern Ireland at a greater rate solely through house sales rate (at 3 per cent per annum) than in Britain through a combination of both house sales and LSVT (just over 2 per cent per annum).

Continued household formation and increased real incomes have also boosted the growth of home ownership. House building has been buoyant and house prices have increased by over 50 per cent during the 1990s. The only significant problems in this sector at present are cyclical: recent interest rate hikes have reduced the affordability of purchase for first-time buyers, but this is likely to be negatively capitalised in house prices, and they are still the most affordable in the UK. We are not aware of any compelling arguments for further assistance to home ownership.

The Executive's strategy anticipates that owner occupation will continue to be the predominant and preferred tenure and that sales to sitting tenants will remain at the current level. The high volume of such sales, however, may be influenced by secondary purchasers, including the children of sitting tenants, to whom the effective discount eventually passes: whether this is an aim of the discounted sale of public assets may be a matter for debate. Private sector construction is expected to fall slightly over the next few years together with a reduction in the rate of house price inflation (NIHE, 1998). Unfitness will continue to decline in certain areas but in other parts there will be little further progress (NIHE, 1998).

NEW DIRECTIONS FOR SOCIAL HOUSING

Tenant participation has not gained much momentum in Northern Ireland, partly due to a fear of the involvement of paramilitaries who maintain their stronghold on public sector estates. Housing associations have shown little interest in tenant participation but the Executive has tried to encourage participation generally and especially within estate based strategies. Fewer than half the Executive's tenants, however, are represented by a tenants' group or association and many tenants show little interest: in one approach to 250 local tenants' groups, for example, only three declared an interest in examining frameworks for greater involvement in the management of their estates (Gray, 1997). Future strategies to assist tenant participation should develop from the expressed wishes of tenants rather than be imposed upon them on the basis of other groups' self-interest.

There is a general recognition both of the move towards a more residualised social housing sector and, at the same time, a need to ensure that social rented housing is acceptable to tenants. Although the province has not yet experienced much demand for LSVT, one association made a substantial bid for Executive property. This did not proceed, but it could pave the way for future bids from associations wishing to expand their activities. The current popularity of the Executive among it own tenants, however, might militate against any such development.

The concept of housing plus has yet to be introduced in Northern Ireland although there has been some diversification of association activity. Some have set up organisations in the Republic of Ireland, particularly along the border counties, to embrace the spirit of regeneration in these vulnerable areas. Belfast Improved Houses, a large association operating in greater Belfast, has set up BIH Holdings which raise money to buy land and build houses to be sold at a profit which can be used to finance the building of social housing. Four foyers have been or are in the process of being built by housing associations, hoping that these will help to encourage labour force participation. There has been growing concern over low investment levels in the west of the province and the need for a major regeneration programme which should also include cross-border initiatives.

The proposals in the housing policy review to transfer the registration, financing and regulatory role of the DoE, during 1998, to the Housing Executive were delayed due to recent political developments. These issues may be determined by the Assembly in its own right. The proposal that virtually all new social housing construction should be transferred to housing associations, effectively doubling their output, may particularly need to be reconsidered. Most associations are very small and therefore the bulk of new build would have to be done by the few larger, more active associations. Mergers are taking place and this process could speed up. Ironically, however, this could result in a situation where fewer regional or province-wide associations more or less mirror the Executive's activities.

In our view it is right that the Executive should be retained due to its vital role within what continues to be a divided society. Its allocation policies have incorporated categories to cater for victims of intimidation and it has purchased private homes from owners having to move as a result of intimidation. The Executive responds quickly to civil disturbances which have resulted in property damage. Despite the relative calm of 1996, for example, the Executive provided temporary accommodation for 260 families forced out after incidents associated with the July Drumcree parade, and met a £2 million bill from property destruction and the need to buy properties from intimidated home owners (Gray and Paris, 1996). Housing associations, both now and in the foreseeable future, have neither the managerial nor the financial resources to accomplish this task, nor do they have full cross-community support. The government, and particularly the new Assembly, should consider the possibility of allowing the Executive to retain a significant new build role.

Other strategic needs are ongoing, especially the need for regeneration policies in urban and country areas, and the building of trust within divided communities. The government must encourage the peaceful development of regeneration policies to suit the needs of the population in a changing economic environment. Inter-agency approaches to housing problems within the wider spectrum of regeneration issues should be given greater importance. The role of housing within wider debates about employment and training also should be addressed, given the high levels of benefit dependency, which is particularly acute in certain parts of the province. The need for economic regeneration should be reflected in both housing investment and consolidating the efforts of the Executive and housing associations over recent years. Increased infrastructural and housing investment is especially required along the north-west corridor stretching from Derry to Sligo as part of an overall policy of reducing levels of deprivation, bad housing conditions and social exclusion.

FINANCE FOR SOCIAL HOUSING

The introduction of mixed funding for housing associations has resulted in an increased supply of social housing stock and has lent support to advocates of transfer of new build to associations. But there could be other means of using private money for social housing provision. The Executive is the obvious candidate to receive extra funding for social housing due to its cross-community acceptance as fair and impartial and also its track record which far outweighs that of the local housing associations. The difficulty, as elsewhere in the

UK, is that Executive activity falls within the confines of the PSBR and it is thus unable to borrow from the private sector. If government would switch from the PSBR to the general government financial deficit mechanism as a borrowing measure, however, it would pave the way for the Executive to become a public corporation (in line with the Treasury's recent announcement that quasi corporations were on the agenda).

Currently, through the private finance initiative (PFI), the Executive maximises the input of private money into the housing market through house sales, land release, facilitating housing associations, developing partnership arrangements with private developers and by providing advice to the private sector. This private sector involvement could go much further if fiscal arrangements were to change. With an asset base of over £1 billion, experienced personnel and a track record of providing and managing housing in a divided community, the Executive would be in an excellent position to attract private finance. It could consolidate the work of the past 27 years and use new finances to enhance its strategic role in meeting housing need throughout the province.

CONCLUSIONS

The reform of housing policy in Northern Ireland has so far resulted in only modest change, and some reforms were delayed with the 1997 election. A number of the Conservatives' commitments remain operative:

- to transfer the Executive's new build role to housing associations leaving only a residual role for the Executive;
- to transfer the DoE's regulatory and monitoring roles in relation to the housing associations and the private rented sector to the Executive; and
- for the Executive to remain the single comprehensive strategic organisation with responsibility for assessing housing need.

New Labour has given a firm commitment that CCT of housing management will not be enforced and that the homeless legislation, which had been introduced to Britain by the previous government, will not be introduced to the province.

The new political agenda following the Agreement, referendum and elections will have a major impact on future decisions. Before the May 1997 election, the Labour Party had published a document setting out its attitude to housing in Northern Ireland. This envisaged the ultimate responsibility for housing being transferred from the Secretary of State to a new Northern Ireland body as part of an agreed settlement. The new Assembly is now in operation, but much remains uncertain, including the operation of the Assembly itself. How will it deal with housing? The planning system, which has remained a DoE bureaucratic closed shop, urgently needs reform and opening up to democratic debate. Should any housing powers be returned to local government? Most councillors have been strongly opposed to this idea, but if local government were reformed, with fewer but larger authorities, this question would need to be reconsidered.

The government, and the Assembly, have to determine who should be the main providers of social housing in the province beyond the millennium. The system which operated after 1971, with the Executive as the main provider and manager of social housing, has been acceptable to all sections of the community. Transferring all new build to housing associations, therefore, is not a satisfactory solution. Nevertheless, the housing association movement should be encouraged to continue to diversify and adapt to the rapid changes that may come about with a political settlement. Given the high levels of segregation that still exist in the province, and the continuing demand for social housing, the government could consider encouraging housing associations to work closely with the Executive to promote integrated housing. Housing associations also could promote cross-border regeneration in the spirit of the peace agreement.

The question of funding must also be addressed and ways should be explored to allow the Executive to utilise its asset base and income stream to borrow from the private sector. This money could then be used to incorporate housing policy within the wider regeneration remit of Northern Ireland. Such additional investment would allow the Executive to consolidate its work by achieving the objectives of its strategy while at the same time encouraging new housing policies in line with the requirements of any new devolved administration.

The future of housing policy in Northern Ireland will depend on the nature of any new administrative framework. New administrative structures, which could include the return of housing and planning powers to local representatives, will set a new context for policy development. It would be important for the government to assess how sustainable a new administrative system might be and the future directions that it should take. This will be strongly influenced by the sectarian divisions that exist particularly within public housing. It is imperative, therefore, that the Executive should remain in existence for the foreseeable future: we should build on the Executive's strengths rather than have them dissipated.

REFERENCES

Bew, P., Patterson, H. and Teague, P. (1997) *Between Peace and War: The Political Future of Northern Ireland* (London: Lawrence and Wishart).

Boal, F. (1996) 'Integration and Division: Sharing and Segregation in Belfast', *Planning Practice and Research*, Vol. 11, No. 2, pp. 151–8.

Brett, C. (1986) *Housing a Divided Community* (Dublin: IPA).

Department of the Environment for Northern Ireland (1996) *Building on Success: The Way Ahead* (Belfast: DoENI).

Gray, P. (1997) 'The Future of Voluntary Housing In Northern Ireland', *Roof*, Vol. 22, No. 1, pp. 14–15.

Gray, P. and Paris, C. (1996) 'A Dangerous Place for Competition', *Inside Housing*, 16 August.

Minton, A. (1996) 'Government Emasculates Ulster Quango', *Inside Housing*, 26 July, p. 1.

Murie A. (1992) *Housing Policy in Northern Ireland: A Review* (Belfast: Centre for Policy Research, University of Ulster, No. 3).

Northern Ireland Housing Executive (1998) *Review of the Northern Ireland Housing Market* (Belfast: NIHE).

Part 3

Stakeholders

Introduction

Tim Brown

Stakeholding is a concept that is closely linked with the third way. Its use has, however, tended to focus on the economy and industry rather than society. Reference is often made, for instance, to the need to extend employee share ownership schemes as a means of increasing the involvement and identification of workers with the firms employing them. But as Hutton (1997) argues:

> The success of a stakeholder economy is dependent on the creation of a stakeholder society. The welfare state is a potentially powerful means of expressing national social solidarity, but is progressively at risk as it becomes organised around means testing and creeping marketisation. (Hutton, 1997, p. 9)

In this respect, Hutton's views tie in with those of Field (1996) who suggests that stakeholder welfare involves a fundamental shift away from means testing towards systems that encourage individual choice. Furthermore, in relation to housing, Hutton (1995) highlighted a litany of the consequences of new right housing policies including, first, a greatly reduced role for local authorities that prevented them from addressing community needs through a successful planning and strategic enabling approach. Second, the powerlessness of tenants to influence the standards of service remained despite creeping marketisation. Third, Hutton pointed out that there were risks and benefits of owner occupation. The volatility of the housing market coupled with insecurity of employment created patterns of inequality in gains and losses for home owners as evidenced by mortgage arrears and repossessions. Fourth, housing associations that have become the main providers of new social housing have been criticised by Hutton for their lack of accountability to local communities as well as for progressively higher rents.

A stakeholding perspective requires that the interests of all these and other groups be incorporated in a socially inclusive manner. The chapters in this section of the book highlight a wide range of ideas on how different interests can be incorporated. It is not, however, as was pointed out in Chapter 1, a comprehensive attempt to define and clarify the role of all stakeholders. The editors acknowledge that there are limitations on coverage as, for example, there is little focus on housing employees as stakeholders. This is a badly neglected area, but the recent work of the Centre for Public Services (1997, 1998) provides an important starting point. Similarly there has been a neglect in mainstream housing literature on the role of women and of specific needs groups such as the disabled. Again, there is a fundamental requirement to develop an analysis of a stakeholder perspective in these areas. The work of the independent living movement, and in particular research by Morris (1993),begins this debate in linking together disability rights and feminist perspectives. The work of Gilroy and Woods (1994) similarly forms the basis for developing a stakeholder perspective for the role of women. Finally, the chapters do not pay specific attention to the construction industry. A useful set of starting points for the debate about stakeholding in the construction industry can be found in Ball (1996) and in *Housing Studies* (1999).

The chapters in this section of the book do provide the beginnings of an analysis of stakeholding in housing. Hood focuses on the role of tenants as stakeholders. She highlights the fact that despite the rhetoric of tenant involvement over the last two decades, they have little real status as stakeholders. Initiatives that improve local authority and registered social landlord accountability to tenants are important, and hence developments such as best value and tenant compacts are to be welcomed. More importantly there is an urgent need to address inequalities in tenants' rights and the lack of legal rights in key areas such as security of tenure. But the most fundamental requirement is for tenants to be able to enforce their rights and hold their landlords to account.

Stoker in Chapter 14 considers the future role of local government. As with many of the contributions to this book, he highlights the tension between a top–down approach and a bottom–up perspective. He argues that there is some evidence of a growing level of trust by central government in the activities of local authorities as illustrated by the willingness to encourage experimentation, to set up pilot schemes and to promote good practice through mechanisms such as best value and beacon status. Nevertheless, this optimism is circumscribed by a concern that some government departments appear less willing to give up a more traditional prescriptive and regulatory style of central–local relations.

In Chapter 15, Clapham suggests a radical way forward for social housing that fits in with third way thinking. He argues that a new vision is required that draws on traditions such as cooperative socialism and communitarianism. And he calls for the further development of community based housing organisations (as developed in parts of urban Scotland) that provide effective housing services while enabling local communities to tackle problems of poverty and social exclusion. This idea is closely linked to many of the other themes within this book including Paterson and Macfarlane's call for a new and wider role for registered social landlords in England for promoting social inclusion, the emphasis by many contributors on the importance of a bottom–up approach, and the significance of learning lessons from other situations. In a number of respects, Tomlins in Chapter 16 also reflects some of these key points. Drawing on a thorough review of the experiences of black and minority ethnic communities, he demonstrates that the third way potentially provides the opportunity for developing a pluralistic form of housing provision that is more responsive and sensitive to the needs of consumers than traditional social democracy or new right approaches. He also argues that despite the constraints imposed by governments over the last two decades, the black and minority ethnic housing movement has been a success story of community involvement and a bottom–up approach. Clearly there are important lessons to be learnt from these developments.

Starting from a different perspective, Wood and Harvey in Chapter 17 also emphasise the importance of a community based local regeneration perspective. They argue that private funders will increasingly require evidence of an holistic approach to tackling social exclusion, with local authorities acting as strategic enablers and bringing together many partners in regeneration projects. This emphasis on the collaboration of a range of stakeholders is at least as important as issues of who provides and manages social housing. Of equal significance, Wood and Harvey state that radical new methods of grant funding are not necessarily required as there is confidence in existing approaches within the financial sector.

Finally, Runnett looks at the issue of regulation. He points out that third way thinking stresses that the dichotomy between public sector management and ownership and the free market is no longer relevant. Instead the emphasis is on combining these two types of approach and ensuring that through regulation (rather than ownership) outcomes are achieved. The nature of regulation is, however, undergoing significant modification with changing patterns of governance. The chapters in Part 2 and Stoker in Chapter 14 summarise the key changes. As Runnett points out, the government needs to give as much attention to developing an appropriate regulatory framework as to substantive housing policies. A comprehensive and integrated approach is needed to overcome the increasingly fragmented and ad hoc approach to regulation.

REFERENCES

Ball, M. (1996) *Housing and Construction: A Troubled Relationship?* (Bristol and York: Policy Press and Joseph Rowntree Foundation).

Centre for Public Services (1997) *Strategy for Best Value* (Sheffield: CPS).

Centre for Public Services (1998) *User/Employee Involvement in Best Value, PFI and Partnerships* (Sheffield: CPS).

Field, F. (1996) *Stakeholder Welfare* (London: Institute of Economic Affairs, Choice in Welfare No. 32).

Gilroy, R. and Woods, R. (eds) (1994) *Housing Women* (London: Routledge).

Housing Studies (1999) 'Focus Issue on Construction', Vol. 14, No. 1.

Hutton, W. (1995) *The State We're In* (London: Jonathan Cape).

Hutton, W. (1997) *Stakeholding and its Critics* (London: Institute of Economic Affairs, Choice in Welfare No. 36).

Morris, J. (1993) *Independent Lives: Community Care and Disabled People* (London: Macmillan).

13

Tenants as Stakeholders

Marianne Hood

INTRODUCTION

This chapter examines the possibilities for social housing tenants fulfilling the role of stakeholders in relation to the management and governance of their housing. Local authorities and registered social landlords (RSLs) have many different stakeholders to consider in relation to their role as landlords. Councils have the Department of the Environment, Transport and the Regions (DETR), elected members and their employees to consider, as well as their tenants and all council taxpayers, the wider local community and particular groups within the community for whom they have a direct obligation to provide housing. Registered social landlords have their funders, the Housing Corporation, their employees and their boards of management to consider in addition to their tenants and residents, the wider community and local authorities in whose areas they work. All of these groups have a stake in the work of social landlords. However, not all get the same status or priority given to their role and position as stakeholders.

Local authorities and RSLs are recipients of public money and, as such, should be as accountable to their tenants as stakeholders as they are to any others. Tenants are important stakeholders in social housing. They have a direct financial interest. Their rents contribute to the provision, management and maintenance of their housing. And they have a direct personal interest because the way in which their housing is provided, managed and maintained has a direct impact on their lives and the quality of their lives.

Getting proper recognition as a stakeholder is about accountability, a word that gets bandied about without being properly defined. Lord Nolan, in his second report, criticised the use of the term accountability as tending to be rather loose and ill defined. Nolan suggested that 'service users and others are truly accountable only to those able to exercise sanctions over them'. If tenants of social housing could take their custom elsewhere they would have a clear sanction over the providers and managers of their housing. However, this option is not open to tenants and therefore other mechanisms are needed to ensure that social landlords are accountable to their tenants as customers and stakeholders.

Local authorities are often perceived as being uniquely democratically accountable through the electoral process, although there is nothing to prevent most housing associations admitting tenants as shareholding members who then have a vote in election of board members. However, this is not the only way that accountability can be achieved. Accountability can be imposed through legislation placing particular obligations and requirements on local authorities and RSLs, it can be created via contractual undertakings by the landlord in tenancy agreements and other local agreements, it can be specifically set up in service standards via consultation, participation and arrangements for monitoring the landlord's performance and instigating any remedial action when agreements and standards are not met.

The opportunity for tenants to play a major role as stakeholders is therefore available and has been for some time. The question to address is whether or not this opportunity has been realised and, if not, what can be done about it.

BACKGROUND

The importance of participation by tenants as customers as a means of increasing the accountability of landlords has been recognised for over 20 years (Goodlad, 1993). All secure and assured tenants in the social housing sector have some rights to be consulted but few rights to actively participate in the matters which affect the provision, management and maintenance of their homes. Some of these rights are contractual via tenancy agreements and some are statutory, although it is only secure tenants who have a statutory right to be consulted and only secure local authority tenants who have a statutory right to manage.

Since the original legislation in 1980 (Housing Act 1980, for England and Wales; The Tenants' Rights Etc., [Scotland] Act 1980) which gave all local authority tenants in England and Wales a right to be consulted (although this legal right was not extended to tenants in Scotland) many changes have been made which have amended the ways in which, and extent to which, tenants have any rights to be consulted. English and Welsh tenants who became housing association tenants from 1988 onwards no longer have a legal right to be consulted. However, new requirements were placed on housing associations by performance standards from the Housing Corporation, Tai Cymru and Scottish Homes, which not only more or less replicate the statutory rights of secure tenants for assured tenants, they go further to encourage housing associations to support the development of tenants' associations, to consult and involve tenants via such associations and to create opportunities for tenants to participate in the management of the association.

Tenants do not have rights to be consulted or involved via tenants' associations. Although leaseholders have legal rights of formal recognition for residents' associations and for residents' associations to be consulted about services and service charges, no such rights are extended via the law to secure tenants of either local authorities or housing associations and RSLs.

Since 1989, English and Welsh local authority tenants, through the Local Government and Housing Act 1989, have been prohibited from taking part as voting members in any main decision making committees of their landlord. Tenants of RSLs and housing associations, on the other hand, are able to take part as full voting members of the main committee or board of management. In Scotland, it is normal for housing associations to be run by the tenants themselves or for tenants to be in the majority of committee members. Housing associations and RSLs who are constituted as industrial and provident societies can invite tenants to become shareholding members with the right to have a say in the development of the organisation and to vote for members of the committee or board of management.

PROBLEMS

The track record of local authorities, housing associations and RSLs in giving their tenants status as stakeholders and fully involving them in decisions which affect them is poor. Although little up-to-date research information is available, findings from the major benchmark study into housing management by the DoE (1993) found that the promotion of tenant participation remained relatively undeveloped in many social landlord organisations, with many tenants criticising arrangements as being little more than lip service. Since that research, many local authorities have had to develop more effective arrangements in order to consult and involve their tenants in the process of compulsory competitive tendering for housing management, and many more housing associations have been created as a result of stock transfers from local authorities requiring high levels of tenant involvement for the transfer to succeed. However, tenants continue to have few rights in law to be fully consulted about all the most relevant aspects of the provision, management and maintenance of their housing.

There are no rights for tenants to be consulted about financial matters or about rent policies and rent levels. This area is specifically excluded from legislation for local authority, housing association and RSL tenants and from any guidance to landlords from the DETR or the Housing Corporation, Tai Cymru or Scottish Homes. Similarly, tenants have no rights to be consulted about policy development or changes to policy. Most of the rights for tenants that do exist via statute or contract are individual rights with no rights of recognition for tenants' associations or rights for tenants to be consulted or involved through tenants' associations. This contrasts starkly with leaseholders that do have such collective rights.

The pattern of changes to tenants' rights over the last ten years reflects government policy and attitude towards tenants in social housing. The major policy objective of the Conservative government was to encourage and promote home ownership and therefore tenants were given increasing rights and incentives to buy their homes and to become owner occupiers. This was coupled, as has been mentioned, with decreases in other rights for both council and housing association tenants, with considerable reduction in the security of tenure of housing association tenants from 1988 onwards.

In spite of government rhetoric about the importance of tenant participation very little has been done to create real rights in this area. On the contrary, since 1988, new housing association tenants have lost their legal right to be consulted. Local authority tenants not only lost their right to be voting members of council committees they also had a severe reduction of their right to be consulted to prevent them from being able to veto the introduction of compulsory competitive tendering of their housing service. Although local authority tenants in England and Wales were given a statutory right to manage, this was not extended to housing association tenants and was in the context of removing control of housing from local authority landlords rather than giving genuine rights of participation to tenants.

Although all tenants are now supposed to be more involved in setting the standards they want for their housing service and in monitoring the delivery of that service, there are few sanctions available to tenants where service delivery is poor and agreed standards and targets are not met. Tenants have no means of enforcing service standards from their landlord and few means available to them apart from court action to enforce any of their rights. Neither the DETR nor the regulators of housing associations and RSLs are required to consult or involve tenants when assessing the performance of social landlords, and tenants have no rights of access to these bodies or rights of representation to them either individually or collectively via their tenants' organisations.

The rights and status of social housing tenants remain below that of leaseholders and well below that of owner occupiers, a status reinforced by legislation in the 1996 Housing Act allowing English and Welsh local authority landlords to use introductory or probationary tenancies for all new tenants. This is a right that is being extended to RSLs through the use of assured shorthold tenancies.

If tenants are to have status and rights as stakeholders, changes will have to be made not only to their rights as tenants but in the balance of power between social housing landlords and tenants and the role which tenants can take in relation to all aspects of the provision, management and maintenance of their homes and estates.

POSSIBILITIES FOR CHANGE

Emphasis continues to be placed by the government on the importance of accountability of service providers to service users as stakeholders. This accountability is at the heart of the proposals for improving local democracy in the best value regime, which will apply to housing associations as well as local authorities. There are a number of opportunities available to social housing landlords to make themselves more accountable to their tenants and thereby give their tenants status as stakeholders. However, some action may also be needed by government to ensure that all tenants have effective opportunities to play a full role as stakeholders.

All Social Landlords Can Make Themselves More Democratically Accountable

Although local authorities have councillors who are elected to represent the interests of the local community, council tenants do not elect the members of their housing committee and cannot take part in that committee as voting members themselves. Councils can, however, allow tenants and tenants' representatives to attend housing committee meetings and take part in all the discussions, even though they cannot vote. Tenants could elect their own representatives to sit on the main housing committee and, at a more local level, providing that no more than 1,500 homes are involved, council tenants can take part in the decision making process including decisions about local rent levels. In housing associations and RSLs, all tenants can be invited to become shareholding members with a vote for who they want to have as the members of their housing committee or board of management. Tenants' associations can also be given rights to elect a number of representatives to sit on the committee or board. All social landlords can set up local committees, forums and panels involving tenants' representatives. Decision making powers can be devolved to local level with clear rights for tenants to be involved in setting and monitoring performance standards.

All Social Landlords Can Give Tenants a Direct Role in Setting, Monitoring and Enforcing All Aspects of Housing Performance and Service Standards

Tenants can be consulted and involved at both an individual and collective level in policy development, in setting standards and performance targets and in monitoring whether or not these are achieved. Social housing landlords can develop in-house arrangements to enable tenants to enforce standards and to ensure that tenants' rights are upheld. Landlords can establish not only comprehensive internal complaints procedures but also arrangements offering independent arbitration or mediation, with arrangements for compensation or redress for tenants.

All Social Landlords Can Introduce Contractual Rights for Tenants to be Informed, Consulted and Involved at Individual and Collective Levels

Legally binding contractual commitments can be given in tenancy agreements to give tenants rights to information, consultation and involvement. These rights can include the right for a tenant to be informed, consulted and involved via a recognised tenants' association and rights for tenants to set up associations which will be recognised by their landlord. Contractual rights can be given to tenants to elect representatives to sit on decision making committees and to take part, via elected representatives, in policy development as well as performance monitoring.

The Government Could Introduce Statutory Rights and a New Single Form of Tenancy for all Social Housing Tenants

Local authority, housing association and RSL tenants and secure and assured tenants have very different rights in law. The rights that they do have are poor with many key areas, such as rights to be consulted about rents or rights of recognition for tenants' organisations, completely missing. Worse still, assured tenants have few rights covered by statute and their security of tenure is much less than that of secure tenants.

The Government Could Introduce a New Single Form of Tenancy to Give the Same Core Statutory Rights, Including Security of Tenure and Consultation and Participation Rights, for all Social Housing Tenants

Statutory rights and regulations could be introduced for all tenants to be informed, consulted and involved at both an individual and collective level in all aspects of the provision, management and maintenance of their housing. Legislation could also be introduced to enable tenants to set up tenants' associations with a statutory right for such associations to be recognised and consulted by social landlords.

Tenants Could be Given Specific Rights to Enforce Service Standards and Their Landlord's Obligations and Contractual Commitments

Statute could introduce specific rights for tenants to ensure that their rights and the obligations of their landlord are properly upheld. This could include specific rights for tenants to have access to, and to make representations to, the bodies responsible for monitoring and inspecting the service performance of their landlord. Tenants could be given the right to call for an independent inspection of their landlord's performance and to be involved in development of plans for remedial action, including rights for tenants to propose that alternative arrangements be made to service provision by their landlord.

CONCLUSION

Although legislation originally gave tenants some rights that could have been developed to enable social housing tenants to have comprehensive rights and to put the landlord–tenant relationship on to a more equal footing, these rights have been severely eroded in the last ten years. Tenants have little real status as stakeholders. They do not have the same status as stakeholders in relation to their housing as that given to leaseholders. Tenants are, nevertheless, important stakeholders in relation to social rented housing and this has been recognised by the government with the introduction of the best value regime for housing.

The government emphasis is on accountability of service providers to customers as stakeholders. However, this presents a particular challenge to local authorities, RSLs and housing associations. Tenants have no sanctions which they can apply to their landlords and they cannot take their custom elsewhere. Other mechanisms and arrangements therefore need to be put in place to create accountability of social housing landlords to their tenants. There are different ways in which such accountability can be developed and maintained. If social housing landlords are going to give tenants importance as stakeholders, and if tenants are to attain that status, then the whole process of consulting and involving tenants in all aspects of the provision, management and maintenance of their housing will have to be reviewed.

All social housing landlords should make themselves more democratically accountable to their tenants by enabling them to have representatives on all the landlord's decision making bodies. RSLs and housing associations can also promote and develop shareholding membership by tenants. Landlords can give tenants a direct role in setting, monitoring and enforcing all aspects of housing performance and service standards with comprehensive internal procedures for dealing with complaints and arrangements for mediation and arbitration. They can introduce contractual rights for tenants to be informed, consulted and involved at individual and collective level. Legally binding contractual commitments can be given in tenancy agreements to allow individual and collective rights to information, consultation and involvement via recognised tenants' associations and groups.

If tenants are going to achieve real status as stakeholders, government will have to address the inequality in tenants' rights and the lack of legal rights for them in key areas such as security of tenure and participation and involvement. All social housing tenants should have the same rights in law and therefore legislation should be introduced to create a new single form of tenancy to give the same core rights to all. However, tenants will not really be able to achieve full status as stakeholders, and social housing landlords will not be fully accountable to them, until they are able to enforce their rights and to have effective sanctions against landlords who fail to meet commitments and agreed performance standards. The challenge for both social housing landlords and the government is to find a way for tenants to have specific rights to hold their landlords to account and to ensure that their rights as stakeholders are finally recognised and properly upheld.

REFERENCES

Department of the Environment (1993) *Managing Social Housing* (London: HMSO).

Goodlad, R. (1993) *The Housing Authority as Enabler* (Coventry and Harlow: CIH and Longman).

Nolan Committe (1996) *Local Public Spending Bodies: Second Report of the Committee on Standards in Public Life* (London: HMSO).

14

Local Governance: What Future?

Gerry Stoker

INTRODUCTION

To understand the future of local government in Britain, it is necessary to first investigate its recent history. Eighteen years of Conservative government from 1979 had a substantial impact on many of the institutions of British society, none more so than local government. The legacy left by the Conservatives is the starting point for the discussion in this chapter. The scope, strengths and weaknesses of the Conservatives' approach are examined first.

When Labour came to power in May 1997, there were some in local government who felt that the pressure for reform would be removed, more money would be liberally sprinkled about and the good old days of municipal socialism would be revived. These people were soon to be disappointed and should have shown greater political understanding and realism. Labour's manifesto and the statements of its leading national figures could not have been clearer. Local government is for 'new Labour' an important target for reform and indeed radical modernisation. Two years or so into its political life few would doubt the scale and substance of Labour's change programme for local government. The second section, therefore, examines the key themes of 'new Labour'. Above all, what marks Labour's programme out is its determination to return political legitimacy and capacity to local government.

The final section of the chapter examines the future prospects for local government under 'new Labour'. It argues that there is a tension between top–down and bottom–up reform strategies that will have to be resolved.

THE INHERITANCE: WHAT THE CONSERVATIVES DID TO LOCAL GOVERNMENT

The Conservatives' 18 years in office saw an unfolding agenda of programmes. There was no grand strategy that was followed through from beginning to end, but a persistent tendency to intervene in local government affairs can be observed throughout the Conservatives' ascendancy.

The first and perhaps dominant theme throughout the period from 1979 to 1997 was a concern to haul back control of local spending. Continuing the challenge to the years of post-war growth that had been launched by Labour in the mid-1970s, the Conservatives tried to make it plain that the party was well and truly over. Grant cuts, capping, removal of the business rate from local control, the debacle of the poll tax, a VAT increase to pay for more of local spending and the arrival of council tax were among the weapons used by the Conservatives. The capital spending regime also saw tighter control and a sustained if not continuous downward pressure.

From the mid-1980s onwards, managerialism also became a key theme for the Conservatives with respect to local government. Managerialism can be defined as the belief that by better management public services should be able to achieve greater efficiency and effectiveness in meeting the public's needs. Through the introduction of competitive tendering, and market type mechanisms in housing, education and social services the Conservatives hoped to ensure that the public got more for less from public spending. Beyond particular instruments there was a growing view that if the public sector followed private management practice, it would greatly improve its efficiency and effectiveness. These practices included:

- emphasis on strategy and business planning;
- streamlined staffing structures;
- IT supported management systems; and
- strong performance culture among staff.

Managerialism was joined in the mid-1980s by the theme of consumerism. For too long it was argued that local government had allowed the voice and interests of its producers, such as professionals and clerical and manual employees, to dominate. Local government needed to get closer to the public, to focus on customer needs and to judge its success by an ability to satisfy the public both in the quality of the service relationship and in the revision of services to match the requirements of users.

A final theme, although one that emerged slightly later than the others so far identified, was a commitment to structural reorganisation. The abolition of the Greater London Council (GLC) and the six metropolitan county councils in 1986 appeared to be driven in part by the then Prime Minister's annoyance with the political posturing of the GLC. The wholesale reorganisation of local government in Wales and Scotland and the meandering shift of England towards unitary status in the early to mid-1990s is more difficult to explain by reference to any one factor. It may be that there was a clear purpose in mind but it has not been unearthed by research.

Four elements in the Conservatives' programmes have been identified: financial constraint, managerialism, customer orientation and structural reorganisation. What were the outcomes? Standstill in broad terms was achieved on the financial side. The picture is, however, complicated by transfers of responsibility both away from and to local government during this period. In 1975, the year of Crosland's 'the party's over' speech, local authority current expenditure was 8.8 per cent of gross domestic product (GDP). It had fallen to 7.7 per cent of GDP by 1993 (Hale, 1997). Current spending increased slightly in real terms but the rate of growth was of a much smaller scale than in the previous decades. Between 1963–64 and 1993–94, it increased by only 5 per cent (Hale, 1997).

The Conservatives' measures may have delivered control over finances but they did so by altering substantially the balance of central and local funding for spending decisions. The removal of the business rate from local control came with the introduction of the poll tax in England in 1990. It was followed by an increase in VAT pushed through in 1991–92 to fund additional central grant aid and reduce the burden of local tax following the miserable failure of the poll tax. The result was that although in 1989–90, 57 per cent of funding came from local taxation by 1996–97 this figure had dropped by 21 per cent (Hale, 1997). The problem created by such a small proportion of local spending being funded from local sources is twofold. First, the gearing effect means that a relatively small increase in spending or shift in grant provision may require a high increase in the council tax that needs to be collected locally. Second, local accountability for spending is limited given the high level of dependence on central funding.

The Conservatives' programme of managerialism can claim to have made an impact. There was and remains a strong commitment to many managerialist themes in the local government community. Particular initiatives, however, have been subject to criticism. Compulsory competitive tendering, for instance, has been seen as inflexible and bureaucratic, encouraging defensive behaviour by local authorities with respect to the services affected rather than a positive partnering attitude to the private sector. Other market type mechanisms are seen as producing some benefits but also undesirable side effects. The customer revolution has also taken hold to a considerable degree. There is some evidence of increased satisfaction with the delivery of public services since the mid-1980s. Customer care training, performance measures and customer charters have become widespread features of local service provision. Reorganisation of local government has been largely completed with the now overwhelming proportion of the population living in unitary authorities, although the wider benefits claimed for reorganisation have yet to be demonstrated.

Without doubt the Conservatives changed local government. They did so in a remarkably sustained statist and centralised manner. Their reform programmes were top–down, dominated by legislative measures and pushed home by a combination of strident ministerial rhetoric and careful and detailed monitoring. But what the Conservatives were never clear about, and the issues reached near farcical dimensions with respect to local government reorganisation, is the purpose and value of local government. There was talk of an enabling role but this was more of a statement about what the government should not do. 'Enabling not providing' was the subtitle of Ridley's pamphlet when he was Secretary of State for the Environment (Ridley, 1988). The Conservatives also neglected the politics of local government. The Widdicombe Committee established by the Conservatives in the mid-1980s in its research brought home the importance of party politics and the increasing politicisation of local government (Widdicombe, 1986). The Conservatives' legislative reaction was to ignore the research and impose a series of restrictions on local politicians and politics. Despite Heseltine's attempts when he was Secretary of State for the Environment for the second time in the early 1990s to raise some serious questions about the political management of local authorities, the Conservatives in practice neglected the issue.

They also neglected to take effective action to stop the sweeping away of the Conservative presence in local government. In 1979 the Conservatives had 53 per cent of all councillors and control of 49 per cent of all authorities. By 1997 these figures had slumped to 20 per cent and 5 per cent respectively. The long-term impact of such a dramatic local decline is seen by many as a contributing factor to the scale of the Conservative Party's defeat in 1997 and the difficulty they are having in rebuilding. The Conservatives may have been able to kick local government but it is possible to argue that local government might have helped to trip them up in the end.

LABOUR'S NEW AGENDA

The Labour Party's landslide general election victory in 1997 brought a new agenda into play for local government. Local government in 1997 was largely Labour with the Labour Party in outright control of about half of all local authorities and involved in the balanced control of nearly another quarter. Labour's stranglehold will be eroded over the next few years but it is likely to remain the dominant party at the local as well as the national level for a number of years, both in terms of the number of councillors and control of local authorities.

The strong presence of Labour at a national and local level has given central–local relations a different tone. There is much talk of partnership with the local authority associations in England, Scotland and Wales undoubtedly enjoying increased access to ministers and real influence over policy. Yet tensions remain in part reflecting the dominance of new Labour at the centre and the presence but not dominance of old Labour in some local authorities. More broadly, the tensions revolve around the challenging and radical nature of the Blair government's agenda for local authorities. As the Prime Minister's pamphlet puts it: 'The people's needs require you to change ... so that you can play your part in helping to modernise Britain and, in partnership with others deliver the policies on which this government was elected' (Blair, 1998, p. 22).

Local government is seen as crucial to delivering key election promises on education, social services, housing and in many other areas. Its modernisation is also seen as part of a broader renewal of the political institutions and constitutional arrangements of Britain. The politics of local government are, thus, important to Labour. Local government as much as national government provides a basis for the public to judge Labour. Failure at either level is regarded as unacceptable. So what is Labour's agenda for local government? The government White Paper, 'Modern Local Government: In Touch with the People', provides the most comprehensive statement (Department of the Environment, Transport and the Regions, 1998).

The heart of the reform package comes in five elements. First, councils are expected to adopt new political structures. Contrary to the fears of some, the approach is not too prescriptive. A number of options are laid out including a directly elected mayor with a cabinet, a cabinet with a leader and what in effect is a city manager system. The White Paper makes it clear that 'councils will choose which of these models they prefer and the detail of how they wish to operate within the broad definition of the model' (paragraph 3.23). Equally, refusing to take forward change is not an option. The White Paper suggests that the government will take a reserve power to tackle councils that fail to develop any reform plans or neglect to implement their reform proposals. In addition, local people are to be given the right to trigger a referendum on the directly elected mayor option. These changes in political structures imply a wider shift in the culture of local authorities. The White Paper suggests less emphasis on council meetings, an enhanced and diverse set of roles for all councillors, a wider range of people attracted to stand for election and, above all, an outward looking style which will make local government easier to access and easier to understand.

The second major element in the reform package is a set of measures to improve local democracy. Again the emphasis is on enhancing the accessibility and legitimacy of local government through 'higher participation in elections and close and regular contact between a council and local people between elections' (paragraph 4.1). Legislation is to be brought forward to enable councils to experiment with electronic voting, new style polling stations, postal voting and the timing of elections. Local authorities are going to be placed under a new statutory duty to consult on best value performance reviews and plans and the broader community plan. Legislation will also be introduced to confirm the power of councils to hold referendums. In terms of electoral arrangements, the government has reconfirmed its commitment to introducing over time a system of annual elections throughout local government. Elections by a third (on a four-yearly cycle) would be the standard pattern in unitary councils. In two tier areas the proposal is that in year one half of the district council would be elected, and in year two half of the county council would be elected.

The third element in the reform package is the introduction of a range of new disciplines on local authorities. A new ethical framework will be provided to be overseen by an internal standards committee but backed up by an independent body to investigate allegations that a council's code of conduct has been breached. The White Paper confirms that surcharging will be abolished.

The fourth, and the most developed, element of the proposals in the White Paper relates to the disciplines associated with best value. Compulsory competitive tendering is to go but in its place there will be a framework designed to encourage clarity about service standards, set targets for continuous improvement, greater involvement for service users and independent audit and inspection procedures. The government is also to give itself powers to intervene in a flexible and constructive way if services and performance failure is persistent or serious.

The final element in the reform package is a set of new powers and responsibilities for local authorities. The White Paper proposes to 'enshrine in law the role of the council as the elected leader of their local community with a responsibility for the well-being and sustainable development of its area' (paragraph 8.9). Along with this responsibility will come a duty on the council to provide a community strategy for its area. Councils are to be given a discretionary power to take steps to promote the well-being of the area (a sort of general competence facility) and a clear power to engage in partnership arrangements of various sorts, including participation in companies. On the financial side, the government proposes a single capital pot, better asset management, the possibility of a supplementary business rate, the abolition of crude and universal capping and more stability in grant provision to councils.

Labour's agenda tackles head on two issues ducked by the Conservatives: the political management and organisation of local government and its core role and purpose. As the Prime minister's pamphlet indicates, the two issues are linked: 'At the heart of local government's new role is leadership – leadership that gives vision, partnership and quality of life to cities, towns and villages all over Britain' (Blair, 1998, p. 13). It continues:

> Local government's credentials to be community leaders are weakened by its poor base of popular support ... Councils need to avoid getting trapped in the secret world of the caucus and the party group. They should let people have their say ... But the heart of the problem is that local government needs recognised leaders if it is to fulfil the community leadership role. (Blair, 1998, pp. 14–16)

Thus at the centre of Labour's agenda is a concern to restore public trust and legitimacy to the political life of councils in order for them to take on a broad community leadership role.

Labour has sustained a commitment to financial constraints although there are signs of relaxation. The announcements on public spending made in June and July 1998 indicate substantially more money for some local government services, especially education and social services, but limited growth in other areas. Capital spending is also likely to be increased above levels achieved under the Conservatives. Yet there is a strong element of caution in the management of local finances. Major levels of control remain in the hands of the centre, although there is considerable scope for local authorities to develop some modest additional revenue streams and some imaginative partnerships that are based on capital projects and release resources through effective asset management.

Labour clearly shares with the Conservatives and many in local government a belief in managerialism and consumerism in a general sense, although its emphasis is rather different. The best value regime carries the potential of being a flexible and effective tool for improvements in local service delivery. There is also a strong theme in government circles on the virtue of developing joined up or holistic approaches for tackling social and economic problems. Local government with its range of responsibilities and leadership roles has a particular contribution to make in this sphere.

THE FUTURE OF REFORM UNDER NEW LABOUR

The Labour government elected in May 1997 has shown a strong interest in continuing the process of change and reform of local government. It has, however, committed itself to developing a different reform style, one that is more experimental and involves more consultation and is less top–down. As Labour's Local Government and Housing Minister has commented:

> It is vital that we lose the skills of battle and find the skills and organisation of partnership ... One of the ways in which we can achieve this is to meet and discuss ideas and policies ... another is through the use of pilot studies to develop and test ideas in the real world. To ensure lessons are learnt before we legislate – not after. (Armstrong, 1997, p. 18)

It would appear that Labour has already latched on to the major lesson of the Conservative period which is that change imposed in an across the board, heavy handed, non consultative manner is prone to considerable implementation failure and the product of unintended effects.

Yet this positive judgement needs to be qualified. The restructured Department of the Environment, Transport and the Regions, which is responsible broadly for local government affairs, is led by ministers committed to a more experimental bottom–up style. But other government departments and ministers appear less willing to give up the prescriptive and regulatory style developed by the Conservatives. In education, employment and welfare policy arenas, legislation and ministerial intervention seem designed to ensure that local government delivers the national objectives of the new government. Local authorities, according to one minister, have to prove they are part of the solution rather than part of the problem. There is thus a more general ministerial concern with achieving action and an impatience with those that appear to be obstructing change.

The substantial shocks to the system of local government in Britain under the Conservatives have under Labour flowered into a reformulated and challenging redefinition of local self-government. The value of local government is not to be judged by the services it delivers (which was the dominant paradigm in the 1970s) but by its capacity to lead to a process of social, economic and political developments in our communities. Local government is above all a political vehicle for communicating, organising and expressing the concerns, visions and problem solving capacity of local people. What is far from clear is whether central government, under the new Labour leadership, is prepared to will the means for local authorities to take on that role. They might, in turn, suggest that it is not clear to them that most local authorities have the will, capacity and imagination to open themselves up in the way the community governance role demands. The debate on local self-government in Britain runs the risk of becoming stuck in a 'catch-22' situation: to perform local authorities need to be trusted but to be trusted they need to perform.

A core proposal in the White Paper (DETR, 1998) may help to resolve the tension. Beacon councils, which will be the very best performing authorities, will set the pace of change and be rewarded with additional powers and freedoms. Beacons will become recognised centres of expertise and excellence to which others in local government will look. They may also become champions for local government capable of persuading uncertain or impatient government ministers that local government can deliver popular, highly effective and legitimate governance.

REFERENCES

Armstrong, H. (1997) 'Five Sides to a New Leaf', *Municipal Journal*, 4 July, pp. 18–19.

Blair, T. (1998) *Leading the Way: A New Vision for Local Government* (London: Institute for Public Policy Research).

Department of the Environment, Transport and the Regions (1998) 'Modern Local Government: In Touch with the People' (London: The Stationery Office).

Hale, R. (1997) 'The Scope and Control of Local Government', in Chisholm, M., Hale, R. and Thomas, D. (eds) *A Fresh Start for Local Government* (London: Chartered Institute of Public Finance and Accountancy).

Ridley, N. (1988) *The Local Right – Enabling not Providing* (London: Centre for Policy Studies).

Widdicombe Report (1986) 'The Conduct of Local Authority Business: Committee of Inquiry into the Conduct of Local Authority Business' (London: HMSO).

15

A Community Perspective

David Clapham

INTRODUCTION

By belonging to a tenants' association I've seen a lot of things I never knew existed and it's made me much more aware of other people's problems. I think it's made me a better person. I feel now that I could go out and cope with a lot of things which I couldn't have done before. For instance, I never could've stood up and spoke in front of people. I would've been too nervous. And I've now joined the school governors and I never would have done that, because I would've thought I wasn't good enough. It's made me realise it's only everyday, ordinary people who do these things.

These words of a tenant activist interviewed some years ago as part of a study of tenant participation show the value of the involvement of tenants through a community based approach. According to Leadbeater (1997), the aim is to find ways of achieving cooperative self-help. He argues that the role of government is to provide the framework to enable people to find mutually advantageous, collaborative solutions. There is little doubt that a new approach is needed in housing. Community based housing organisations provide a real third way which enables people to get together to help themselves. They are an effective partnership involving private finance, public subsidy and regulation, and community self-help.

There is increasing concern over the state of public rented housing in Britain today and a search for a vision which can guide the future of the sector and help to stem its decline. This chapter argues that the key to that vision, and the implementation of a third way, lies in the strong traditions of cooperative socialism and communitarian thought which lead to models of community based housing organisations which can provide effective housing services while enabling local communities to help themselves to tackle their housing problems and social exclusion.

PUBLIC RENTED HOUSING

Over the years of Conservative housing policy, public rented housing (by which I mean both council and housing association owned housing) has become the home of those who have no other choice. The single minded pursuit of the expansion of owner occupation has left a public sector in poor condition which is stigmatised and is seen by many as a badge of failure. Despite the housing market recession of the early 1990s and the increased financial risk associated with a more flexible labour market, the vast majority of the population see themselves as home owners and associate this status with success. Home ownership is perceived as giving more control over one's life as well as providing a good financial investment especially a nest egg for old age or something to leave the children or grandchildren. There is no denying the financial benefits to many people of home ownership, although it must be stressed that some people, particularly the more marginal home owners, do not enjoy the benefit of increasing prices and struggle to repay the mortgage, keep the house in good repair and still make ends meet. The financial benefits in old age may also be illusory as the house is sold to pay for nursing home or care costs. Nevertheless, whatever the actual position, home ownership is seen as the status to be achieved by the vast majority of households.

The financial benefits of home ownership have been accentuated by the system of finance for public rented housing. The reductions in subsidies and the introduction of private finance for housing associations has resulted in large increases in rents with the resultant pressure on housing benefit. There have been two major impacts of this trend. The first is to accentuate the financial benefits of home ownership for those in work who would have to pay the full rent. The second has been a strong financial disincentive to work for tenants who would see their benefits withdrawn as their income increased.

The extent of the disincentive varies according to the rent level as well as the size of the family, but in some circumstances it can result in the loss of up to 98 pence in an extra pound earned. This financial structure has reinforced the perception of public rented housing as being for those who cannot or will not work.

Policy towards public rented housing during the Conservative years concentrated on restricting the development and landlord role of councils and creating a competitive regime among housing associations which it was believed would raise efficiency and make the best use of the declining public resources for new building. The result has been the continued growth of the housing association sector and of individual housing associations. The need for efficiency and the attraction of private finance have shaped the sector over the past few years. The trend has been for associations to grow larger in order to acquire the asset base to attract finance and absorb risk as well as searching for economies of scale in management. Large associations with a business ethic and a regional or national sphere of operation now dominate this sector in England. In Wales and particularly in Scotland, associations have not grown so large but the trend has been in the same direction with the financial regime fostering both an increase in scale and a dilution of the link with local communities which was particularly strong in Scotland.

Policy towards council housing has been focused around the transfer of stock towards housing associations or other forms of landlord. Clearly this has partly been pursued out of a political dislike of local authorities, but it has also been advocated as a way of bringing private finance into public rented housing. Thus the Chartered Institute of Housing (Hawksworth and Wilcox, 1995) has advocated the model of a local housing company in order to circumvent the constraints on capital expenditure designed to manage the size of the public sector borrowing requirement (PSBR). Other models of local housing corporations have been promoted and many voluntary transfers of stock have taken place by local authorities of all political persuasions.

WHERE DO WE GO FROM HERE?

During the years of opposition, the Labour Party did not seem to have come up with a coherent alternative to the Conservative vision of public rented housing and this shaped the first year of the Labour government.

All that has been offered is a slight change of emphasis with the core of policy intact. There is no perceptible softening of the commitment to home ownership and no sign of increased resources for public rented housing beyond the limited freeing of capital receipts from the right to buy. What has changed has been a slight shift in emphasis towards local authorities who are to play a larger role in the allocation of funding to housing associations. There has been a more pragmatic approach to transfers of stock from local authorities, but little sign of easing the financial pressures which have caused many local authorities to move in this direction.

One noticeable change has been the added emphasis given to tenant participation in both local authority and housing associations. In the latter case there has also been a related concern with the democratic deficit in associations, with more emphasis being given to account-ability to tenants and bringing them more within the remit of a strengthened local democracy.

A further change has been the adoption of social exclusion as the primary target of social policy. Housing seems to have no higher a political priority than in the Conservative years. It no longer seems to be regarded as an end in itself. Rather it is recognised that social exclusion is concentrated in particular locations many of which (although by no means all) are public sector estates. As a consequence housing organisations are seen as one element in the partnership approach towards these areas.

In summary, the approach of the Labour government has been to tilt the balance of advantage back towards local authorities and away from housing associations without tackling the overall problems of the public rented sector. At the local authority level there is evidence in some places of a desire to re-exert the primacy of local authorities over housing associations, but without a clear idea of what should be achieved. There is no vision to guide policy towards the structure and role of the public rented sector. Without this vision the likelihood is that it will continue its drift into decline with the physical condition of the stock and the social and economic infrastructure of the estates deteriorating. The public sector will continue to be seen as a ghetto for those with no choice and the phenomenon, present in many areas of Britain, of empty public rented houses among an overall housing shortage will continue.

TOWARDS A COMMUNITY VISION

There is a vision which can provide the much needed guide to policy towards public rented housing. It is based on a long and valuable tradition of socialist thought which stretches back to the communitarian philosophers, Kropotkin and Proudhon, writing in the last century, and the guild socialism of G. D. H. Cole (for a review see Birchall, 1988). It has been reflected in the Labour movement through the self-help tradition of mutual organisations of the friendly societies and cooperatives. There is a general case to be made for this political tradition, but the emphasis here is on the importance of this approach in tackling social exclusion which is at the heart of the Labour government's social priorities. The case for a community vision in housing can also be made by referring to the success of housing organisations based on this vision in meeting the needs and aspirations of tenants for an efficient and an effective housing service. Therefore, the case for a community based vision for public rented housing has two strands. The first is the political argument that community solutions are necessary elements of a political vision which attempts to tackle social exclusion by empowering people and giving them control over their lives. The second is the pragmatic argument that community based solutions in housing work in the sense that they can provide good quality housing and housing services. Both of these will be considered in turn.

The Political Case

The concept of social exclusion has dominated debates over social policy in the Labour government and housing has been considered to be a major factor in its creation and in its alleviation. Despite the importance attached to the concept, it is very difficult to define. For example, a report from the Chartered Institute of Housing in Scotland entitled 'Unlocking the Future: Tackling Social Exclusion' (CIH, 1998) contains six different definitions of the term which vary in their precise meaning. One of these is: 'Social exclusion is the combination of poverty and institutional discrimination, both of which helps to create unfavourable life chances and chronic exclusion from normal citizenship' (cited in Mignione, 1997).

The report does not choose one definition of social exclusion and this adds to the confusion over exactly what it is. Nevertheless, there are certain elements which recur in different definitions. Social exclusion is more than just material poverty, but incorporates many elements of multiple deprivation, the precise mix of which may vary considerably from one area to another. There is a concern with the causation of exclusion which is seen to lie in a mixture of institutional discrimination and personal behaviour. It is argued that the welfare state, in particular the social security system, has helped to create and sustain a dependency culture and the solution lies in the reform of state welfare systems, through, for example, welfare to work, designed to change the behaviour of the excluded.

In discussing social exclusion there is concern over what people are excluded from, and this is often phrased in terms of an exclusion from citizenship. For example, 'The term social exclusion is intended to recognise not only the material deprivation of the poor, but also their inability to fully exercise their social and political rights as citizens' (Geddes, 1997, p. 10) and 'notions such as social exclusion focus on ... inadequate social participation, lack of social integration and power' (Room, 1995, p. 105). Social exclusion is said to involve a lack of citizenship rights and the power to exercise them and to participate in political and social life. Attention is directed towards the lack of control which excluded people have over their lives and over the actions of public services which impact on them. The term 'empowerment' is often used in discussion of appropriate strategies to combat social exclusion.

Recent debates on citizenship have stressed the interrelatedness of rights and obligations (for a review see Clapham et al., 1996). Marshall (1950), in putting forward the concept of citizenship, stressed that every right brought with it a corresponding obligation, but the emphasis until the last few years has been on the advocacy of rights and it is only recently that the focus has shifted on to the appropriate place of obligations. Etzioni (1995) argues that many current social problems arise because of an excessive individualism and an over-concentration on rights compared to social obligations. He argues for a moratorium on the creation of new social rights which he claims have been devalued, and for a new emphasis on shared moral responsibilities. People should not wait for their lives to be made better through social rights given by the state, but should actively take responsibility themselves:

people have a moral responsibility to help themselves as best they can ... the laying of a claim to participate actively in advancing their lives on those who are disadvantaged ... rather than lay back and be compensated ... is based, first of all, on a concept of human dignity. There is ... something deeply degrading about being dependent on others. It is respectful of human dignity to encourage people to control their fate the best they can. (Etzioni, 1995, p. 144)

Porter (1993) has argued that there are three elements of citizenship. The first is the rights and respect that people have in the society. The second is the skills and abilities that people and communities have in order to exercise those rights. The third, following Etzioni's concern with obligations, is the attitudes and behaviour of people towards other citizens and the willingness to adopt the obligations of citizenship and act fraternally towards other citizens and the community.

The argument here is that community based housing organisations are effective vehicles for helping to achieve the aims of citizenship and so to help overcome social exclusion. Clearly housing organisations cannot achieve this by themselves, but what community based organisations do is to provide excluded communities with the opportunity to take more control over a central part of their lives and from this base to reach out into other elements of community life. This can offer individuals and communities both self-respect and the status and respect of the wider society. It provides a structure and resources which can lead to increased skills and abilities which can be used for the good of the individual and community in a wide range of settings. For example, a number of people have used the experience of being involved in the running of a community based housing organisation to develop the confidence and skills to find employment whether in housing or other work. At the same time community based housing organisations provide a focus for concerns about the obligations towards the community. By involving people and overcoming feelings of powerlessness they can enable them to realise that they have a stake in the community and that their behaviour influences the health of that community.

A community based housing organisation can provide an effective focus for community involvement in the wide ranging issues and problems of social exclusion. The interrelatedness of the problems of socially excluded communities is widely recognised as is the need for solutions which involve the community and are steered by them. The range of locally based initiatives is very wide and many housing organisations have begun to be involved in partnerships involving local schools, health professionals, the police, voluntary organisations and many others (for reviews see Clapham and Evans, 1998; Brown and Passmore, 1998). A community based housing organisation can provide a way into these partnerships for the community and a way of coordinating the meeting of the wide range of community needs.

The Service Case

There is now considerable evidence that community based housing organisations provide more effective services to tenants than other kinds of organisation. For example, a review of the evidence on the success of housing management measured by performance indicators and tenant satisfaction showed that small, locally based and community controlled organisations provided a better service than other types of landlord and there was no evidence that this improved effectiveness was bought through higher management costs (Clapham, 1992). There is further evidence that the transfer of former council housing to community based housing organisations results in a better quality of service to tenants. This has been shown in a Department of the Environment report on cooperatives in England (Price Waterhouse, 1995) and in a report based on research in Scotland where such transfers have been undertaken for over ten years (Clapham et al., 1998). The evidence from the Scottish study was that this improvement in service delivery can be sustained over a ten-year period and so is no flash in the pan. The irony of the policy of the Conservative governments was that they ostensibly supported voluntary transfer to housing associations on the basis that they provided a better service than local authorities. However, this better service was achieved largely because associations were smaller than local authorities and because they spent more on management. The outcome of the governments' policies was that the associations grew larger and spent less on management so that they more closely resembled the local authorities they were designed to replace.

The interesting question is why the evidence favouring community based housing organisations has been ignored. Clearly it does not suit housing officers who gauge their status and salary by the number of houses they manage or local councillors concerned to retain control over their council housing empires.

HOW DO COMMUNITY BASED HOUSING ORGANISATIONS WORK?

There is a wide range of community based housing organisations and the intention here is not to advocate any one particular form. Rather the choice will depend on local circumstances and the wishes of the community and others involved. The research evidence is that many different forms of organisation can provide the benefits outlined earlier.

The spectrum includes fully mutual cooperatives where membership is synonymous with being a resident or other structures where residents are only one party involved. Examples of other parties who may be involved are local councillors or other community leaders, or people with a particular skill which may be useful such as accountants, solicitors, architects, community workers, housing officers, etc. Residents may own the property through a housing association which they control or they may manage or maintain the property for another party such as the local authority under a management agreement, perhaps as a tenant management cooperative. Other forms could include local housing companies with strong tenant representation or an estate management board. All of these forms differ in the scope of their responsibilities and the formal influence that residents have. Each form has its advantages and disadvantages which may weigh differently in different circumstances. For example, the ownership options such as the housing associations or local housing company offer more scope for control and responsibility, and perhaps crucially in some circumstances, provide access to central government grants and private finance which can enable improvement of the houses and their environs. However, in some circumstances these extra opportunities may be perceived as burdens which the community does not want to, or is unable to shoulder.

The key elements of a community based organisation in the sense that I use the term are that it is small (say, up to 1,000 houses), is locally based and allows substantial influence to residents. Of course all of those elements are imprecisely defined, but this is not a problem. What is important is the implementation of the spirit of community control in particular circumstances. The difficulties of definition are illustrated by the problems in deciding what influence tenants have in any situation. The formal structure of the powers that tenants have is only one factor in many which influence outcomes. For example, tenants may in some circumstances achieve more where they seek to influence their landlords through the press or other form of public campaign than if they are part of a formal structure of tenant participation. Just because some forms of community based organisation offer residents fewer formal powers does not mean that the residents do not achieve what they want. So much depends on the attitudes of other parties such as the landlord or particular councillors or housing officers.

An example of successful community based organisations is the cooperatives and community based housing associations formed on council housing estates in Scotland as part of the community ownership programme. This was first started in the mid-1980s and had support across the political spectrum. It involved a local authority transferring the ownership of housing to a new cooperative or community based housing association, usually these days after a ballot among tenants. Financial support for the purchase and improvement of the housing comes in the form of grants from Scottish Homes and from private sector loans. Community ownership organisations are small (usually between 100 and 500 dwellings) and are managed by a committee of residents, which is elected by the membership. The committee is responsible for devising and implementing the development programme and for all aspects of housing management, and the committee employs staff to carry out this work. Scottish Homes has a key role of funder and of regulator as it does with all housing associations in Scotland.

Research on the first community ownership schemes (Clapham et al., 1998) has shown that residents have consistently supported the organisations and are happy with the developments undertaken and the services provided. The general view is that the community ownership schemes have been sensitive to the needs of the local area and its residents and have been effective and efficient when compared with other forms of public landlord. They have managed to sustain a high level of participation from local residents and have given them substantial influence over the running of their community. In a survey of four of the original schemes about ten years after their inception, three-quarters of residents said that they trusted the community ownership organisation to do what is right for the residents and levels of confidence were high. The schemes had achieved substantial change in their areas which often extended well beyond the housing itself and spread into many aspects of community life. They had done this without compromising their position in meeting housing need and catering for the poorest of the population and were accountable to Scottish Homes for the use of public money and for the fairness of their allocations policies and other housing management policies and practices.

CONCLUSION

Public sector housing is in a difficult position. Starved of money to provide decent conditions, shrinking in size with much of the best stock having been sold, it has become the sector of last resort for those unable to afford home ownership. It is stigmatised and synonymous with failure and social exclusion. Vision is needed if this decline is to be reversed and social exclusion effectively tackled. The roots of this vision lie in the strong traditions of cooperative socialism which have led to the existence of community based housing organisations which can provide a model for the public housing sector as a whole. They can provide a way of enabling individuals and communities to take more control over their own lives and in so doing help them to gain self-respect and the respect of the society as a whole which comes with full citizenship. At the same time they are a cost effective way of providing housing services which are attuned to the needs of particular areas. They can achieve this while providing communities with access to private and public sector resources in the same way that current methods of large-scale voluntary transfer or local housing companies do.

The problems of public sector housing are not just confined to a lack of financial resources, and transfer of council stock to large unaccountable housing companies will do little to counter the underlying problems of status, dependency and social exclusion. However, transfer to community based housing organisations can provide access to the financial resources while offering a way of tackling the underlying problems.

REFERENCES

Birchall, J. (1988) *Building Communities the Co-operative Way* (London: Routledge and Kegan Paul).

Brown, T. and Passmore, J. (1998) *Housing and Anti-Poverty Strategies* (Coventry and York: Chartered Institute of Housing and Joseph Rowntree Foundation).

Chartered Institute of Housing (1998) 'Unlocking the Future: Tackling Social Exclusion' (Edinburgh: CIH).

Clapham, D. (1992) 'The Effectiveness of Housing Management', *Social Policy and Administration*, Vol. 26, No, 3, pp. 209–25.

Clapham, D. and Evans, A. (1998) *From Exclusion to Inclusion* (London: Hastoe HA).

Clapham, D., Dix, T. and Griffiths, M. (1996) *Citizenship and Housing: Shaping the Debate* (Coventry: Chartered Institute of Housing).

Clapham, D., Kintrea, K. and Kay, H. (1998) 'Sustainability and Maturity of Community Based Housing Organisations', *Journal of Co-operative Studies*, Vol. 31, No.1, pp. 30–8.

Etzioni, A. (1995) *The Spirit of Community* (London: HarperCollins).

Geddes, M. (1997) *Partnership against Poverty and Exclusion: Local Regeneration Strategies and Excluded Communities in the UK* (Bristol: Policy Press).

Hawksworth, J. and Wilcox, S. (1995) *Challenging the Conventions: Public Borrowing Rules and Housing Investment* (Coventry: Chartered Institute of Housing).

Leadbeater, C. (1997) *Civic Spirit: the Big Idea for a New Political Era* (London: Demos).

Marshall, T. (1950) *Citizenship and Social Class* (Cambridge: Cambridge University Press).

Mignione, E. (1997) 'Enterprise and Exclusion', in *Demos Collection*, Issue 12.

Porter, K. (1993) *Impoverished Concepts of Citizenship in the Debate on the National Curriculum* (London: University of London, Centre for Multi-cultural Education, Institute of Education Occasional Paper No. 8).

Price Waterhouse (1995) *Tenants in Control: An Evaluation of Tenant-Led Housing Management Organisations* (London: HMSO).

Room, G. (1995) 'Poverty in Europe: Completing Paradigms of Analysis', *Policy and Politics*, Vol. 23, No. 2, pp. 103–13.

16

The Empowerment of Black and Minority Ethnic Stakeholders

Richard Tomlins

INTRODUCTION

Etzioni's (1995) emphasis on the importance of self, community and society has been used to characterise the third way in this book. Similarly, Brown, above, has referred to the significance of Hutton's ideas (1995, 1997) and the importance of social and economic inclusion, rather than simplistic conceptions of equality, in the stakeholding debate. These discussions provide opportunities for the empowerment of black and minority ethnic stakeholders, for example through renewed support for the role of the black and minority ethnic housing movement in tackling the housing, employment and social interests of black and minority ethnic communities in Britain. Indeed, the debate concerning the third way provides a more receptive environment for developing a pluralistic form of housing provision, which is more sensitive and responsive to its consumers' needs, than old style social democracy or neoliberal approaches. This chapter will discuss these potential policy developments in the context of the current housing outcomes of black and minority ethnic communities in Britain, and the historic role of the free market and the social sector in meeting black and minority ethnic housing need. It will also note the potential for the realisation of a pluralistic ethnic housing policy, with specific reference to the practical example of the black and minority ethnic housing movement in Britain.

CURRENT HOUSING OUTCOMES IN BRITAIN

The 1991 Census has allowed a relatively up-to-date picture to be constructed of the differences between the housing experiences of the white majority community and black and minority ethnic communities. However, we should note the limitations of any generalisations given the considerable heterogeneity in the housing outcomes of black and minority ethnic communities. There are also problems with reliance on Census data because of limitations in its scope; for example, it does not include data on homelessness (see Tomlins, 1999, for a fuller overview).

The Census portrays, generally, a growing concentration of black and minority ethnic communities in urban areas (Robinson, 1993), although there is segregation between black and minority ethnic communities as well as between black and minority ethnic communities and the white majority community (Peach and Rossiter, 1996). Harrison et al. (1996) suggest that the increasing geographical concentration of black and minority ethnic communities reflects 'White out-migration from areas of [minority] ethnic group residence, the in-migration of new arrivals to the country, the higher fertility rates of [minority] ethnic groups and new household formation among the [minority] ethnic groups' (Harrison et al., 1996, p. 54). However, within the cities and towns in which this growing concentration has occurred, there are also some modest examples of suburbanisation among particular black and minority ethnic communities, although as Owen (1996) notes, the extent of these trends should become more apparent when data from the 2001 Census are made available.

The tenure data from the 1991 Census demonstrate that households from the white majority community are more likely to be owner occupiers than black and minority ethnic communities, that they rent from local authorities in similar numbers to black and minority ethnic communities, but are less likely to be renting properties from housing associations or private landlords (Owen, 1993). But, these broad generalisations once again conceal a diversity of outcomes with, for example, South Asian households far more likely to be owner occupiers than white communities, despite the low proportion of owner occupiers among Bangladeshi households living in London (Harrison et al., 1996).

Indeed, in general, black and minority ethnic communities are increasingly concentrated in poor quality districts of cities in comparison with the white majority community. This includes the owner occupied sector (Phillips, 1997; Ratcliffe, 1997) which should, therefore, not automatically be equated with a privileged housing position. The English House Condition Survey (1991) indicates that it is the Pakistani and Bangladeshi communities which are particularly likely to be in the worst housing conditions, and the greatest divergence in the housing outcomes of the white majority and black and minority ethnic communities can be observed in measures of overcrowding assessed on the number of persons per room:

> The national average is 2.2 per cent of all households ... However the figure for ethnic minorities is 13.1 per cent; more than an eighth of all ethnic minority households ... More than a fifth of all South Asian households and nearly a tenth of Chinese and other households live at a density of more than one person per room. (Owen, 1993, p. 9)

It should, nevertheless, be emphasised that while South Asian communities contain larger than average household sizes, these snapshots of overcrowding are also a reflection of the housing options which are available to those households.

Social characteristics such as age, gender and disability will also have an impact on the housing outcomes of all ethnic groups. The Sample of Anonymised Records available to Harrison et al. (1996) was only sufficient to allow consideration of differential outcomes by sex of head of household for white, indian and black caribbean households. Nevertheless, they indicated that for each of these ethnic groups, female headed households were more likely to be represented in local authority housing and less likely to be owner occupiers. Differential rates of the formation of female headed households by ethnic group will, therefore, influence housing outcomes measured by ethnicity, as Peach and Byron (1992) have demonstrated with respect to the African Caribbean community. Ratcliffe (1996) emphasises the importance of considering disability in assessing housing need, and draws attention to particularly high levels of long-term illness and impairment among black and minority ethnic households in Bradford.

He adds that these rates could be expected to increase as black and minority ethnic communities move from a relatively young age structure to an older one more commonly associated with disability and long-term illness.

The explanation of these housing outcomes has tended to focus on the relative importance of housing choice and housing constraints. A consensus has developed that black and minority ethnic communities have housing choice within a greater system of housing constraints than those faced by the white majority community. However, it is also useful to examine the ethnic breakdown of housing outcomes in terms of possible political and policy solutions, beginning with the operation of the free market and contrasting this with approaches which rely on municipal socialism and paternalistic provision.

THE ROLE OF THE FREE MARKET

A number of writers have argued that the private sector offers the best opportunity for success in improving the housing outcomes of black and minority ethnic communities. Indeed, a number of writers have argued that the housing outcomes of Asian communities, in particular, represent a success story, demonstrating the benefits of the free market system, which should be celebrated rather than pathologised. This school of writing disputes the proposition that black and minority ethnic housing experiences, which differ from a white norm such as concentration within a poor area, greater overcrowding or lack of access to a particular tenure, are necessarily the product of discrimination. Writers from the choice school, such as Davies (1985), suggest that black and minority ethnic communities have become the 'objects' of study, with their freedom of action and cultural preferences at best undervalued, and at worst ignored.

Reliance on the free market, in theory, allows black and minority ethnic communities to ignore the paternalistic constraints of white majority policy makers, exercise tenure choice and benefit from the resource of community which, as James notes (1993), residential concentration offers. It allows minority ethnic groups to express identity through residence.

Dahya (1974) and Ratcliffe (1981) have suggested that Asian communities have expressed strong preferences for owner occupation and viewed local authority rented housing, in particular, in a negative way as a welfare tenure. Habeebullah and Slater (1990) have also highlighted the way in which Indian, Pakistani and Chinese households have been deterred from seeking local authority housing by a perception of it as a tenure of last resort. Indeed, Modood (1990) argues that Dahya's premise of Asian housing preference is now a commonplace truth despite being initially received with unease.

However, we might note that these trends are not static and economic factors make continuing reliance on the free market problematic as an effective way of meeting all black and minority ethnic housing needs. In addition, social sector housing providers have in some instances been able to change their style of provision to provide an enhanced housing choice for black and minority ethnic communities beyond the private market.

Robinson's (1980) study of housing outcomes in Blackburn notes the growing access of some Asian communities to the local authority housing sector while acknowledging the continuing role played by housing choice in those outcomes. He notes that the gradual development of local authority accommodation in areas of Asian residence, coupled with the arrival of East African Asians who did not harbour a desire to return to a homeland, explain the apparent changing tenure preference of the Asian community. More recent research reports have also suggested a growing demand for social sector housing among black and minority ethnic communities, which have been presumed to have an overwhelming preference for owner occupation. Ratcliffe (1996) identified that in Bradford there was now a significant expectation among Asian households that they would need the help of the social rented sector to be able to afford to gain access to bigger properties. He also noted that while the ethnic composition of the area was not a crucial influence upon housing demand for almost a third of Asian households, and indeed for relatively few African Caribbean households, it was a particularly important influence for younger South Asian households. These findings suggest that the concentration and geographical separation of ethnic groups will continue if not increase. Similarly, the University of Salford's (1996) housing needs study in Peterborough demonstrated a demand for social rented housing alongside the demand for owner occupied property, although this was largely confined to existing areas of residence.

Housing associations may play an important role in these changing trends, perhaps due to the size and location of properties, greater speed of access to accommodation for those who are able to access the waiting list and perceived greater sensitivity to specific needs (Bowes et al., 1997). Indeed Law et al. (1996) not only note a particular demand for housing association property among some black and minority ethnic communities, but also a demand for the shared ownership properties which housing associations commonly provide. However, Law (1996) also argues that the ethnicity of the housing provider is important, suggesting that it is the growth of black and minority ethnic housing associations which has provided an accessible doorway into social housing for black and minority ethnic communities by challenging community perceptions of housing options. Therefore, it may be a reflection of historic weaknesses in social sector provision, which are now being overcome, rather than a purely positive choice for free market solutions, which has led some black and minority ethnic communities to show a preference for owner occupation.

There are also practical difficulties for black and minority ethnic households to realise tenure preference and the potential resources of spatial concentration through the free market. For example, there have been widely documented examples of discrimination within the private rented sector. While it seems as if the more overt forms of discrimination have generally disappeared, the Commission for Racial Equality (1990) suggests, on the basis of its sample survey, that one in five accommodation agencies and one in 20 private landlords and landladies discriminate against black and minority ethnic households seeking accommodation. Law (1996) notes that high profile private landlords such as the Church Commissioners, the Crown Estates Commissioners and the Duchy of Cornwall have been held to demonstrate 'quite shocking ignorance and complacency towards anti-racism and equal opportunities' (London Against Racism in Housing, 1988, p. 34). Skellington (1996) adds that the London Housing Unit argues that racism in the private rented sector is a major cause of the disproportionate levels of homelessness experienced by black and minority ethnic communities.

There are also continuing instances of organisational barriers in gaining access to owner occupation through discrimination by estate agents (CRE, 1988, 1989), in addition to earlier barriers in obtaining mortgages (Karn et al., 1985) which it is now believed have been largely eradicated, albeit leaving a legacy of disproportionate reliance on high cost home loans in black and minority ethnic communities.

We should also stress that it is not clear how far the success thesis of the free market approach can be applied to all black and minority ethnic communities. This limitation to the comprehensiveness of the choice argument reflects the overwhelming focus of housing choice researchers on Asian communities.

THE ROLE OF THE SOCIAL RENTED SECTOR

The social housing sector has until recently been dominated by municipal provision and, it might be argued, remains characterised by the paternalism which has historically typified that sector. This might be seen as leading to the absence of culturally competent provision, despite the relatively high levels of representation of some black and minority ethnic communities, such as the African Caribbean community, in the social rented sector. Indeed, the weaknesses of provision can be characterised as reflecting the actions of individuals, organisations and the state.

The Actions of Individual Gatekeepers

The actions of individual gatekeepers to resources have played a significant part in restricting the housing opportunities available to black and minority ethnic communities in the social sector, (see for example CRE, 1983; Phillips, 1986; Henderson and Karn, 1987; Niner, 1987; Dalton and Daghlian, 1989; Sarre et al., 1989; Hickman and Walter, 1997). However, this generalisation disguises a variety of processes, which range from the deliberate discrimination of the racist officer through to the benevolent, but still discriminatory practices, of the officer seeking to meet housing need.

Some of these processes in the social sector may simply be an extension of the distinctions that have historically been made by some housing workers, and indeed their organisations, between those who are deserving of having their housing need recognised by access to a waiting list or by an offer of accommodation, and those that are undeserving of this privilege. There is a wide literature on these practices (for example Damer, 1976; Gray, 1976), which, it might be argued, is becoming topical again because of the promotion of sensitive allocations (for example, Page, 1993) to create sustainable communities on housing estates. While it has been common to suggest that the discriminatory actions of housing managers result from a lack of professionalism or everyday prejudices (CRE, 1983), Sarre et al. (1989) show that, at least in part, they may also be the result of workplace culture.

It might be suggested that discriminatory assessments of housing need are historic processes, which have now been successfully tackled by a greater awareness of equality issues among housing organisations. However, the work of Jeffers and Hoggett (1995) is important in demonstrating that discriminatory stereotypes which disadvantage minority ethnic communities continue to exist even in organisations with highly developed equality programmes and high numbers of officers from black and minority ethnic communities. Despite active programmes of organisational hygiene (Jeffers and Hoggett, 1995) to increase formalisation and tackle bias and stereotyping, discretion, albeit within organisational procedures, continued to disadvantage black and minority ethnic households.

The Actions of Organisations and the Local State

A number of the prejudicial actions of individuals in the social sector have seemed to exist within an organisational structure which implicitly, if not explicitly, sanctions those actions. In addition, there are a host of relatively common organisational practices which, while seemingly objective and impartial, prevent the housing needs of black and minority ethnic communities from being met. For example, a refusal by social housing providers to accept waiting list applications from owner occupiers, irrespective of the condition of that property and the amount of equity which might be released from its sale, ignores the difficulties of black and minority ethnic communities living in poor quality owner occupied property. Other practices, which might disguise housing need or prevent it from being met, include eligibility criteria such as residence qualifications to gain access to accommodation and a failure to advertise available housing services (Dalton and Daghlian, 1989) or policies of preferential access for daughters and sons of existing tenants (CRE, 1993).

In addition, there is evidence that the most desperate households are offered the worst housing. This can be indirectly discriminatory if black and minority ethnic households are in the greatest housing

need. As Henderson and Karn have noted with respect to local authorities: 'Contrary to the public's view, the day-to-day process of allocations in any local authority does not involve finding properties to "suit" people but rather finding people to "suit" properties' (Henderson and Karn, 1987, p. 216). However, the social rented sector, despite its paternalistic provision, has had limited success in tackling racial harassment and it still seems to be more common for the victim of racial harassment to be moved rather than the perpetrator to be evicted (CRE, 1993; Skellington, 1996). This preference seems to reflect organisational pressures on staff time and perceived difficulties in successfully undertaking court action.

Julienne identifies the lack of cultural competence in social sector provision in discussing the extent to which sheltered housing provision addresses the needs of black and minority ethnic elders:

> black and minority ethnic elders ... do not know about these services and where they do, these services are not sensitive to their particular needs. The accommodation is located in an area away from the communities they feel comfortable in, away from shops catering for their needs and places of worship; staff and residents don't understand and are often hostile to their language or customs, diets are not catered for, and publicity about the schemes is targeted in areas in which they do not live and in a language they cannot read. (Julienne in Jeffery and Seagar, 1993, pp. vii–viii)

Law et al. (1996) and Mullings (1992) add that black and minority ethnic communities do not benefit from investment in social sector housing stock, even when they are represented within the tenure, because of the large-scale and long-term investment needed on many of the estates where black and minority ethnic communities are concentrated. The relatively good quality estates where the white majority ethnic community is concentrated appear to have gained disproportionate funding because they allow limited sums of capital investment to be spent quickly to achieve visible improvement.

Structural Influences

In essence, the social rented sector is most able to meet the housir needs of black and minority ethnic communities where those nee

mirror the housing needs within the white majority ethnic community. Indeed, regulating the free market can also be seen as a prescriptive spatial model for black and minority ethnic communities:

> Our white liberal 'friends' of the time knew of course what was best for us; they knew that it was in our best interest to be dispersed; that our aggregation was synonymous with ghettoization; that as black people we will obviously be flattered to be placed among white people rather than having to live in communities in which the majority of people are black. They knew our needs better than we ourselves did. Our 'friends' and enemies were at one in ignoring alternative views. (James, 1993, p. 261)

However, despite this paternalistic approach to spatial location, there has historically been a failure to be positively interventionist and link housing policy with wider socioeconomic policy objectives at a national policy making level to meet the needs of black and minority ethnic communities.

Nevertheless, positive policy initiatives do operate within these constraints. The black and minority ethnic housing movement in England provides one positive example of community initiatives being empowered by innovative national policy making and indicates, in part, the way in which a third way of housing policy which is sensitive to housing need and difference could be developed.

THE BLACK AND MINORITY ETHNIC HOUSING MOVEMENT

Black and minority ethnic housing associations are identified by the Housing Corporation (1998) as those where 80 per cent of the organisation's governing body are from black and minority ethnic communities. As Crawley and Lemos (1993) note, they are essentially a community response to the inequalities which black and minority ethnic communities experience in gaining access to accommodation and employment opportunities within the social housing sector. Indeed, the National Federation of Housing Associations (NFHA) was still finding distrust in the 1980s among black and minority ethnic communities concerning the commitment of mainstream housing associations to meeting their housing needs:

associations were either irrelevant or actually detrimental to their needs ... the housing associations generally ... thought they were doing a good job for those in the black community ... the black groups thought that housing associations were insensitive to their needs and they had little influence on, and no control over, what housing associations were doing in their area. (NFHA, 1983, p. 13)

Schemes designed by and for black and minority ethnic communities can meet cultural and social needs that would otherwise go unmet by mainstream provision. They highlight housing need among black and minority ethnic communities, rather than hiding housing needs, which are different from those traditionally found within the white majority community, although it should be noted that housing schemes developed by black and minority ethnic housing associations will typically house residents from the white majority community (Jones, 1994) in addition to households from minority ethnic communities. Black and minority ethnic housing associations can also play an important community role which goes beyond simple bricks and mortar housing needs and begin to address the wider socioeconomic needs which have been articulated as the target of 'housing plus' services.

The black and minority ethnic housing movement achieved significant growth during the Housing Corporation black and minority ethnic housing strategies between 1986 and 1996. For example, as Harrison et al. (1996) note, the sector grew from approximately 4,000 properties in ownership or management in 1992 to over 17,000 properties in ownership and management by 1996. However, the changing funding systems for all housing associations, coupled with government reductions in capital housing expenditure have provided difficulties for all relatively small organisations, including the majority of black and minority ethnic housing associations (Singh, 1991; Crawley and Lemos, 1993). This is demonstrated by the reduction in the funding for social rented housing received by black and minority housing associations from £96 million in 1994/95 to £46.04 million in 1998/99 (Housing Corporation, 1998). Nevertheless, black and minority ethnic housing associations continue to receive a notable share of state funding for new social rented housing, with a slight increase in the share of funding from 9.12 per cent in 1994/95 to 9.95 per cent in 1998/99, although it should be noted that this represented a fall in the proportion of rented units produced in the whole housing association sector.

The difficulties of black and minority ethnic housing associations reflect:

> an inconsistency of official policy ... On the one hand was the desire from the mid-1980s onwards to encourage the emergence of housing organisations more representative of black and minority ethnic communities. On the other hand there was awareness (post-1988) that the new economic climate made viability and potential rent levels more problematic. (Harrison, 1992, p. 429)

While mainstream housing associations have improved their race equality performance in response to the development of black and minority housing associations (Harrison, 1992), the long-term future of the black and minority ethnic housing movement has been unclear. This reflects the tensions in Housing Corporation policies outlined above and its decision to end its strategy of ring fencing capital funding for the black and minority ethnic housing movement in 1996 in favour of a looser and less proactive enabling framework.

However, the Labour government has encouraged the Housing Corporation to introduce a new strategy (Housing Corporation, 1998) which addresses a number of the movement's problems. There is now, once again, hope that unregistered black and minority ethnic housing associations can move to registration and the greater organisational and property development opportunities that this offers.

There has been no parallel black and minority ethnic housing strategy in Northern Ireland, Scotland and Wales. Indeed, it is only recently that the Race Relations Act has been extended to cover Northern Ireland. In Wales, the emphasis of Tai Cymru, the former national regulatory body, has been on the role of mainstream housing associations in meeting the needs of black and ethnic minority communities, although the strategy has been relatively ineffective (Franklin and Passmore, 1998). Similarly, in Scotland, Scottish Homes, the regulatory body for housing associations, has focused on provision by mainstream associations. Strong lobbying by black and minority ethnic communities has, however, resulted in a change in this position including the formation of Scotland's first black and minority ethnic housing association.

In England, the growing Housing Corporation emphasis on housing plus services and tackling social exclusion closely parallels the agendas of black and minority ethnic housing associations and, therefore, provides opportunities for mutually beneficial growth. It is clear, as Beider (1998b, p. 20) has argued, that 'black-led organisations could be in the first wave of social housing organisations that implement new ideas on social regeneration'. Nevertheless, it is not clear that the new strategy, and its renewed emphasis on stock transfers will fully address the viability problems of black and minority ethnic housing associations and the pressure on rent levels resulting from their stock profile (Soares, 1997). Indeed, failure to address this issue has a potentially wide impact, including issues of welfare dependency and the operation of the Labour government's welfare to work strategy. However, the new black and minority ethnic housing strategy, despite its limitation, does offer the opportunity for us to consider a pluralistic ethnic housing policy which offers a third way to the free market and municipal socialist approaches outlined above.

THE THIRD WAY

The third way can empower black and minority ethnic stakeholders by drawing on and developing the successes of free market and social sector policies. These successes can only be maintained through a continuing commitment to tackle direct and indirect discrimination within the housing system, coupled with an assessment of the housing preferences and opportunities available to black and minority ethnic communities and the promotion of a healthy private sector. It is important that we do not forget the important role of mainstream organisations in this process. For example, Charlesworth (1998, p. 22) notes that local authorities are not subject to the same assessments of race equality performance as housing associations and suggests that the best value regime could be adapted to remedy this policy weakness.

Black and minority ethnic housing associations have an important role to play in third way approaches, since they assert the primacy of empowerment and self-help over paternalism, and question the validity of the social engineering which may emanate from top–down policy implementation. Third way housing policy has the opportunity to embrace a bottom–up and diverse model of housing policy making which offers a less prescriptive view of service provision and housing outcomes. In this model, the choices of black and minority ethnic communities to spatially concentrate are not simply associated with marginalisation, but can be supported by policies and financial resources to ensure that the life chances within those spatially differentiated areas are comparable with those within mainstream society. In this example, the third way takes the form of a pluralistic housing policy which is likely to be most successful when it is developed as part of a pluralistic social policy, addressing structural inequality and assessing all governmental measures for their impact upon black and minority ethnic communities. For example, in the context of housing, funding for property improvement and new building in areas of black and minority ethnic residence must be linked to the employment of local labour. Positive action should also be taken to ensure that employment opportunities within the wider urban area are available to black and minority ethnic communities, and social welfare services must be proportionate to need across the urban milieu. Through a combination of measures social contact on the grounds of ethnicity need not be constrained, should there be a black and minority ethnic preference for residential segregation.

Further community empowerment can be achieved by ensuring that at least some of the services targeted upon areas of black and minority ethnic residence are controlled by the communities receiving the service. While this might occur through representation within mainstream organisations, the provision of services by separate organisations controlled by particular black and minority ethnic communities also has an important role to play. Ensuring continuing improvements in access to mainstream provision, alongside the development of separate organisations, will prevent the development of an apartheid system of provision. In any case, Johnson and Ward (1985) note in their study of the effectiveness of the Birmingham Inner City Partnership that black-led organisations are frequently more inclusive than white-led organisations.

The community action of black and minority ethnic communities has a critical role to play in achieving pluralism through demanding influence in housing policy and local politics, in addition to arguing for improved housing conditions. It is clear from the issues addressed above, that the black and minority ethnic housing movement offers the potential to address social exclusion and the wider socioeconomic agenda which many mainstream organisations have neglected in their dash for growth.

CONCLUSION

The essential condition of any housing policy is the recognition of, and provision for, black and minority ethnic housing need. This should mean pluralism and universalism, with the opportunities to exercise choice in the free market augmented by sensitive provision from the social sector in order to meet weaknesses in the market.

The free market offers the potential to meet many of the housing aspirations of black and minority ethnic communities in terms of tenure and spatial choice. However, there are barriers to the market (outlined above) which require market regulation and, in addition, economic barriers which place owner occupation, and indeed, private renting out of the reach of some communities.

These difficulties and shortfalls have historically been met by state intervention, which has traditionally involved paternalistic white majority 'solutions' on behalf of and for 'the other'. An alternative approach is offered by the grass-roots activism within black and minority ethnic communities which has led to the development of the black and minority ethnic housing movement. It is critical that this is not seen as a short-term policy solution, which was suggested by the decision to replace the black and minority ethnic housing strategy in 1996 with an enabling framework, but as the foundation for a more fundamental policy change. Demands for greater resources, but also significantly for more community control over resources, provide an important challenge to the future construction of social policy.

The increased involvement of black and minority ethnic communities within mainstream housing organisations, particularly at senior organisational levels, has a key part to play in more sensitive provision. But there is also a need for generous ring fenced funding for black and minority ethnic organisations in order to effectively support community initiatives and respond to the disproportionate vulnerability of relatively small organisations to external factors. As Beider (1998a) notes, the prize to national policy makers is the ability of black and minority ethnic housing associations to go beyond narrow bricks and mortar issues and to address wider socioeconomic objectives such as social exclusion.

Nevertheless, it is still essential that mainstream social sector provision be non discriminatory and meet any particular needs of black and minority ethnic communities. The British experience has been that even where direct discrimination has been eliminated, a litany of rules and regulations (for example, residence qualifications, preference given to sons and daughters of existing residents, dwelling type and design) act as barriers to black and minority ethnic access to good quality housing. However, a number of mainstream providers have started to recognise that some black and minority ethnic communities may have specific requirements of properties which will increase their satisfaction with the dwelling. In so far as these innovations increase the variety of the total housing stock, they are also likely to directly benefit white majority communities. Social housing organisations have also sought to develop more sensitive management policies through training, monitoring and the provision of translated material. This is not to say that all black and minority ethnic communities will have specific requirements of dwelling design and/or management, or that particular black and minority ethnic communities will always have specific requirements. However, in a genuinely pluralistic system, responsive provision is essential. Therefore, it seems essential to advocate greater research into the housing needs and preferences of black and minority ethnic communities.

Individual initiatives such as the development of the black and minority ethnic housing movement can be seen as empowering black and minority ethnic communities. These have represented fragile gains which, at times, have seemed at odds with the philosophy of national housing policy. In contrast, we now have the potential to develop the black and minority ethnic housing movement alongside the mainstream, underpinned by a pluralistic philosophy which values and celebrates difference and empowers black and minority ethnic stakeholders.

REFERENCES

Beider, H. (1998a) 'Progress Report on Consultations', *Black Housing*, February/March, pp. 8–9.

Beider, H. (1998b) 'Black Housing Futures', *Black Housing*, April/June, pp. 19–20.

Bowes, A., Dar, N. and Sim, D. (1997) *Too White, Too Rough, and Too Many Problems: A Study of Pakistani Housing in Britain* (Stirling: University of Stirling, Department of Applied Social Science, Research Report No. 3).

Charlesworth, J. (1998) 'BME Housing Policy – CRE Response', *Black Housing*, July/September, p. 22.

Commission for Racial Equality (1983) *Collingwood Housing Association* (London: CRE).

Commission for Racial Equality (1988) *Homelessness and Discrimination* (London: CRE).

Commission for Racial Equality (1989) *Racial Discrimination in Liverpool City Council* (London: CRE).

Commission for Racial Equality (1990) *'Sorry, It's Gone' – Testing for Racial Discrimination in the Private Rented Sector* (London: CRE).

Commission for Racial Equality (1993) *Housing Associations and Racial Equality* (London: CRE).

Crawley, R. and Lemos, G. (1993) *Training Needs Analysis of Existing and Emerging Black and Minority Ethnic Housing Associations in the Midlands* (Leicester: BASE Trust/WMHTS).

Dahya, B. (1974) 'The Nature of Pakistani Ethnicity in Industrial Cities in Britain', in Cohen, A. (ed.) *Urban Ethnicity* (London: Tavistock), pp. 77–118.

Dalton, M. and Daghlian, S. (1989) *Race and Housing in Glasgow – The Role of Housing Associations* (London: CRE).

Damer, S. (1976) 'A Note on Housing Allocation', in Edwards, M., Gray, F., Merrett, S. and Swann, J. (eds) *Housing and Class in Britain* (London: Political Economy of Housing Workshop, pp. 72–4).

Davies, J. G. (1985) *Asian Housing in Britain* (London: Social Affairs Unit, Research Report 6).

Etzioni, A. (1995) *The Spirit of Community* (London: Fontana Press).

Franklin, B. and Passmore, J. (1998) *Developing for Diversity: the Needs of Minority Ethnic Communities* (Cardiff: Taff Housing Association).

Gray, F. (1976) 'The Management of Local Authority Housing', in Edwards, M., Gray, F., Merrett, S. and Swann, J. (eds) *Housing and Class in Britain* (London: Political Economy of Housing Workshop), pp. 75–86.

Habeebullah, M. and Slater, D. (1990) *Equal Access to Council Housing in Rochdale* (London: Community Development Foundation Publications).

Harrison, M. (1992) 'Black-led Housing Organisations and the Housing Association Movement', *New Community*, Vol. 18, No. 3, pp. 427–37.

Harrison, M. L., Karmani, A., Law, I., Phillips, D. and Ravetz, A. (1996) *Black and Minority Ethnic Housing Associations: An Evaluation of the Housing Corporation's Black and Minority Ethnic Housing Association Strategies* (London: Housing Corporation).

Henderson, J. and Karn, V. (1987) *Race, Class and State Housing: Inequality and the Allocation of Public Housing in Britain* (Aldershot: Gower).

Hickman, M. and Walter, B. (1997) *Discrimination and the Irish Community in Britain* (London: CRE).

Housing Corporation (1998) *Black and Minority Ethnic Housing Policy* (London: Housing Corporation).

Hutton, W. (1995) *The State We're In* (London: Jonathan Cape).

Hutton, W. (1997) *Stakeholding and its Critics* (London: Institute for Economic Affairs, Choices in Welfare No. 36).

James, W. (1993) 'Migration, Racism and Identity Formation: The Caribbean Experience in Britain', in James, W. and Harris, C. (eds) *Inside Babylon: The Caribbean Diaspora in Britain* (London: Verso), pp. 231–87.

Jeffers, S. and Hoggett, P. (1995) 'Like Counting Deckchairs on the Titanic: A Study of Institutional Racism and Housing Allocations in Haringey and Lambeth', *Housing Studies*, Vol. 10, No. 3, pp. 325–44.

Jeffery, J. and Seagar, R. with Williams, J. and Julienne, J. (1993) *Housing Black and Minority Ethnic Elders* (London: Federation of Black Housing Organisations).

Johnson, M. R. D. and Ward, R. (1985) *Five Year Review of Birmingham Inner City Partnership* (London: Department of the Environment/ Aston University Management Centre).

Jones, A. (1994) *The Numbers Game: Black and Minority Ethnic Elders and Sheltered Accommodation* (Oxford: Anchor Housing Trust).

Karn, V., Kemeny, J. and Williams, P. (1985) *Home Ownership in the Inner City: Salvation or Despair?* (Aldershot: Gower).

Law, I. (1996) *Racism, Ethnicity and Social Policy* (Hemel Hempstead: Harvester Wheatsheaf).

Law, I., Davies, J., Phillips, D. and Harrison, M. (1996) *Equity and Difference: Racial and Ethnic Inequalities in Housing Needs and Housing Investment in Leeds* (Leeds: University of Leeds).

London Against Racism in Housing (1988) *Anti-Racism and the Private Sector* (London: LARH).

Modood, T. (1990) 'Catching up with Jesse Jackson: Being Oppressed and Being Somebody', *New Community*, Vol. 17, No. 1, pp. 85–96.

Mullings, B. (1992) 'Investing in Public Housing and Racial Discrimination Implications in the 1990s', *New Community*, Vol. 18, No. 3, pp. 415–25.

NFHA (National Federation of Housing Associations) (1983) *Race and Housing ... Still a Cause for Concern* (London: NFHA).

Niner, P. (1987) 'Housing Associations and Ethnic Minorities', in Smith, S. J. and Mercer, J. (eds) *New Perspectives on Race and Housing* (Glasgow: Centre for Housing Research, Studies in Housing 2), pp. 219–47.

Owen, D. (1993) *Ethnic Minorities in Great Britain: Housing and Family Characteristics* (Coventry: University of Warwick, CRER, 1991 Census Statistical Paper No. 4).

Owen, D. (1996) 'Size, Structure and Growth of the Ethnic Minority Populations', in Coleman, D. and Salt, J. (eds) *Ethnicity in the 1991 Census: Volume One: Demographic Characteristics of the Ethnic Minority Populations* (London: HMSO), pp. 80–123.

Page, D. (1993) *Building for Communities* (York: Joseph Rowntree Foundation).

Peach, C. and Byron, M. (1992) 'Caribbean Tenants in Council Housing: "Race", Class and Gender', *New Community*, Vol. 19, No. 3, pp. 407–24.

Peach, C. and Rossiter, D. (1996) 'Level and Nature of Spatial Concentration and Segregation of Minority Ethnic Populations in Great Britain, 1991', in Ratcliffe, P. (ed.) *Ethnicity in the 1991 Census: Volume Three: Social Geography and Ethnicity in Britain: Geographical Spread, Spatial Concentration and Internal Migration* (London: HMSO), pp. 111–34.

Phillips, D. (1986) *What Price Equality? A Report on the Allocation of GLC Housing in Tower Hamlets* (London: GLC).

Phillips, D. (1997) 'The Housing Position of Ethnic Minority Group Home Owners', in Karn, V. (ed.) *Ethnicity in the 1991 Census: Volume Four: Employment, Education and Housing among the Ethnic Minority Populations of Britain* (London: HMSO), pp. 170–88.

Ratcliffe, P. (1981) *Racism and Reaction: A Profile of Handsworth* (London: Routledge and Kegan Paul).

Ratcliffe, P. (1996) *'Race' and Housing in Bradford* (Bradford: Bradford Housing Forum).

Ratcliffe, P. (1997) ' "Race", Ethnicity and Housing Differentials in Britain', in Karn, V. (ed.) *Ethnicity in the 1991 Census: Volume Four:*

Employment, Education and Housing among the Ethnic Minority Populations of Britain (London: HMSO), pp. 130–46.

Robinson, V. (1980) 'Asians and Council Housing', *Urban Studies*, Vol.17, pp. 323–31.

Robinson, V. (1993) 'Ethnic Minorities and the Enduring Geography of Settlement', *Town and Country Planning*, March, pp. 53–6.

Sarre, P., Phillips, D. and Skellington, R. (1989) *Ethnic Minority Housing: Explanations and Policies* (Aldershot: Avebury).

Singh, L. (1991) 'Current Issues of Concern for Black HAs', *Black Housing*, Vol. 7, No. 9/10, p. 8.

Skellington, R. (1996) *'Race' in Britain Today* (London: Sage).

Soares, T. (1997) 'Black HA Rents', *Black Housing*, July/September, pp. 6–7.

Tomlins, R. (1999) *Housing Experiences of Minority Ethnic Communities in Britain: An Academic Literature Review and Annotated Bibliography* (Coventry: University of Warwick, Centre for Research in Ethnic Relations).

University of Salford (1996) *Study of the Housing Needs of the Asian and African/Caribbean Communities in Peterborough* (Salford: University of Salford).

17

A Financial Perspective

Jeremy Wood and John Harvey

INTRODUCTION

Housing professionals are aware that almost £12 billion of private finance has been raised in just over ten years to fund either the building or running of affordable housing projects by registered social landlords (RSLs). This is an exceptional achievement; a practical demonstration of effective and successful private and public sector partnership. However, compared to other privatisation activity it has received little recognition or publicity outside the housing sector.

Despite this success the focus of housing development activity has centred on playing the numbers game, concentrating on maximising the number of properties built. The driver for this approach is a response to housing need statistics. Statistics certainly have their place in determining what is developed and how this is implemented. Placing too much emphasis on the numbers developed may satisfy short-term needs, but may not be the best option for long-term provision.

Social housing regulators have also been keen to maximise the number of houses developed by RSLs. This has been influenced by their need to account for every penny spent as well as ensuring that best value is obtained from public subsidy. The amount of public subsidy to support RSL development has, and continues to be, reduced year on year. Regulators have responded to this by changing how they allocate these limited resources. Alternative approaches to maximise the number of houses developed have included an increased emphasis on the low cost home ownership programme (such as shared ownership) as well as the introduction of competitive bidding for public sector grant.

BACKGROUND

When private finance was first introduced to RSLs, lenders and their associated professional advisers went through steep learning curves. Over time the loan facilities made available by funders have evolved. Lending instruments and products were originally based on low start finance such as index linked and deferred interest loans. Now RSLs can obtain complex and flexible funding arrangements to meet their treasury and risk management needs. The market for RSL finance has matured and is now supported by both the capital markets and a wide range of competing financial institutions.

The RSL sector has demonstrated an exceptional debt repayment track record having incurred insignificant losses and this performance has encouraged increasing numbers of lenders to enter the market. This has created fierce competition between funders, yet the reduced allocation of public subsidy has reduced demand for finance at a time when supply is in abundance. The inevitable result, to the benefit of RSLs, is reduced borrowing margins. Moreover, RSLs' overall borrowing costs have been substantially improved by the beneficial economic circumstances prevailing over the last few years.

The introduction of competitive bidding for social housing grant in England and rent benchmarking in Wales has impacted on the long-term sustainability of development activity by RSLs. Both approaches have encouraged RSLs to cross-subsidise new scheme development. This is achieved by utilising unencumbered assets and cashflow to support development activity. However, this is a finite resource. Once used it will cease to be available. The speed at which an RSL curtails its development activity and becomes a management only organisation therefore depends on the size of its development programme.

FUTURE ISSUES

The late 1980s and early 1990s saw RSLs concentrate on new build activity. Future housing issues will centre on the regeneration of existing urban areas. Existing public sector housing has a repairs bill in excess of £20 billion. Dealing with this will include an element of clearance and rebuild but the emphasis needs to switch to the regeneration of existing communities.

Housing may be a crucial driver for successful regeneration but it cannot achieve it in isolation. Regeneration is about the whole community. If there are no employment prospects, leisure and recreational facilities, educational establishments, medical centres or retail outlets there will be little demand or desire to inhabit housing accommodation within that location regardless of the quality and suitability of the units provided. Conversely, if the infrastructure is in place but there is insufficient or unsuitable housing, people will not want to live in that area. It is the integration of these issues that provides a stimulus to the creation and sustainability of communities.

More focus needs to be applied to the whole regeneration issue. Funders may only be directly involved in the provision of housing whether it be social housing, private rented housing or housing for sale but we also want a sustainable community structure. Funding for housing is long term: 25 years or even 35 years. Repayment of the debt raised depends upon continued demand and occupancy of the houses. If a strategy for wholesale community regeneration is not part of the project there must be a question mark over future demand. This will restrict future rental income which ultimately will affect both the cost and availability of finance.

Effective regeneration requires radical and novel responses. This may include stakeholder involvement from employers, mixed tenure development, integrating different client groups and wider use of housing plus. RSLs who focus their activities on housing plus will need to quickly develop a wide range of skills to understand and manage the increased risks that regeneration and renewal activity involves. These activities will be centred on housing provision but are likely to move away from traditional grant funded social housing. Value for money will continue to be crucial and producing affordable housing at the lowest unit cost will be the key to flourishing RSLs.

These pressures are encouraging diversification as a means of ongoing development. But development without social housing grant carries additional risks. RSLs which focus on housing management can survive and continue to play an important part in housing provision, providing management services to other bodies. By diversifying its activities a RSL may be able to cross-subsidise the provision of social housing from alternative income streams. Risk management of these activities will be crucial otherwise the RSL may find its mainstream social housing actually begins to subsidise the diversified activities.

Cost control pressure will lead to bigger and fewer RSLs, to ensure effective asset management and that a sustainable development programme is delivered. Despite reduced numbers and unit growth, RSLs will need to retain local identity and local accountability to continue productive relationships with tenants and local authorities. Many RSLs are currently exploring the benefits of group structures to retain local accountability and to obtain economies of scale. For example, group borrowing facilities provide financial benefits as the costs to a larger stronger parent may be to the benefit of a smaller weaker subsidiary.

Fundamental to regeneration and renewal of existing stock and urban areas is partnership with stakeholders. Partnerships will involve local authorities as enablers, central government, funders, contractors and developers, other agencies as required, as well as RSLs and crucially the existing community. It is essential that each and every partner be accountable for their role in the provision not only of housing units but also its role within the wider regeneration context. Partnership processes will require innovative thinking and this may combine with innovative financing. Funding models based on the design, build, finance and operate (DBFO) approach of the private finance initiative (PFI) are being developed as means of funding existing stock needs.

Under a straightforward PFI scheme undertaken under DBFO rules, the private sector has to provide all the DBFO activity and they have to take some risk. If we look at a typical PFI, the local authority will, in all probability, want to refurbish some assets and build some new ones or extend some existing ones. What does the local authority need to do?

- It must convince a lender that there will be enough money paid by the local authority over the whole lending term to secure the loan sufficiently to get a competitive rate of interest. Now clearly if the local authority does not think it will need the substantial part of the asset for the term of lending it calls into question whether it is worthwhile doing at all. In most cases they have to convince the lender that there is sufficient collateral to support the borrowing.

- It has to face the fact that most, if not all, of the people and organisations making the primary supplies that comprise design, build, fund and operate are not doing it for altruistic reasons and are risk averse (except when extra risk can be justified by extra profit).
- It has to face the fact that the complete deal has to be arranged in advance to cover the whole term of lending with a single or consortium provider. If you need to borrow over 30 years, you need to contract with the operator for 30 years.

Assuming the local authority passes hurdle one and has a good business case, it faces hurdle two which is the nature of the suppliers. The great majority of the private sector exists to fulfil a perfectly laudable objective which is to maximise the return to shareholders. The public sector's objective is to maximise the value of services for the community. These are not naturally compatible and no amount of goodwill or openness will avoid the fundamental difference.

The final problem faced by the local authority is the borrowing. This usually establishes the term of the deal and it needs to be long and aim to ensure the combined interest and repayment is affordable. Local authorities would not normally contract with a builder for 30 years to build a building or an architect to design a building or a facilities management company to manage a building. Builders mostly want to finish the building, get paid and get on to the next contract. Facilities managers on the other hand do like very long contract arrangements which, sensibly, most clients are unwilling to provide.

There are some organisations, however, that seem to have good long-term track records of both survival and consistency of operational objectives. It cannot be accidental that most housing transfers and many residential home transfers have been to not for profit organisations: they make sense. The local authority can have some comfort in a long contract with an organisation which does not have the maximisation of profit as an objective and whose survival depends on continuing to provide the services which its local authority client requires as efficiently as possible. The organisation does not have to do anything directly, though it may. Its primary business is to ensure that the services are provided. It can procure each part of the DBFO requirement appropriately: finance, long; facilities management, medium; new build services, short term. There are no downside cost implications in using an intermediate organisation and the potential for procurement at more competitive prices than in a turnkey deal.

Two potential concerns are that voluntary sector PFI is untried and that non profit making bodies may be commercially unsound. However, although the circumstances are different with residential homes transfer and large-scale voluntary transfer of housing, they are not that different. As to survivability the track record of the not for profit sector seems to compare rather well when contrasted with the commercial sector and spectacularly well when compared with the developer sector. How many of them were around in their current form 30 years ago and how many of them are likely to be around in another 30 years?

There is no perfect way to safeguard value over 20 or 30 years. Local authority stewardship of assets has hardly been a model. The keys to the most secure and value providing ways of using PFI involve some simple rules:

- a sound business plan which isn't fudged in the hope that the future will bale out weaknesses;
- a primary contractor for the whole deal which is not for profit and committed to the same objectives as the local authority;
- effective competitive procurement and management of primary services; and
- sound management in the primary contractor.

Once those principles are established and developed properly the corporate legal and financial issues can be relegated to their proper place in the process.

A WAY FORWARD

One alternative approach is, in effect, a hybrid. It incorporates elements from PFI and experience to date from housing transfers and the delegation of housing management functions to estate management boards (EMBs) and tenant management organisations (TMOs). It involves raising private finance legitimately without devices or the once and for all transfer of stock by the local authority. It could facilitate innovations in management of housing services. More importantly it introduces the necessary imperative and obligation of a long-term approach to reinvestment strategy through specifying performance and outputs in a private sector funded and monitored business plan.

This approach is based on the incorporation of a community based not for profit company, in which the local authority would be a minority shareholder. This body would take either a long lease on the houses and flats or a freehold with a buy back option for the local authority. It would enter into a formal contract with the local authority to provide housing management services in return for a fee. This means that the public sector could retain a freehold interest but would have engaged in a genuine transfer of risk to the new company in terms of the contracted commitments.

The company would then borrow money in the private sector (using its assured fee income and interest in the property as security) to undertake necessary catch up repairs and improvements. It would also establish a long-term reinvestment strategy as part of its business plan, funded over, say, 20 to 30 years. The company could be an operating company undertaking repairs and improvements and grounds maintenance. It might also provide energy services directly to tenants under the new deregulated energy supply regime.

POSITIVE RESULTS

The outcome of this approach would be the following:

- The reinvestment backlog is tackled.
- Long-term maintenance and improvement would be guaranteed and outside the control of the local authority (that is, it could not be influenced by short-term calculations in relation to rents).
- The local authority would remain the tenants' landlord, but the whole range of tenant services and housing management would be out sourced to the company under contract (in a way similar to EMBs and other TMOs now).
- The local authority would remain the long-term owner of the stock.
- Tenants would not be confronted with the once and for all choice of transfer (which is often seen as threatening, leading to lack of sufficient support on a ballot).

- Rents could be kept lower than with traditional transfer because no purchase price would be payable and delegation of day-to-day management would be accompanied by rigorous attention to securing reductions in the local authority's management costs.
- A community based company would provide a direct and expert focus on the landlord services being provided.
- Lenders would ensure that the stock would be brought up to and maintained in good condition.
- The company might wish to take a wider range of functions including housing plus type activities.

COSTS AND BENEFITS

The principal cost would be that of servicing the loans from the private sector. This is likely to have some impact on rents and hence on housing benefit expenditure. Some estimates suggest that these costs will be lower than those arising on large-scale voluntary transfers (LSVTs) and far less than those on transfers supported under the ERCF (Estate Renewal Challenge Funding).

Significant savings may be achieved by reducing costs of housing management and securing better value from existing expenditure, such as that on repairs, as indicated in research into the effectiveness of TMOs published by the Department of the Environment, Transport and the Regions. Taken over, say, a 20- or 30-year business planning period savings secured in year one are recurrent and significant.

The government can control the rate at which such companies are created because of the need for permission to be given before local authorities can grant a long lease on their rented housing. Other advantages of this approach are that it accommodates rather than denies the emotional attachment which many local authority councillors have towards the ownership of their housing. It puts the customer in a position where effective choices over costs, quality and standards can be made.

BASIC LENDING PRINCIPLES

Whatever structures and mechanisms are developed to deliver the funding requirements of the future, basic lending principles will need to be observed to ensure lenders' confidence is retained. Without this the opportunities to raise private finance will become not only more limited but undoubtedly more expensive.

Management capability is an important ingredient for a lender. If there is no track record the assessment of management must be based on experience, qualifications and certain subjective criteria. This may vary from detailed research into an individual's background to a view about the ability to achieve the objectives set. After all, even poor financial disciplines may take time to impact to an extent which requires a lender to act.

Another important area on which a lender will focus its analysis is the financial strength of the business being scrutinised and the robustness of any business plan provided. The business plan must show the ability to repay any loan within the agreed term using sensitivity analysis that satisfies viability using a funder's assumptions. These may differ between funders and will almost certainly vary from the RSLs' own base case assumptions which will usually tend to be optimistic. The greater the scope for adverse sensitivity then the greater the comfort afforded to a lender. This obviously impacts on risk, repayment and ultimately pricing issues. Comfort may be taken from the financial strength of existing operations if the RSL is not a start-up organisation and may be strengthened if guarantees or cross-collateralisation is allowed from the balance sheet strength of the borrower.

To date, housing providers have found it relatively easy to raise private finance due to a combination of a competitive market place and a fall in the cost of borrowing through reductions in the general level of interest rates. In order to be able to continue to raise private finance when market conditions are not so favourable RSLs need to ensure their business plans are robust to cope with both the good and bad times.

CONCLUSION

In concluding it is probably safe to say that the search is still on for a PFI model that will allow the government to ensure that there is both suitable and sufficient access to housing for all those in need at the same time as reducing both capital and revenue subsidy. Given limited access to funds the role of the local authority is likely to change. Whether or not it continues to be a housing provider is probably incidental. Crucial will be the promotion of community regeneration projects. Successful regeneration will demand that the local authority creates a focused corporate strategy for implementation that creates partnerships but above all is driven by the need to be accountable to the local community. Community regeneration can only succeed if the community is a fully participating partner.

Actual provision will be undertaken by those who demonstrate best value, affordability and community accessibility. In the past this has been proved possible in part through the introduction of private finance to RSLs and more latterly large-scale voluntary transfer (LSVT) transactions. The current grant funding model has been a proven success. Too much tampering may be dangerous and threaten the funding possibilities of the future. It is essential that the funder's confidence be retained to ensure an adequate supply of finance is available by maintaining the exemplary track record that has been demonstrated over the last ten years.

18

A Regulation Perspective

Selwyn Runnett

INTRODUCTION

Regulation in social housing is now a key issue. It is all part of the transformation in centre-left thinking in recent years about the role of the state and the question of how it should intervene in society and the economy. In many fields, we have seen decisive moves away from a model of the state as provider towards that of regulator and this has, in turn, generated new debate about the boundaries between public and private, and about what should remain uniquely the role of the state.

Regulation also fits neatly into the debate on the third way which allows an escape from the dichotomy of new right markets and pseudo markets on the one hand and uniform state provision on the other. The debate is moving away from the simple divisions of the past: public versus private, state versus market, collective versus individual. The emphasis is shifting instead to ways of combining these seemingly irreconcilable ways of working, often in quite pragmatic ways in different policy circumstances, rather than choosing between them. This debate is just beginning in housing.

It is refreshing that we are moving away from the new right inspired view that in some way social housing should be seen as a commercial business to be run on the same lines as a successful supermarket group. Tenants and those in housing need are seen as customers with choices and social housing organisations sell their services according to carefully crafted business plans. This approach is now largely discredited. Those who need housing are clearly not in the same position as supermarket customers who have genuine choice on which brand to buy or who can take their goods back for a refund. Nor are social housing organisations commercial companies whose main concern is shareholder value; rather, they are organisations with social objectives and a commitment to a variety of key stakeholders.

BACKGROUND

Despite the new right attempt to slot social housing into a free market framework, successive Tory governments recognised the need for regulation. Indeed, the classic case for regulation is where an industry has a monopoly or quasi-monopoly. In this situation, it has excessive and unfair power over consumers, who cannot shop elsewhere or can do so only with difficulty. In these cases, regulation is essential in order that consumers can get good quality service at a fair price. Social housing organisations, as landlords, are just such quasi monopoly providers: traditionally their housing has been in short supply (indeed rationed), the consumers of the service have little effective choice, and in general they are further disempowered by coming from those sections of our society that are generally social excluded.

As we know, regulation has, in fact, been with us for a long period and took on its current familiar form during the Industrial Revolution. In its early phases it primarily concerned itself with the issue of minimum standards within a market economy. A mixture of regulatory standards backed by statute and self-regulation emerged with some of the excesses of the Victorian free market system being ameliorated not by regulation but by the work of charities and voluntary organisations. The alternatives to regulation of a market economy came from two directions. One was the creation of self-help membership based organisations such as friendly societies, trade unions and producer and consumer cooperatives. The regulation element here was provided by direct democratic accountability to the membership. The second alternative was government, local and central, backed by the power to tax. Both tiers of government provided services and facilities directly in the form of state provision. Regulation in this case was by way of the accountability of directly elected representatives and in the statutory relationship between local and central government.

This history is worth recounting because the general split in regulatory approach that developed from the Industrial Revolution onwards has applied equally to social housing. The charitable housing trusts and societies that were established during this period were regulated by a mixture of self-regulation through, for instance, trust deeds, and statutory regulation through either the Charity Commission or the Registrar of Friendly Societies. The new wave of housing associations and societies established in the 1960s and 1970s followed a similar pattern with the important difference of the creation of the Housing Corporation in 1964. It introduced much strengthened statutory monitoring and regulation in order to oversee and safeguard substantial amounts of public money that were being pumped into a voluntary sector structure.

By contrast, council housing was state provided housing created by a partnership of central and local government. It was not based on ameliorating free markets but on replacing them with the planned provision of affordable housing based on need. Regulation came through the accountability of local councillors to local electorates by means of regular elections with some value for money controls operating between central and local government. It is interesting that the third way of provision through friendly and mutual societies and cooperatives hardly developed in the field of social rented housing (in contrast to the mutual building societies involved in house building and ownership).

THE CURRENT REGULATORY FRAMEWORK

So what is the current structure of social housing regulation across Britain? Council housing in England, Scotland and Wales has perhaps seen the greatest changes, and faces even greater change in the period ahead. Inevitably, the debate on regulation of council housing is tied up with the general debate about the role and status of local government. Clearly, the view under the Tories was of local government primarily as an agent of central government with the narrow remit of responsibility for procuring specified public services. This was the end result of a process which saw more and more functions being removed and the resulting fragmentation of its strategic role. It became a body primarily looking after a collection of local public services with plans being developed in the 1980s for it to become a shell purchasing services on a client contractor basis. In housing this approach manifested itself in the creation of LSVT (large-scale voluntary transfer) housing associations and an emphasis on the enabling role.

With local authorities now raising only 15–20 per cent of their overall expenditure from local taxes, local government has become very weak, has low public approval ratings, and is perceived to be inefficient and unresponsive in its task of managing and delivering local services, particularly in the management of council housing. Its democratic role has been weakened not just by central government but by low turnouts in local elections, elections being fought primarily on national issues, and the poor public image of local councillors. Many argue that this perception is unjustified but, nonetheless, there has been an increasing trend for central government to regulate local government through central regulatory bodies. Accountability through local councillors has therefore been supplemented by an increasingly proactive Accounts Commission for Scotland founded in 1974 and, in the case of England and of Wales, the Audit Commission established in 1983. A key role for both organisations has been to promote the best use of public money by seeking to achieve economy, efficiency and effectiveness through value for money studies.

In the case of housing associations and other registered social landlords (RSLs), regulation has been undertaken by the Housing Corporation in England, Scottish Homes in Scotland and until recently Tai Cymru in Wales. Each has had a different approach to regulation and the scale of operation has varied significantly. The Housing Corporation regulates over 2,000 RSLs, Scottish Homes under 300 and Tai Cymru less than 100. Tai Cymru was widely regarded as adopting an approach of detailed scrutiny although it did produce topic audits that considered sector-wide issues. Recent examples included stock condition surveys and tenant participation. This produced a management consultancy style of audit and regulation which neither the Housing Corporation nor Scottish Homes have adopted.

It is interesting that all three regulators made explicit links between investment decisions and regulatory outcomes. This is not surprising given the fact that RSLs now draw heavily on private finance supplied by lending institutions in a highly successful example of a type of public–private partnership. Funders want proper and consistent regulation of RSLs as a prerequisite to creating and maintaining the confidence necessary to attract private investment in social rented housing.

In Wales, Tai Cymru used a poor audit outcome to stop an RSL from bidding for capital grant. Both Tai Cymru and the Housing Corporation also notified RSLs if they were considered ineligible to receive capital grants. One particular difference between Scottish Homes and the other two regulators is that in Scotland a grading system has been adopted. Tai Cymru, however, took the view that the publication of league tables was unproductive and diverted energy away from tackling the issues identified in an adverse regulatory report. The issue of grading and league tables is of course tied in with the current trend towards benchmarking and performance classification.

One thing stands out clearly from the social housing regulation debate. It is that traditionally the systems for regulation of council housing and for RSLs have been and still are quite different. At its core, the debate on regulation is concerned with the three issues of standards, finance and accountability. One model works on the basis of primary accountability to statutory regulators and the other works on primary accountability through the ballot box to a local electorate.

THE FUTURE REGULATORY FRAMEWORK

So how is the debate likely to develop and what are the key issues for the Labour Party? One thing is certain; we need to stay focused on the political issues involved in the three key areas of regulation identified above. There are calls being made now for harmonisation of standards, financing and a new and growing debate not just about the accountability and internal governance of both council housing and RSLs but on the regulation of the newly developing forms of social housing organisations in the shape of local housing companies and local housing corporations. These new organisations have an echo in the debate at the beginning of this century about the creation of public utility societies. If social housing organisations are to develop into utilities, there is now a growing body of experience and debate on the merits and demerits of a variety of regulatory regimes in this field.

In the area of housing finance, there are regular calls for the dual capital funding streams of credit approvals and approved developed programmes to be merged and for revenue regimes to be brought together. The same logic applies with even greater force when it comes to service and performance standards. Why should basic housing management standards vary as between a local authority housing service and local RSLs when they operate in the same area, sometimes on adjacent sites? Why are rent levels different? The pressure to streamline and unify is inexorable and, in some cases, unanswerable.

There is, however, a serious problem in respect of accountability. The changing context within which RSLs and council housing work, and a changed underlying assumption about the role of housing associations, has brought about the problem. RSLs are independent voluntary bodies and distinct independent legal entities. They are not part of the state. In recent years, the housing association movements in England, Scotland and Wales have been at pains to point out that associations are not quangos. The problem is that the statutory framework of registration, finance and regulation laid down in the relevant Housing Acts and the Housing Associations Act makes them de facto state controlled bodies even if this is not the strict legal position. The view among many key opinion formers is that for all intents and purposes housing associations are state controlled bodies funded by the state with the three regulators acting as buffers between central government per se and individual associations and RSLs. Once this argument is accepted, logic leads to the view that, as council housing is state provided and controlled, why not merge the two types of state controlled social housing into one? It will surely lead to cost savings and to greater efficiency and effectiveness. It is then a simple step to argue for accountability through a unified system of regulation.

The result of these shifts in the position of housing associations and local authorities is that the argument for combining what are seen as two state controlled systems of social housing is now very persuasive. However, if the argument for a unified system is accepted, the problem, of course, then lies in the principle and form of regulation. Regulation could take the following forms:

- by government department
- a regulator accountable to a government department
- a regulator accountable to a minister
- a regulator accountable directly to Parliament
- an independent regulator established by statute
- accountability to local councils
- direct accountability to tenants
- some combination of the above.

How, therefore, could a unified system of accountability by regulation work and what model should be employed? The problem is the different forms of internal governance. RSLs have no element of direct democratic accountability unlike that still present in the internal governance of council housing. A unified system implies introducing local democratic accountability into RSLs or removing it from council housing. Alternatively, a new mixed system could be developed. Now that the issue of unified accountability in standards, finance and internal governance has been raised the key question is how the debate will develop to a conclusion. Will that conclusion apply across the whole of Britain or, given the Labour Party's programme of devolution, will it be different in each of the three countries?

In England, regulation is shared by the Housing Corporation, the Audit Commission and local democratic accountability through local councils. On the finance side of the equation, there have even been the beginnings of joint work by the Housing Corporation and local councils in the joint commissioning initiative. There is no short-term prospect of devolved regional government across England and the government is committed to reform and to a future for local government based on a best value regime, elected mayors, changes in internal management and reform of electoral arrangements.

In Scotland and Wales, the new Scottish Parliament and National Assembly for Wales will create what in European terms is a regional tier of government. This introduces an entirely new dimension into the equation within these two countries. Both the Parliament and the Assembly will have direct responsibility for housing and local government. Even given the fact of the continued existence of the Accounts Commission for Scotland and the increasingly anomalous position of the Audit Commission in Wales, it will be within the remit of each body and its government to take its own view on the regulation of social housing. Indeed, uniquely in Wales, Tai Cymru was merged with the Housing Division of the Welsh Office to form an integrated Housing Department for the National Assembly and its government. It will therefore be essential for the Scottish and Welsh Labour Parties to think through the relevant issues and reach conclusions on future policy based on their distinctive needs.

CONCLUSIONS

So where is the debate on regulation likely to take us and is talk of unified regulation realistic? The fundamental divide between social housing organisations that are subject to direct democratic account-ability (council housing) and those that are not (RSLs) will remain. The different legislative framework for each is set to remain and that inevitably means that separate formal regulatory regimes for each sector will need to be retained. This, however, should not preclude the need for change and new thinking. In Wales, for example, a new framework for quality social landlords is being developed jointly by the Welsh Federation of Housing Associations and the Welsh Local Government Association. It involves agreed performance indicators, the development of a series of principles to define a quality social landlord, an examination of how achievement of these principles can be measured, and also how an external regulator can undertake an assessment.

However, as argued above, the three issues of standards, finance and accountability are key political issues for the Labour Party. This was emphasised by the Chancellor of the Exchequer, in his statement to the House of Commons on the economic and fiscal strategy report in June 1998. He stated quite clearly that the government was determined to ensure best value for money and the most efficient possible use of resources. He also introduced the guiding ethos behind the comprehensive spending review that there is no place for new spending unless there is reform through clear targets, standards and rigour in the use of money. As part of this, he announced the creation of a new inspectorate for housing which will form part of the Audit Commission. Its brief will be to improve the management of council housing, set new standards of performance and guarantee high quality investment.

In May 1998 the Housing Minister in the Department of the Environment, Transport and the Regions set out the government's 'principles for a new housing policy' in which there was a strong call for a more comprehensive and integrated approach to housing issues. This approach needs to be carried forward into the area of regulation. The outline of the debate is now clear. The way we approach the three key issues involved in social housing regulation should also reflect the principal themes of the third way. As Hilary Armstrong (see Chapter 9) has stated, 'Housing is at the centre of the government's social policy.' New and creative regulatory frameworks in England, Scotland and Wales can make a major contribution to fulfilling Labour's policy agenda. Regulation needs to be at the heart of new Labour's housing policy.

19

Conclusions

Tim Brown

INTRODUCTION

Discussions on the third way as a political ideology underpinning new Labour show no sign of diminishing. There continues to be considerable attention in academic journals and the media on the concept of stakeholding: some of this material is supportive and descriptive (Kellner, 1998), while other coverage is much more critical (MacGregor, 1999; *Marxism Today*, 1998). The third way is an evolving concept and it is therefore not intended to provide a definitive statement of its general propositions or its implications for housing. The aim of this final chapter is merely to illustrate and reiterate how stakeholding and the third way relate to debates on housing issues. This is itself a somewhat problematic exercise since housing, as many of the contributors have noted, unlike other aspects of social policy such as education and health, is not regarded as a high priority. The Labour government in consultation and discussion papers has stressed the significance of new thinking, and the Green Paper on public health states, 'To achieve these aims, the Government is setting out a third way between the old extremes of individual victim blaming on the one hand and nanny state social engineering on the other' (Department of Health, 1998, p. 5).

The forthcoming Government Green Paper on Housing in England provides opportunities for change. These must be based on a wide debate that ensures governemt policy achieves joined-up thinking as well as creating an innovative approach which puts consumers first.

Many of the contributors have highlighted how policies should be developed to reflect important issues associated with the third way.

The first section of this chapter attempts to draw together these themes and relate them to some of the underpinning principles of the third way as emphasised by Giddens (1998) and covered in Chapter 2. The second section takes a more critical perspective and summarises some of the key arguments that challenge the notion of the third way. It might be suggested, of course, that such debates are not especially relevant for housing as they tend to focus on abstract notions and other areas of welfare policy. But the author would argue that it is essential for housing debates to be aware of such discussions since housing, as many contributions, especially in Part 1, note, should be regarded as part of an holistic approach. Furthermore, a failure on the part of housing academics and practitioners to appreciate and participate in these wider debates is likely to reinforce the marginalisation of housing as part of social policy. Nevertheless, unless links are made between the big ideas of stakeholding and the third way and housing issues, there is unlikely to be a useful engagement between underpinning concepts and housing practice. This is illustrated in the final section of this chapter.

PRINCIPLES AND POLICIES

Chapter 2 emphasised five key themes associated with the third way as developed by Giddens (1998):

- politics as issue based as well as cross-cutting traditional patterns of governance and popular support;
- a new mixed economy of welfare provision with an emphasis, through regulation if necessary, on achieving outcomes rather than focusing on who provides services;
- democratising democracy by emphasising the devolution of responsibilities from traditional centres of power to lower tiers including national assemblies, local government, communities and individuals;
- an emphasis on a social inclusive one nation approach to tackling issues in an holistic manner but with a willingness to be active

> participants in transnational governance such as the European Union;
> • a focus on the social investment state with an emphasis on welfare policy as a means for restoring a balance between rights and responsibilities.

Many writers have placed the emphasis on new politics and changing governance over the last two decades (see, for example, Rhodes, 1997; Stoker, 1999). Contributors to this book emphasise the relevance of these debates for housing and a third way. Oxley highlights the importance of the European Union in terms of its impact on housing policies, while the authors in Part 2 emphasise a wide range of issues associated with changing patterns of governance including national assemblies for Scotland and Wales and the emerging regional dimension in England. In addition, traditional political allegiances are breaking down and being replaced by new social movements based around, for instance, green issues. As Bhatti shows in Chapter 3, there is a growing concern over environmental issues and the main political parties have incorporated a green dimension into their policies. Furthermore, many current housing policies raise interesting dilemmas from a green perspective. These include green field versus brown field development and whether protectioniist policies merely reinforce the vested interests of powerful elites who, by adopting an environmental agenda, hide a more reactionary approach based on nimbyism ('not in my backyard' perspective). Yet it is often easy to forget that traditional political allegiances can remain highly powerful forces that will shape future housing policies, as Gray and Paris highlight in their chapter on Northern Ireland.

Many contributors discuss the new mixed economy of welfare. An effective strategic enabling role for local government is stressed by Stoker and by Wood and Harvey among others. At the same time, both Clapham and Tomlins point to the possibilities of developing more radical and new approaches to social housing provision such as community based housing organisation (following the Scottish community based housing association model) and the emerging black and minority ethnic housing movement. Clearly these types of ideas move the debate about the provision of services away from the rather stale and traditional antagonisms between free market supporters and the state provision lobby. Nevertheless, this is not to suggest that there is no role for traditional providers. As Hood points out, many council and housing association tenants wish to remain with their existing landlords, but they want to do so on the basis of a much greater degree of control over and accountability of their landlord. Similarly, Tomlins identifies that home ownership may provide important opportunities for black and minority ethnic households. Overall, therefore, the emphasis is on a diverse and pluralistic range of provision but, as Runnett indicates, it is essential that relevant and appropriate means of regulation be developed. There are obvious dangers in the continued development of a fragmented and ad hoc system of regulation, while what is required is a comprehensive approach which reflects the changing patterns of governance identified by the contributors in Part 2 and by Stoker.

Democratising democracy is a phrase that Giddens (1998) uses frequently and refers to a greater transparency and openness in decision making and governance. Many of the contributors have emphasised the significance of these developments including:

- the establishment of national assemblies in Scotland and Wales with responsibility for key but not all aspects of housing policy;
- the possibility of the devolution of power over housing and planning issues in Northern Ireland;
- stronger autonomy for local government;
- encouraging local bodies such as community based organisations and the black and minority ethnic housing movement; and
- greater control and influence by tenants over their landlords.

To these we could add other relevant examples such as the growing interest in regional governance in England and ongoing debates about a more relaxed regime for the activities of housing associations and registered social landlords. However, there still remain many unanswered questions. For example, do these changes cumulatively create a more open and transparent society enabling individuals and communities to have a greater influence on housing policies and practices? Or, are these developments merely reordering the top–down power relationships in society rather than creating a bottom–up approach?

An emphasis on how to achieve social inclusion has been a recurring theme throughout the book. The contributors to Part 1 stressed the significance of housing as part of an holistic approach for promoting social inclusion. Joined up thinking is required so that the links between, for instance, housing, health, education and the environment are acknowledged. Furthermore, many of the chapters suggest how either housing organisations ought to expand their activities in partnership with other bodies (see Paterson and Macfarlane) or new types of bodies should be encouraged (see Clapham) to develop these links. Additionally, there are lessons to be learnt from other countries, and some of the projects highlighted by Goetz in his chapter on the USA are particularly interesting in this respect. Nevertheless, in the medium term, the possibilities of promoting social inclusion may, as Oxley shows, be as strongly influenced by the European Union.

Finally, a fundamental theme throughout the discussions on the third way and stakeholding is the debate about the balance between rights and responsibilities. Many of the contributors emphasise the significance of this aspect including Armstrong, Hood and Tomlins, but changing this balance may prove difficult. Goetz, for example, provides a salutary case study of how the good intentions of the new Democrats in the USA became sidelined in the mid-1990s by the changing balance of political forces.

A CRITICAL PERSPECTIVE

The concept of the third way, as was shown in Chapter 2, has been criticised from both the left and the right of the political spectrum. Although it is not the intention to provide a thoroughgoing analysis of these viewpoints, it is important to appreciate that concerns are wide ranging and include, first, that the third way has not been sufficiently radical to break the links with neoliberalism. Burchardt and Hills (1999), for example, comment that welfare provision continues to evolve with a slow but steady shift towards private provision and private finance. Secondly, and on the other hand, there is a belief in some quarters that the third way is still rooted within traditional social democracy. At the same time, other commentators have argued that the third way ignores some honourable traditions within social democracy such as the attempts at community action and popular planning in the early 1980s by Labour controlled local authorities. Thus, these critical perspectives have contributed to a rethinking and reworking of ideas about welfare and social policy. MacGregor (1999), for instance, acknowledges that the third way is different from traditional social democratic welfare as well as neoliberalism, but remains unconvinced by what she calls the new paternalism. Instead, she argues for a fourth way based on the principles of radical democracy with an emphasis on equality.

The third way and stakeholding is therefore likely to remain a focus of continuing debate. This is likely to continue to generate a wide range of ideas and perspectives, some of which will be critical while others will explore individual principles in depth. The third way, as Giddens (1998) points out, is not yet a fully worked out philosophy, but out of current discussions a dialogue is emerging within the social democratic movement about renewal. Of course, it might be suggested that there are serious problems for any government that argues it is constructing a new path without having a developed and formulated political ideology. The third way could become merely the sum of whatever policies and practices the government adopts, leading to an incremental and fragmented set of ideas with no clear underpinning principles. However, the editor believes that this viewpoint is overplayed. The previous government, for example, did not have a fully developed new right perspective prior to 1979 and, indeed, it can be argued that many of the principles underlining much of its social policy did not emerge until the late 1980s. Thus it is highly likely that the third way will evolve into a more fully developed and cohesive framework only in the medium term.

HOUSING PRACTICE

The concepts of the third way and stakeholding are therefore at an interesting stage. A critical debate is taking place on broad ideas and principles, while at the same time government policies are beginning to emerge. In addition, there are innovative practices developing at a local level. A useful and thought provoking illustration of these complex trends relates to the balance between rights and responsibilities, the promotion of sustainable communities and tenancy agreements.

There is considerable interest in transforming so-called problem estates as well as creating new balanced communities. Many different ideas are being promoted including the promotion of mutual aid and support. Burns and Taylor (1998), for example, argue that social cohesion can be encouraged through the development of loose networks that support a wide range of informal activities such as neighbourhood care and self-help groups. Effective initiatives, however, do not require formal intervention and can best be developed by supporting mediating organisations working with local communities. Ideas such as promoting civic and social entrepreneurship are thus particularly relevant. These suggestions clearly link in with many of the themes underpinning the third way, including the emphasis on mutuality (Kellner, 1998), citizenship, and a mixed economy which embraces an enhanced role for voluntary organisations and local community based agencies. At the same time, such thinking also draws attention to some of the neglected roots of the labour and trade union movement including self-help, friendly societies, cooperatives and voluntary organisations. But how are these new responsibilities of mutual support, for instance, going to be developed in practice on rundown social housing estates with, say, high levels of anti-social behaviour and a breakdown of community? Dwyer (1998) suggests that a new welfare consensus is emerging that is built on notions of duty or responsibility rather than rights. In relation to housing, the increasing use of probationary tenancies may be illustrative of this process, as is the growing interest in community lettings or placement policies on allocations. But equally significant are innovative approaches that are being piloted by a number of registered social landlords. These include:

- a mutual aid scheme developed by Manningham Housing Association in Bradford, which involves potential new tenants in a recently completed project agreeing to provide help to neighbours; and
- Irwell Valley Housing Association in Greater Manchester providing different standards of service including a gold service (incorporating a quicker repairs service) as an incentive for good behaviour.

These ideas and approaches have not necessarily been received with universal enthusiasm. There are concerns as to whether groups such as the homeless might be excluded from the benefits of such schemes. Furthermore, there are worries that the negative aspects might take precedence over the more positive elements. The emphasis could be on excluding certain groups and individuals rather than promoting of social inclusion. Indeed, it is interesting to note that there is a growing emphasis in social housing on dealing with the symptoms of anti-social behaviour and conflicting lifestyles among tenants by operating social exclusion practices. In the education field, however, there is now an emphasis on reducing exclusions from school and investigating the causes rather than dealing with the symptoms of the problem. Such differences in policies and practices, possibly within the same community, pose a challenge to holistic thinking in tackling social exclusion.

REFERENCES

Burchardt, T. and Hills, J. (1999) *Private Welfare and Public Policy* (York: York Publishing Services).

Burns, D. and Taylor, M. (1998) *Mutual Aid and Self-Help: Coping Strategies for Excluded Communities* (Bristol: Policy Press).

Dwyer, P. (1998) 'Conditional Citizens? Welfare Rights and Responsibilities in the Late 1990s', *Critical Social Policy*, Vol. 18, No. 4, pp. 493–517.

Department of Health (1998) 'Our Healthier Nation: A Contract for Health' (London: The Stationery Office).

Giddens, A. (1998) *The Third Way* (Cambridge: Polity Press).

Kellner, P. (1998) *New Mutualism: The Third Way* (London: The Co-operative Party).

MacGregor, S. (1999) 'Welfare, Neo-Liberalism and New Paternalism', *Capital and Class*, No. 67, pp. 91–118.

Marxism Today (1998) 'Special Issue', November/December.

Rhodes, R. (1997) *Understanding Governance* (Buckingham: Open University Press).

Stoker, G. (ed.) (1999) *The New Management of British Local Governance* (London: Macmillan).

List of Contributors

EDITOR

Tim Brown is a Principal Lecturer in Housing Studies in the Centre for Comparative Housing Studies at De Montfort University, Leicester. He is a coordinator of the Housing Management Working Group for the European Network for Housing Research. He has published widely on a range of topics including social exclusion, housing needs studies and black and minority ethnic housing requirements.

CONTRIBUTORS

Hilary Armstrong MP has been the Minister for Housing and Local Government since May 1997.

Mark Bhatti is a Senior Lecturer in the School of Applied Social Science at the University of Brighton.

David Clapham is a Professor of Housing Studies at the University of Wales in Cardiff.

Jean Conway was a Senior Lecturer in Housing Studies at Sheffield Hallam University.

Edward G. Goetz is Associate Professor of Urban and Regional Planning at the Hubert H. Humphrey Institute of Public Affairs at the University of Minnesota.

Robina Goodlad is a Professor of Housing and Urban Studies in the Centre for Housing Research and Urban Studies at the University of Glasgow.

Paddy Gray is a Senior Lecturer in Housing in the Housing Research Centre at the University of Ulster.

John Harvey is a Consultant with the Barony Group, an independent management consultancy practice.

Marianne Hood is Vice Chair of the Labour Housing Group and an independent consultant specialising in tenant participation.

Richard Macfarlane is an independent researcher and consultant specialising in community based economic development.

Angela Maye-Banbury is a Research Fellow in the Centre for Comparative Housing Studies at De Montfort University, Leicester.

Mike Oxley is a Professor of Housing Studies in the Centre for Comparative Housing Studies at De Montfort University, Leicester.

Chris Paris is a Professor of Housing in the Housing Research Centre at the University of Ulster.

Bob Paterson is a Visiting Research Fellow at the University of Salford.

Selwyn Runnett is a consultant on housing issues.

Tamsin Stirling is an independent housing research and policy consultant.

Gerry Stoker is a Professor of Politics in the Department of Government at the University of Strathclyde.

Richard Tomlins is a Senior Lecturer in Housing Studies in the Centre for Comparative Housing Studies at De Montfort University, Leicester.

Jeremy Wood is based in the Housing Department of the Nationwide Building Society.

Index